The
FINAL
SCROLL

The

FINAL
SCROLL

JAMES W. COOK

THE FINAL SCROLL

iUniverse books may be ordered through booksellers or by contacting:

iUniverse
1663 Liberty Drive
Bloomington, IN 47403
www.iuniverse.com
1-800-Authors (1-800-288-4677)

Because of the dynamic nature of the Internet, any web addresses or links contained in this book may have changed since publication and may no longer be valid. The views expressed in this work are solely those of the author and do not necessarily reflect the views of the publisher, and the publisher hereby disclaims any responsibility for them.

Any people depicted in stock imagery provided by Thinkstock are models, and such images are being used for illustrative purposes only.
Certain stock imagery © Thinkstock.

ISBN: 978-1-4917-7999-6 (sc)
ISBN: 978-1-4917-7998-9 (hc)
ISBN: 978-1-4917-8000-8 (e)

Library of Congress Control Number: 2015916929

Print information available on the last page.

iUniverse rev. date: 10/19/2015

This book is dedicated to my mother, Thelma, whose inspiration made this story possible.

CHAPTER 1

Today is the fourth day of the fourth month of the seventh year. It has been seven years since millions of people vanished off the earth, or so it seemed. My name is Sue Chamberlain. I'm a reporter for the New York Herald. I'm standing here close to the Jewish Temple waiting for the world leader and the religious leader to enter the plaza for an announcement. It is Sunday, Apr4th, 8am. Easter Sunday.

I have no idea what lays in store, not only for the world, but for me personally as well. My story begins nine months ago. I was at work in my office at the Herald when I received a call from an old friend of mine during our college years. He's an archeologist from the university. His name is Pedro Gonzolas. His specialty is Middle Eastern religious artifacts. He was calling me from Peru, and I found it strange that he would be there rather than Israel or Jordan. With anticipation Pedro said, "Sue, you better come down here. There's something I want to show you." I knew that if Pedro wanted me there, it had to be for a very good reason, so with anticipation I went home, packed a suitcase and left for the airport, a passport in hand.

The flight was long, New York to Lima, Peru seemed like it would take forever, but in no time, there I was in Lima. Pedro met me at the airport and drove me to my hotel to unpack and rest for an hour before heading out. I asked him what was so important that I had to be in Lima. He said, "Sue, wait till I show you what I found."

After unpacking, I waited for Pedro to return to have a late dinner and perhaps find out what all the fuss is about. It wasn't like Pedro to call and ask me to come to him on such short notice, so I knew whatever it was, it was very important.

At precisely seven o'clock, Pedro knocked on my door, wearing a dashing blue suit. God, I thought, it must really be important for Pedro to go all out and dress so formal. As we walked through the corridor, Pedro whispered, "Sue, I found what could be the most important archeological discovery ever, even better than the dead sea scrolls." Now my curiosity was beginning to surface. I thought to myself, "What could be a better find than the dead sea scrolls?" As we ate our dinner at one of the most exclusive eating establishments in Lima, Pedro began to give me a hint at what he discovered. Pedro asked me, "How good are you at deciphering Hebrew, ancient Hebrew to be exact?" I was aghast. How could ancient Hebrew be discovered in Peru?

After dinner, Pedro and I walked throughout the city, all the while Pedro, without telling me exactly what I was about to see, became so excited I thought he'd jump straight out of his pants. I always knew Pedro to be somewhat excitable, but this was one for the books. I never, in all the years I knew him, was Pedro ever this excited.

As we walked inside the hotel, Pedro held my hand, gave me a warm kiss, and told me he'd be at the hotel at six in the morning. I wondered why so early, but all Pedro said was, "You'll find out tomorrow." By this time my curiosity was full blown, but I still had no clue of what Pedro had found or how ancient Hebrew was involved. Laying under the covers, all I could do was think about what Pedro had said, causing me to drift off to sleep.

At six o'clock, Pedro was knocking on my door, causing me to rise from my slumber, but not quite fully awake. Putting on my housecoat and slippers, I yelled out, "Ok, ok, I'm coming." When I opened the door, much to my surprise, there stood Pedro, dressed as though he was going on a safari. Excited, Pedro said, "Hurry up. We have a long day ahead of us and I want to be in the village of Puna before it gets too late." Puna, I thought. Where the heck is Puna?

After a very long drive that seemed to take forever, we arrived at the outskirts of Puna. Although Puna is a small city, it does have some of the finest restaurants and boutiques, but it also had a quaint little shop that sold souvenirs depicting the history of the region. Grabbing our gear from the jeep, we checked into the hotel, spread our suitcases down, and just relaxed for a couple hours. During this time, Pedro explained that what he had found was probably the greatest discovery in Peru for all time. Based on his excitement, I knew he stumbled unto something quite interesting, but I had no clue what his discovery existed of, at least until he took me to one of the numerous caves in the region.

On our way to the caves, we stopped in the small village of Tarma to purchase some supplies and food for what would become a very long day.

Walking for several miles, we arrived at our first destination. Looking at his map, Pedro showed me that we were at cave number 67. What that meant I didn't know, but at least Pedro knew where he was. Cautiously entering cave 67, it was dark, damp, and wet. Water was pouring from the roof of the cave and dripping into some sort of waterway. The ground was dry, but I still felt that we would get wet or at least dirty from the dust created by the cascading water.

Once we had gone about two hundred feet, we came to an area that was huge, somewhat appearing as though nature had created this massive formation.

Taking his flashlight, Pedro strolled toward the rear of the cave, showing me what he had discovered. Propped against the wall sat an object that appeared to be a scroll, an ancient looking one at that. It appeared that it had been in the cave a very long time, perhaps even centuries. With great care and precision, Pedro opened the first page, showing me the text of the document.

Pedro said, "It appears to be ancient Hebrew, but I'm not exactly sure." Carefully placing the scroll in my hands, I looked it over and realized that Pedro had found something unique. It sure appeared to be Hebrew or even Latin. Pedro insisted it was Hebrew and although he wasn't fluent in the language, he said he had seen similar text many years ago outside Jerusalem. Using his flashlight, Pedro slowly scanned the page and noticed a word that could mean temples, but what temple or where? As he continued reading the document, I decided to investigate the cave further. As I walked around, I came to what appeared to be a sub wall, perhaps indented. I yelled over to Pedro, "Pedro, come look at this." As Pedro walked over, I noticed that it was an indented wall, but how did it get that way and what could be behind it?

"Wait here', Pedro said. Going over to his magical bag of tricks as I called it, he grabbed a military style shovel, unfolded it, and returned. I said, "Are you crazy. That wall could be several feet thick, and besides would it be worth all the trouble to find out if anything was behind it." Undeterred, Pedro began the tedious task of digging around the indentation. I thought at this pace he'd probably get through in several days or weeks, but never any mind. When Pedro had a streak of determination, nothing could stop him.

After shoveling an enormous amount of dirt, Pedro struck something on the other side. At first I thought it was only more rocks, but as I looked, I saw what appeared to be some sort of wooden chest. Stretching his arm across, Pedro managed to grab the chest by its old, rusty handle.

Pulling it toward him, Pedro tried as best he could to remove the chest from it's hiding place, but it was too large to retrieve it from behind the small opening that Pedro made.

Undeterred, Pedro once again grabbed the shovel and started the long, meticulous job of removing as much dirt as possible in order to grab the chest and pull it over to our side, but the chest was extremely heavy and I knew I didn't have the strength necessary to pull it over. At the rate Pedro was working, it would take another two hours of digging to retrieve what he hoped was another set of scrolls. Although we had one scroll, somehow we both felt there were more of them, hidden away in the mountain.

Feeling exhausted, Pedro dropped the shovel and said, "Perhaps tomorrow we can get the chest out." Pedro was so tired I thought I'd have to carry him back to town and our comfortable room. As we walked, what seemed to take forever, Pedro and I knew we were onto something, and it was probably to become the most famous story of my career. Nobody else knew of this place but us, and I wanted to keep it that way for as long as possible. Pedro and I had one scroll, but we knew there were more of them hidden away, and it was possibly to be the largest treasure trove ever discovered, even more than the Dead Sea Scrolls.

As the sun began to set, Pedro and I sat on the balcony of our hotel room, enjoying the cool breeze and the sights and sounds of a busy street. I was in my glory. I was far from New York City, and I was fortunate to be a part of history. My boss at the New York Herald will be proud of me and perhaps I'll get that long awaited raise I've been asking for.

As the sun began to rise, the day was already beginning to become warm. As I rose to my feet, I shoved Pedro's body, trying to get him awake for the long day ahead, but Pedro wasn't the type of guy one could awaken so easily. He definitely needed some encouragement to rise and shine.

What will we discover today, I thought, as I put makeup on my face and put on my black leather boots.

As we sat down to have breakfast, I asked Pedro whether he had tried to interpret the first scroll. "God help me," I don't have a clue as to what the scroll says and I'm afraid to have anybody take a look for fear it would bring other archeologists to Peru, and rob us of this historical discovery. I could see the look in his eye that he was worried, so I said to him, "Pedro, listen. We'll have to find somebody able to read the scroll in order to find out what it says." Pedro knew that I was right, but who could be trusted to translate the scroll without raising any red flags.

With the first scroll tucked away in its leather bag, Pedro and I began our journey back to the cave and began the long, tedious task of removing the large, heavy, wooden chest that has been hidden, perhaps for centuries. As I walked, I thought to myself, "What could the chest contain and could it be something that would bring us notoriety.." Unknown to me, the chest would only reveal another mystery.

Finally arriving at the mouth of the cave, Pedro and I began the long trek inside, darkened by pitch blackness, and the smell that only a deep cave can have. Our flashlights seemed to become lost in the vast blackness of the cave, yet we continued until we finally arrived at the spot we left yesterday. Once again, Pedro began the task of shoveling the dirt away from what appeared to be some sort of chamber hidden behind the rocky dirt that kept it hidden for many years.

Finally, Pedro and I were able to grab the handle and retrieve the wooden chest. It appeared that it had been hidden for centuries, but how could a wooden chest survive for so long, I wondered. Raising his flashlight, Pedro inspected the chest and discovered that it had been sealed with a nickel plate. Pedro said, "Where in God's name did this come from?" To me it didn't matter. What mattered to me was what is inside and is it something that will bring us a fortune.

Now that we had the chest out from it's hiding place, our next problem was trying to figure a way to open it. The seal was tight and held firmly in place. All I could think of was whether the chest held more scrolls or perhaps gold and precious stones. Pedro said, "I'll have to return to town and buy something to pry open the chest, but is the seal so tight nothing will open it?" Peering inside the chamber, Pedro noticed something else. In the far side of the chamber there appeared to be more treasures. Holding his flashlight steady, Pedro scanned the chamber noticing it's vast reaches. It seemed as though it continued forever and even deeper than we had expected.

Pedro decided to enter the chamber, but danger lurked with every crawl and step. Stooping right behind Pedro, I scanned the chamber and was in awe of its vastness. The air inside was thin unlike the air at the cave's entrance. I felt that perhaps we should return another time with air packs, just to be sure we'd have enough oxygen. Pedro insisted there was nothing to worry about, and besides, we wouldn't be inside the chamber for long.

As Pedro and I searched the chamber, we came across yet another chest, but this chest was broken apart, revealing it's content. Scattered around were several more scrolls, all containing what appeared to be ancient Hebrew text. As I opened one of the scrolls, my eyes led me toward the first paragraph. I wasn't sure exactly what it said, but it appeared to be written in Latin. The first thing I wondered was how could Latin and Hebrew texts be in this cave together. I was sure it would take lots of research to discover why both texts would be together inside this chamber.

Above the first sentence was in Latin, the name Abraham. Surely it must be ancient writing about the father of all nations, Abraham, straight from the Old Testament. I didn't understand much Latin, but I knew it was a very important discovery.

As Pedro gathered the remaining scrolls, I left the chamber and with the scroll in hand, I went outside the cave to call my editor back in New York City. I knew I had the story of a lifetime right in my hands, perhaps even gaining a Pulitzer Prize. Without revealing too much information, I told my editor, Ronald Silfies, that I'd be staying in Peru for perhaps a few more weeks. At first Ronald wasn't very keen on my being away from the office for so long, but I assured him that my absence will be worth the wait.

By this time Pedro was leaving the cave, but without our booty. Exclaiming, Pedro said, "Sue, we must go see Father Michael Ligouri before we drag out the remaining scrolls. We must be sure that what we have here is worth the effort." I must admit I agreed with Pedro, but somehow I had a funny suspicion that we had stumbled unto something far bigger than we could imagine.

By the time we returned to Puna, we were so tired that all we wanted was to get something to eat and rest. Even I thought to myself that tomorrow is another day. As the sun began its journey from the sky, I had visions of grandeur. I imagined myself standing before the Pope, being blessed, and given the keys to Saint Peter's Square. Drifting off, my mind seemed to know I was onto something bigger than myself.

With the morning rain came the realization that Pedro and I would find out today what we had discovered, or should I say Pedro discovered. Running down the street trying to hold a bagel in one hand, coffee in the other, I placed the first scroll under my armpits and ran to Pedro's car. I was so excited I nearly spilled the coffee all over the scroll, but reassuring Pedro that all was well, I placed the scroll in the backseat and off we drove. The church was several miles outside of Puna and the road wasn't paved in some spots, but after a bumpy ride, we arrived at Saint Vincente, the local Catholic Church. Inside, waiting for us, was Father Ligouri. Having no idea what my excitement was, the Priest led us into his office, and asking how he could help us, I showed him the scroll. Father Ligouri asked, "What is this, my child? What have you found?" Having no clue I said, "Father, we were hoping you could tell us."

Carefully opening the scroll, Father Ligouri's eyes focused on the writings. Father Ligouri said, "What you have here are texts written in Latin, perhaps from the first century after Christ, or even before the birth of Christ." By this time my knees were shaking from excitement. I thought to myself, "How lucky can a girl get, especially from New York City." This is the kind of thing that only experienced archeologists discover. Father Ligouri asked, "Where in God's blessed name did you get this?" I wasn't very sure whether or not to reveal where we found it, but knowing that if one can't trust a Priest, who can you trust.

As I looked at Pedro with inquisitive eyes, I decided to trust Father Ligouri. I explained that we had found the treasure in a cave a few miles from town. I didn't tell him that there were more of these scrolls since I wasn't very sure whether we found anything of significance anyway. Father Ligouri began reading the scroll and told us that what it was, was some type of document describing what the other scrolls contained. Apparently, it stated that the Hebrew texts were several thousand years old and that they contained scripture from the Book of Abraham. "Perhaps," Father Ligouri said, "the scroll described the lost Book of Abraham, possibly written several centuries before Christ." I thought, that would make the other scrolls even more important than the scroll we were showing Father Ligouri. I did have one question to ask and that was, "If this scroll describes the lost Book of Abraham, how did it find it's way to Peru and who could have taken it here?" Father Ligouri said, "That my dear child, is the sixty four-thousand dollar question." I knew our investigation was going to take not just weeks, but perhaps months or even years to decipher.

According to the Latin scroll, the Book of Abraham had disappeared after Babylon had taken Jerusalem, but it didn't say exactly who hid the treasure and most importantly how it found its way to South America. Placing the scroll back in my hands, Father Ligouri suggested we find the ancient writings and return them to him, perhaps he'd discover what their contents were saying as well as how they made their way to a cave in Peru.

Pedro and I drove back to the hotel and began sifting through the three scrolls we brought back from the caves. Although there were more of the scrolls, we decided to only reveal the first two or three before making our discovery public. I knew nothing of Hebrew text and Pedro knew only a few words he had learned from a Rabbi he knew in Lima. I said, "Well, let's take one scroll to Lima and see your Jewish friend, perhaps he'd be able to explain what it said and how and why it was hidden in Peru." Agreeing, Pedro placed one scroll in a velvet cloth, handling it with care. Loading supplies in our truck, we began the journey to Lima and hopefully the first scroll will reveal something of historical significance.

As we drove into Lima, I noticed that the citizens were about to celebrate a festival. Buildings were adorned in flags and banners, and there was a jolly atmosphere in the air. Pedro, always in the mood for celebrating, decided to get a hotel room for the night and tomorrow morning we would go to the main synagogue in Lima. Although the Jewish community was quite small considering the total population of Lima, they were a close tight knit community, heaped in tradition. If anyone would be able to decipher the scroll, it would be the head Rabbi whose name was Peter Caldero. Rabbi Caldero was in his eighties and very knowledgeable in ancient scripture and was quite fluent in ancient Hebrew. Before we'd get to see Rabbi Caldero, we first would have to request an audience through Rabbi Jacob Berman. Rabbi Berman was in his fifties and spent most of his life in the United States, only having been in Lima for about three years. Even Rabbi Berman was no stranger to ancient texts but not as well as Rabbi Caldero.

The most important question I had was, how did these ancient writings end up here, in Peru? I was sure Rabbi Caldero would have the answer to that question.

Having got myself ready for tonight's festivities, I met Pedro in the hotel lobby for a night on the town. The festival was some sort of celebration commemorating the founding of the town. As we strolled through the assorted avenues, I was able to catch a glimpse of the variety of homespun yarn, crafts, and even some delicacies known for their quality in this area of Peru. As we turned a corner, I noticed something in the air that reminded me of my grandmothers cooking, but I never expected the aroma to represent what it was. Pedro informed me that the dish I was smelling was rattlesnake heads soup, a fine dish for the locals. That's when my stomach began to churn like I was going to puke, but Pedro insisted I try a small bite so I wouldn't embarrass myself. Walking up to the counter, Pedro made the request for two servings. I wasn't sure whether I could get myself to try this dish, but it did smell good I must admit. Taking the spoon, I took a small amount, brought it to my lips, and although hesitant, I placed the soup in my mouth, savoring the juices. It was rather delicious so I consumed the entire serving. I never thought the day would come when I'd be eating rattlesnake head soup.

As the sun began to set, Pedro and I sat down under a tree, on a blanket, and enjoyed the live music performed by local bands. It was so romantic, but I tried not to become too emotionally attached to Pedro, although he was quite handsome.

Finally the day came when we might have an answer from Rabbi Berman whether or not Rabbi Caldero would see us. Rabbi Berman was just as curious as we were and without hesitation escorted us into the tabernacle, and had us sit and wait. What seemed like a lifetime had passed, Rabbi Berman returned with the good news that Rabbi Caldero would see us.

As we slowly entered the Rabbi's private office, Pedro and I started to feel nervous. Had we brought the Rabbi anything of significance or were we showing him something of a fake? Having only the first scroll I'm sure wouldn't be enough, but Pedro decided not to play all our cards at once, so to speak.

After several minutes had passed, Rabbi Caldero came into the room. Sitting down behind his huge oak desk, the Rabbi asked, "How may I help you?" Pedro asked Rabbi Caldero if he would read a scroll for him, one written in ancient Hebrew text. Rabbi Caldero said, "Let me see what you have and I will tell you exactly what you have." As Pedro handed Rabbi Caldero the scroll, I began to get quite nervous. Had we really found anything of importance, I wondered.

As we watched the Rabbi unfold the scroll and began to read, he temporarily stopped reading to ask us the same question Father Ligouri had asked. "Where in God's name did you find this scroll?" All Pedro could say was that several weeks ago he was out near the mountains exploring, hoping to find some archeological discovery when he found a cave, entering, and after some time had passed he found the scroll.

Rabbi Caldero excitedly said, "Do you two know what you have found?" We must have had a dumb look on our faces as Rabbi Caldero said, "You have found a scroll that has been missing for thousands of years." Perplexed, I asked him what it contained and it was then that we found out what we had found. According to Rabbi Caldero, we had found what could only be described as the lost Book of Abraham. Rabbi Caldero informed us that although the Talmud contained the first five books of the Old Testament, it was believed that a sixth book should have been included but was never found.

Calling out for Rabbi Berman, Rabbi Caldero said, "I want to show this scroll to Rabbi Berman and get his take on this." As Rabbi Caldero showed Rabbi Berman the scroll, I could see the excitement on both their faces. Rabbi Berman said that it was believed there were several scrolls missing and wondered if we had found more scrolls. Pedro reluctantly said yes, that we had found five more scrolls in the rear of the cave. Both Rabbi Caldero and Rabbi Berman suggested we bring the scrolls to them for further translation. Agreeing to do so, we left for the hotel, packed two small suitcases, and drove out to the cave to retrieve the five scrolls. We had left them in the back of the cave, as if to hide them from prying eyes should anyone else venture inside.

As we entered the cave, I told Pedro that we must search for more scrolls, that perhaps there were more than the five we have also found.

Just as we picked up the scrolls, the ground started to shake, the ceiling of the cave began to fall to the ground, so we ran as fast as we could to prevent being trapped inside the cave and perhaps dying from lack of air.

Driving as fast as he could, Pedro was just as excited as I was, not to mention Rabbi Caldero and Rabbi Berman. I was so happy that I was playing a part in this discovery. I knew that this story could possibly enrich me with that evasive Pulitzer Prize I had always longed for, just as any other journalist. Before taking the scrolls to the Rabbi's, I suggested we photograph our little discovery. Returning to the hotel, I grabbed my camera from it's hiding place and began to snap photo after photo, just to have a record as proof of our find. Not to say that the Rabbi's would steal from us, but as anyone would do, I wanted to have the proof.

The synagogue was only several blocks from the hotel so we decided to walk there. Along the way we encountered an unusual person. She had come out from her house just as we approached. She stood in front of us never allowing us to pass. She peered into my eyes, and with a calm, yet stern voice said, "You will both die if you continue on your quest." I thought it was strange that this woman would say that, not to mention the fact that how would she know we were on a quest.

Pedro just said, "Never mind her. She's loony tunes, and not a very reliable person." "Besides," he said. "She's the local soothsayer, and not a very reliable one at that." I could tell she was quite spooky, but yet harmless I'm sure.

As we approached the synagogue, I felt nervous and shaky. What, I wondered, would we do if what we possessed was something other than old scrolls full of nonsense. Then I realized that the scrolls must be authentic if two Rabbis were interested. As we entered, Pedro insisted he do most of the talking since I wasn't a native to the country and there could be a degree of mistrust. Knowing that Pedro knew more than I did, I let him do most of the talking accept if I felt there was a need to know more.

Rabbi Berman entered the foyer asking if we had the other five scrolls. Pedro only brought two scrolls, not wanting to risk losing all five should we have been mugged along the way. Pedro knew there were thieves in town that looked for anyone not considered a local. He was sure that if someone else possessed the five scrolls, they could barter them for a huge amount of cash on the black market, so just to be safe, Pedro only came with two of the scrolls. At first Rabbi Berman was upset that Pedro had only brought two scrolls, but Pedro assured him that once the two scrolls plus the first scroll were translated, he would bring the other three.

Rabbi Berman led us to the office of Rabbi Caldero having us wait for his arrival. Rabbi Caldero was away and would return soon, the Rabbi said. As Pedro and I waited, we discussed whether we should return to the cave. Perhaps, he said that there are more scrolls yet to be found. I felt uneasy about that since the roof of the cave seemed to crack and fall, yet I was just as curious myself. The danger didn't consume my psyche so I agreed.

After about a half hour, in walked Rabbi Caldero. Sitting in his large chair behind his massive desk, Rabbi Caldero asked if we brought the other scrolls. Handing the Rabbi one of the scrolls, Rabbi Caldero, along with Rabbi Berman opened the first scroll. As Rabbi Caldero ran his eyes across the scroll, he began to explain that what we had was actually a verbal map to other scrolls, possibly as many as twenty or more. He went on to say it was as if whoever wrote the scroll didn't want the entire message to be contained in one scroll.

Rabbi Caldero began to translate and when he read the first few sentences, I was shocked by what he said. The Rabbi continued saying, "What you have is, like I said before, the lost biblical Book of Abraham, thought to be lost forever and never included in either the Talmud or the Christian bible. When I asked him how ancient Hebrew and Latin text could have made their way to

Peru from Palestine, all he could say was, "My dear, that's what's confusing me. Perhaps through the centuries, ancient Hebrew's hid them from the vast armies that invaded Palestine, killing Jews and then Christians, perhaps to get these scrolls into their hands. Perhaps, these sacred scrolls were first hidden much like the dead sea scrolls, preventing them from ending in the hands of the enemies of Jerusalem." I had to admit, it sure made sense, but, who took them from the middle east all the way through South America, ending in what would become modern day Peru? Also, how was it that a small village like Puna or even the larger city of Tarma ends up possessing the scrolls.

As Rabbi Caldero translated, he read that the first scroll contained messages that predicted the future. It did have the words, Book of Abraham, and did describe Abraham to a tee, but started with Jacob, then Joseph. It also had words of the great flood that occurred during the time of Noah. It predicted the life of Abraham and his loyalty to God, as well as the sons of Jacob with emphasis on Joseph and his brothers. The Book of Abraham even mentioned Egypt and the tribes of Israel. The Jews, according to the Book of Abraham would reject God and then be subject to years of slavery and domination.

The first scroll ended with the rise of the prophet Daniel. All it mentioned was that Daniel would possess the power to interpret dreams and bring wonder to the people of Israel.

Rabbi Caldero folded the scroll shut and said, "There must certainly be more scrolls to discover." It seems that perhaps the scrolls give a portrait of not just the history dating back roughly five thousand years, but may even conclude with what my generation is experiencing. Pedro and I excused ourselves and promised we would return with another scroll very soon.

As we sat in the hotel, Pedro opened the second scroll to see if it contained even more chapters. The first scroll had twenty chapters so we assumed that each scroll could have the same amount of chapters with even more information. Pedro, closing the scroll, said that we must return to the caves of Puna as soon as possible. He was certain that there was more treasure to be found, and who knows, we could even discover the ark of the covenant. That has also disappeared from history so perhaps these scrolls could indicate where that could be found. No matter, it confused me on how these scrolls made such a long journey from modern day Israel all the way to Peru, but I was certain I would discover a very important clue during my search.

Pedro, having three more scrolls in his knapsack, told me he had to return to Lima to have Father Ligouri decipher the scroll in Latin. Perhaps that scroll would give up even more information. I myself would return to New York City to place all the information we have already discovered on my computer. The article I was working on would surely give me the recognition I've desired for so long. Even the New York Herald could earn a place of notoriety, and that would please the editor I'm sure. Nobody else in the country had such an earth moving story as I had, but still, there was a long way to go. Soon Christmas would come and I wanted to return to Peru to check the caves of Puna with Pedro and see if we can find even more scrolls, but I had a feeling that such a task would take me farther than Peru.

As I boarded the plane for South America, I wondered how the world will react to such a discovery, but once the plane landed in Lima, all I could do was embrace the warm sun as soon the autumn air would find it's place in the sky and make searching for more scrolls even more difficult. Once winter arrives, trekking the small hills would prove difficult if not impossible.

As I returned to the town of Puna, I called Pedro to let him know of my return and that all I had was four more weeks before Christmas to continue our adventure. The smell of food surrounded the hotel as the kitchen prepared the evening meal. Although I wasn't pleased with most dishes, I managed to find a few that I would eat. As I wasted the time waiting for Pedro to return from Lima, I double checked my camera and made sure there was enough film to document every thing I discovered. As they say, a picture is worth a thousand words and I certainly had enough pictures and words already.

Within a couple hours, Pedro gingerly came strolling to me in the hotels dining hall. With the excitement of a child, Pedro said, "Sue, wait until you what I've found out, you'll be ecstatic." Now I am certainly confused. What could Pedro have discovered during my two-week absence? As we ordered our meal, which by the way consisted of lamb, which I normally wouldn't eat, Pedro told me that Father Ligouri deciphered the Latin scroll, however, he also found out from the translation, that there could be even more scrolls written in Latin. That peaked my curiosity even further. If there were more scrolls written in both Hebrew and Latin, we were possible sitting on the most important discovery since the dead sea scrolls were found.

According to Pedro, Father Ligouri said the scroll could have been written on the Island of Patmos where Saint John wrote the Book of Revelation. Could he have written the scrolls in addition to the last book of the New Testament or perhaps Saint Paul? Then I thought to myself that perhaps someone unknown in history could be responsible. Still, I knew there was a connection. I told Pedro I wanted to return to the Saint Stevens Monastery in Lima to find out for myself what Father Ligouri knew or at least could also be on to something. Pedro knew more than I did, but I wanted more information before returning to the caves of Puna. I only had four weeks before I hade to return to New York City for the holidays and I wanted to also check with Cardinal Metzger at the largest Roman Catholic Cathedral in New York to ask him his opinion about the scrolls. I didn't want to give out too much information, but I decided to trust Cardinal Metzger since I knew he had a confidential policy, much like the confessional. I thought if I dig and prod, I might find out some more about our discovery or at least if anybody else knew of the existence of the scrolls or a perhaps any suspicion.

Lima is a large city and there were various ways to get information from a variety of sources. There was, of course, Father Ligouri, but I felt that even a psychic might reveal anything that would shed light on our archeological adventure. As I strolled around Lima, I came across a house, with a sign that read, Madam Zara, Fortune Teller. I usually wouldn't resort to such stuff, but what the heck, I might as well give it a try.

Madam Zara turned out to be an elderly lady, around seventy-six years old with flowing black hair that cascaded down her back. Madam Zara led me into her so-called chamber where she held court. It was dimly lit, a smell of burning incense, and drapery hanging from the walls. As I sat before her, I had a feeling that I shouldn't be here, but I also thought that madam Zara might be able to guide me through this adventure. As she laid out her deck of cards, she explained that the cards will reveal to me what I want to know. Having been raised in a strict Christian home, I felt somewhat uncomfortable with the idea of seeing Madam Zara. I was always taught that such people were satanic, but something came over me, like I was being guided somehow.

With the deck now spread, Madam Zara had split the deck, and began to spread the cards in a cross like fashion. Taking the cards one by one, Madam Zara began to read the meaning of each card to me. She began the reading by saying what I already knew. She said I have come from far away in search of answers. As she continued, I thought I was wasting my time, but just as she revealed the second last card, Madam Zara's face turned white, almost as though she had seen a ghost. Madam Zara told me that there was extreme danger ahead and that I should proceed cautiously in my endeavor. That may have been correct, but when she revealed the final card, Madam Zara trembled, her hands shaking, and sweat pouring from her brow.

As I sat waiting to hear what she had to say, I wondered whether or not I wanted to know what the card revealed. As she showed me the card, I saw it was the death card. With her head bowed, Madam Zara said, "You are in extreme danger. There are those who will find out about your discovery and will try to kill you to prevent its location from being revealed and it's meaning. Beware," she said. I suddenly began to feel scared, but I knew I must continue no matter what kind of danger would present itself. Thanking her for my reading, I left for the hotel to wait for Pedro to return. Perhaps he would have good news for me although I wasn't feeling there would be.

Hours had passed before Pedro returned. I asked Pedro, "Where have you been all this time?" Pedro went on to explain that he had returned to the caves at Puna, searching for more scrolls and a few clues. Pedro went on to say, "Sue, I think there could be more scrolls somewhere else. I don't think they're all together in Puna." I knew in my heart this was going to become an adventure of a lifetime, but at what cost. I informed him of my reading at Madam Zara's and that she said people will want to find our scrolls and kill us. Pedro, fearing the worse said, "This is why we must trust no one except the Father Ligouri and the two Rabbis. Anyone else could bring us danger."

As the days passed, Pedro returned to Tarma to find the famed American archeologist, Robert Calisi. Pedro had learned that Calisi was in Tarma searching throughout the city for historical artifacts and if anyone could tell us the meaning of the scrolls and could be trusted, it was Calisis. Three days after Pedro left for Parma, I returned to New York City. My editor was quite upset that I had been gone for so long. He wanted to know why I was spending so much time in Peru, but all I told him was that I was on to something that would be worth the time. I pleaded with him for more time and that it would be worth it. I said, "Bill, believe me when I say that what I'm discovering will bring the New York Herald the story of the century, just give me more time." After thinking it through, he agreed. Bill knew I wasn't the type of person who would waste time on a story that wouldn't be worth the wait. What I didn't know was where this journey would take me and what laid ahead. One thing that didn't cross my mind was that it would involve treachery, murder, and pure evil.

As the days came and went, I was no closer to the truth than when I first started this project. I continued to be in contact with Pedro despite our long distance. Apparently, Pedro was told by Father Ligouri to take the Latin scrolls to the Vatican Emissary in New York, Cardinal Manci. If anyone could decipher the scrolls, it would be him. Father Ligouri was no slouch, but for something this important, it would have to be Cardinal Manci. I assured Pedro I would give this a chance. Gaining an audience with Cardinal Manci was no easy feat. He was a very busy man and it could take days, perhaps weeks before I could see him. One thing, I was no quitter, and that was a good thing, especially once

I learned that Cardinal Manci was in Rome and wouldn't return to New York for several more weeks.

Within days, my editor called me into his office. He had a very important assignment for me that would prevent me returning to Peru. I was chosen to represent the New York Herald in Rome to cover a story concerning the leader of the W.F.C. short for World Federation Council. The President of that council was named Adrian, and his meeting with the ailing Pope Thomas I was possibly their last meeting and it's widely believed that the summit would result in an important agreement between the Vatican and the W.F.C. According to my sources there would be hundreds of reporters from around the world covering this story and although I wasn't very keen at first about going to Rome, I knew I was being honored by my editor for being chosen for this assignment.

As I packed by suitcases, I received a call from Pedro. According to Pedro, an archeologist from Lima had heard a rumor that Pedro and I had discovered something incredible and Pedro was worried that perhaps this man would jeopardize our discovery. Having remembered what Madam Zara had told me about danger surrounding my discovery, I warned Pedro to be aware of anyone trying to grab the scrolls for their own fortune to be made on the black market. I knew how trusting Pedro could be at times, but at the same time he also could be the suspicious type. For now, all that was on my mind was this important meeting between Pope Thomas and Adrian. It was rare that these two leaders would meet, so figuring this could be a one chance in a lifetime I agreed to go to Rome.

As I packed my suitcases, I gently placed the one Latin scroll I brought back to New York, thinking perhaps I would be able to have a one on one meeting with Cardinal Manci. I thought if I couldn't see him in New York, perhaps I'd be able to meet Cardinal Manci and have a really good interpretation of the first Latin scroll.

As my flight made the journey to Rome, I took out my notes, wanting to see if I jotted everything down I wanted to ask Cardinal Manci. I had no idea what I'd learn, but soon I would find out I was a long way off from finding out what the Latin scrolls said and how they were connected to the ancient Hebrew scrolls.

Four days after arriving in Rome, I took my place in Saint Peters square where all journalists had to take their place. From my angle, I would have the perfect spot to get a glimpse of the two leaders. My cameraman, Josh Eddinger, managed to get a great spot without having anyone in the way of the camera lens. Waiting with anticipation, I couldn't get what Pedro told me the last time we talked. I was worried that if too many people find out what Pedro and I have been doing, I'd never get the story of the century and could also possibly lose getting that Pulitzer Prize.

As the crowd waited for the curtains to open, the anticipation grew to a fever pitch. Finally, after waiting for more than two hours, Pope Peter II and President Adrian appeared on the balcony. As the two men waved to the massive crowd, everyone was waiting for that special moment when the two would shake hands and give each other a gentle hug, signifying their unity. It was something that had been wanted since Adrian became the leader of the World Federation Council. It has been seven years in the making and the world waited with bated breath for this historical moment. We learned that the two would meet in Jerusalem in a few months to meet with the Muslim cleric, Imam Mehrdad. That also has been something the world has been waiting for. It would mark the official unification of the three major religions of the world and herald in the dawn of a new era, a new world order. That in itself was remarkable, but the thought that only two years ago, a would be assassin would shoot President Adrian in the head, and although severely wounded, President Adrian made the most remarkable recovery ever for a person who took a head shot and survived.

As the crowd dispersed, I made my way through the streets of Vatican City toward the main office for a journalist pass to see Cardinal Manci. As I showed the guard at the office my credentials, I peered around, noticing the numerous photographs of popes from the past. Nervously waiting, I was given a security pass and sent on my way. The guard instructed me to only go see Cardinal Manci at his office, number 16. Searching the vastness of Vatican City, I wondered whether Cardinal Manci could even help, but I needed answers and I'd take a shot at trying almost anybody.

As I went through the massive door of office number 16, I made my way to the priest who managed the office and the Cardinal's daily affairs. Standing before him, I said, "My name is Sue Chamberlain and I represent the New York Herald. I'm requesting a few moments with Cardinal Manci." All the priest would say was, "Cardinal Manci is very busy. Come back another time." Not wanting to miss this golden opportunity, I graciously asked once again, "May I please see Cardinal Manci, it is of the greatest importance." As expected the priest suggested I return another time, but I he told me that, the huge door leading to Cardinal Manci's office opened. Standing there before me was Cardinal Manci himself. Pondering what to do, I quickly said, "Your excellency, may I have a few moments of your time?" I wasn't expecting him to notice me, but unbelievable to me,

Cardinal Manci said with a look of pleasantly on his face, "Young lady, how may I help you?"

As I stood before him shaking from my nerves, told him that I had something of great importance to show him and that I had been told by Father Ligouri in Lima, Peru that he could help me with my dilemma. Cardinal Manci responded, "Surely my child, enter." As we made our way into his office, Cardinal Manci said, "I know Father Ligouri well. We served together in Latin America for many years in my early years as a priest. How may I help you?"

As I sat down, I opened the case containing the scroll and showed it to him. As he looked at the scroll, he asked, "Where in God's blessed name did you find this?" Hesitantly I informed him that I was doing research in Peru and came across the scroll during an archeological excavation. As he continued unraveling the scroll, he began to interpret its contents, but not before he said, "Sue, you have no idea what you have here, do you?" I had to admit that I didn't realize it's importance but I also knew it had to be of great value, at least on a historical basis.

Cardinal Manci read the scroll informing me that it was only the first of possibly three to five scrolls. The one I found described first century Jerusalem and with pinpoint accuracy described events of that period of history, but it also contained writings of past events. According to the scroll, there is written a portion describing a vast amount of Hebrew texts that has been hidden to prevent its contents from falling into the hands of the Romans. It certainly was written in Latin with a cursive element. It may have started with the first century, but the scroll ended it' part describing events dating back to the time of Daniel. After glancing over the scroll, Cardinal Manci said, "You must return to Peru and search for the rest of the scrolls."

Before leaving his office, I asked him, "How could scrolls written in ancient Jerusalem end up in South America?" Cardinal Manci responded. "When you find the final scroll, it will have your answer, but please take caution, the scrolls contain valuable information that were they to fall into the hands of scrupulous people, it could cost you your life." That certainly sounded familiar. That's exactly what Madam Zara told me. Feeling nervous, I placed the scroll back into my suitcase, thanked Cardinal Manci for his time and started walking towards the door when suddenly the Cardinal said, "My child, when you find the other scrolls, please bring them to me so I can see for myself what the church through the ages had thought were lost long ago." I agreed, since I needed his translation to get the full picture of what Pedro and I had discovered. Not only did we have to search for more scrolls written in Latin, but we also had the problem of the ancient Hebrew texts to contend with.

After spending another day in Rome, I returned to New York City and my apartment. As I grabbed a bite to eat, I sat at my computer and transcribed the information Cardinal Manci had translated so I'd have a record of the events should something happen to me or the scrolls. I even went as far as to encode my transcripts, giving Pedro the passwords to my records.

Before returning to Peru, I spent the next several days spending time with my family. It was my father's birthday and I needed to be with my parents, brothers and sisters, and their extended families. I wasn't sure how long I would be gone so I needed the quality time. Before leaving for my father's birthday party, I wrote a letter to my mother, sealed it shut, and gave her valuable instructions not to open the letter unless something happens to me. All my mother could say was, "What could happen to you? You're a journalist covering stories about America." All I could tell her was that I was returning to Peru and that there could be danger. My mother promised that she wouldn't open the letter unless something did happen to me. I didn't let her know what Madam Zara and Cardinal Manci warned me about, but I just wanted her to know the truth should something bad happen.

Several days after the birthday party, I was on my way to the airport when a sudden feeling came over me. Perhaps it was woman's intuition, but something was bothering my conscience. As I waited to depart, I went over my notes on my laptop. I wasn't sure how long I'd be away from New York so I transferred my files from my home computer to the laptop. I made a password up hoping that could prevent somebody from seeing my notes. As I began checking my notes, I realized that I hadn't heard from Pedro in a few days so grabbing my cell phone I placed the call to his house. Not getting an answer made me feel somewhat scared, but Pedro has been known to disappear for days at a time, and besides, soon I'd be landing in Lima, then take the taxi to the hotel, change clothes, and wait for Pedro. I wanted to convey to him what Cardinal Manci had told me and I really wanted to search for the second and perhaps third scrolls.

Hours passed and still no Pedro. Now I was beginning to become concerned. Fearing danger may have fallen to him, I grabbed my bag and left for the train station to take me close to where the cave is located.

An hour later I was walking towards the hillside, wondering to myself whether or not to continue this discovery. Perhaps there was danger lurking at every turn, but who would want to harm or even kill me over a few ancient scrolls, I wondered. Nevertheless, I decided my curiosity was worth taking a chance.

As I entered the mouth of the cave I called out, "Pedro, Pedro, are you in here?" Hearing no response, I continued going deeper into the cave. Once again I called out, "Pedro, are you in here?" Suddenly I heard a muffled sound, coming from deep inside the cave. Taking my lantern, I cautiously walked closer towards the sound. It was Pedro, trapped behind a mountain of dirt. Somehow while he was searching the cave, he managed to cause the cave to collapse, trapping him deep inside. I yelled, hoping he would hear me, "Pedro, keep calm. I'm going to go get help." I had no idea who could help dig Pedro out, but I knew I couldn't do it alone. It was now that I had concerns. Who could I trust and will this be the thing that brings danger to Pedro and myself? NO matter, I needed help so I waited at the train stop, and within an hour I was back on the train headed for the town of Puna.

Knowing nobody, I went to the reception desk and asked the clerk whether he knew somebody who could help me dig out Pedro, especially if he was running out of air. Within an hour, I had a team of men, pickaxes and shovels in hand, we loaded up on trucks and headed out of town and to the cave. As we drove there, a man by the name of Hansi struck up a conversation. Asking me why I was in the caves in the first place, all I said was that Pedro and I were exploring, looking for artifacts from the early days of settlements in Peru, but that perked his interest. Had I made a grave mistake telling Hansi what we were doing, I thought. Too late, Hansi's curiosity came to the surface. Could I trust Hansi or would he be the one to betray and kill us?

It took two hours of digging to get to Pedro, and as the hole widened, I saw Pedro, standing there holding another scroll. This time Pedro hit pay dirt. It turned out to be the second scroll written in Latin. Once he saw the team of men, he quickly shoved the scroll behind his back, walked toward us, and thanked everybody for coming to his assistance. Thankfully the men who dug for two hours weren't concerned with what Pedro had discovered, but I can't say the same thing about Hansi.

As the men dispersed, Hansi stayed behind which caused me some concern. Hansi even offered to help in any way possible, but I insisted Pedro and I could handle things ourselves. Having failed to gain our trust, Hansi walked away with a look of defeat, yet at the same time seeming to be quite spooky. Pedro then showed me the second scroll. As expected, it was written in Latin. We wasted no time getting to Lima to show Father Ligouri our latest discovery. If only Pedro or I could read Latin, but would we be able to grasp the importance of the text.

Two days later we arrived in Lima, excited as though we were children opening our Christmas presents. As we entered the church, Father Ligouri had just finished his daily routine of hearing confessions. Sitting in his office, we took out the scroll and handed it to him. Once he knew this was the second scroll even he was filled with excitement. Taking it out of the velvet cloth surrounding it, Father Ligouri began to look it over, reading out loud and Latin what the scroll said.

According to Father Ligouri, this scroll held important significance. It was actually a blueprint to the scrolls written in ancient Hebrew. Apparently, the Latin scroll was most likely written either in the first or second century's and did describe in detail the location of the Hebrew scrolls and what they contained. The scroll mentioned that the Hebrew scrolls were hidden outside of Jerusalem and even Nazareth and Bethlehem, the birthplace of Jesus Christ. The scroll went on to say that there were actually seven scrolls, hidden to prevent the Romans from discovering them, using them for their own agenda and also went on to mention the Babylonians, the

Persians, and other enemies of the Jews living in what became Palestine close to the period of the New Testament's years.

By the time Father Ligouri completed reading the scroll, we discovered that the final Latin scroll would most likely say how the scrolls began their journey from Palestine to South America. Father Ligouri told Pedro and I that the scrolls, both Latin and Hebrew consisted of writings predicting the future with the inclusion of names and places, right up to the time of the anti-Christ. Amazing, I thought. Now I knew the importance these scrolls had and how through the ages people were murdered in order to obtain them. It was clear to me what Madam Zara and Cardinal Manci had warned me about. There was more danger than I could comprehend, and perhaps it would all begin with the mysterious Hansi.

Leaving Father Ligouri keep the two Latin scrolls, Pedro and I left to catch the final train to first Tarma, then Puna before settling in the hotel to discuss our next move.

As we prepared for our venture, I couldn't help but think that something terrible was about to unfold. Taking our bags to the jeep, Pedro saw Hansi approaching from the pub across the street. That guy gave me the chills and I knew that I had to investigate why Hansi, a German, was living here in Peru and took a liking to us. Perhaps it was nothing to be concerned about, but I had a funny suspicion that something about Hansi was too strange not to be dangerous.

Just as I was getting into the jeep, Hansi came over, placed an arm on top of the roof, and began asking questions, such as, "Where are you two headed?" I felt it was none of his business so I abruptly said, "Going to the countryside." Now that was the wrong thing to say because it only perked Hansi's interest. Stunningly, Hansi asked, "Mind if I come along for the ride?" I gave one look at Pedro with fearful eyes, then turned and told Hansi that we'd be gone for hours and that I had only packed enough food for Pedro and I for the rest of the day. Surprisingly, Hansi said, "Ok, I guess I'll go another time, perhaps." Thankfully the idea of Hansi coming along left me, at least for now. As Pedro and I left, I noticed from the side mirror that Hansi was watching closely and that made me quite nervous. Suppose, I thought, Hansi is suspicious of Pedro and I, and perhaps he might have some connection between the scrolls being hidden away and could even be a black market entrepreneur, trying to cheat us out of our discovery for his own financial reasons. Could Hansi even resort to murder?

With my mind racing about Hansi, I didn't realize that we had arrived at the summit of the cave. The time flew by so fast that I hadn't even thought of whether or not we would have a new discovery.

Taking a few of the bags, Pedro and I entered the cave wondering if it was safe since Pedro was trapped a couple days ago. Taking a shovel, Pedro decided to search the right side of the cave, and began to dig. I asked Pedro, "Why are you digging over there?" Pedro explained that when he was trapped, he noticed a small amount of light coming through that area. "I'm sure there's something behind all this dirt" Pedro stated. Ok, I thought, let's get cracking. Taking the other shovel, I started to dig a few feet away from Pedro. After digging for close to an hour, we managed to dig a small opening and Pedro, using his flashlight, saw what he perceived, was a treasure trove. He noticed a rather large chest deep inside the cave like chamber and also what appeared to be weapons and digging equipment. Who, he thought, could have been here before us?

Working feverishly, we began to shovel the huge amount of dirt in front of the chamber. Once we were able to crawl through, Pedro went first, then I, as our flashlights lit up the chamber. When I saw what was there, I screamed, "Oh man, have we found something beautiful and I'm sure very valuable." Cautiously walking towards the chest, I took my flashlight and aimed it straight towards it. It glistened in the light and as I approached, I saw the chest was covered in precious stones and diamonds. I yelled to Pedro, "God almighty, this thing must be very valuable, but who could have put it here and why."

By this time my nerves were on edge. I was sure that if the wrong people found out about this chamber and what it held, they'd sure want to kill us for this discovery. Strangely, the first person to come to my mind was Hansi.

As Pedro and I inspected the chest, Pedro gently broke the seal, opened the lid, and unbelievably, there was even more to unfold right before our eyes. Inside the top portion of the chest were four more scrolls, folded and sealed. The mystery of the scrolls would have to be deciphered by either Father Ligouri or perhaps Rabbi Caldero and Rabbi Berman. Pedro lightly took the scrolls out of the chest and laid them on top of a tablecloth we had packed. Looking down, we saw that there was another lid that the scrolls had hidden. Pedro was just as curious as I, but yet I was concerned about how we would get the chest and it's contents to either the monastery in Lima or the Jewish temple for further analysis.

Taking the second lid out, we discovered more precious stones and what grabbed my attention the most was a brass cup. Who could have owned the cup, used it, then stashed it into the chest for safekeeping, I wondered. Pedro insisted we leave the chest behind but take the four scrolls to town and return another time for the chest and it's valuable cargo. We certainly didn't want to have eyes watching our every move, and besides, there could be others who would be interested in what we had discovered. I remember what Madam Zara told me when she read my fortune, telling me that there was danger ahead and that we should trust nobody.

Closing the lid of the chest, Pedro placed the scrolls in his satchel, and as we left the chamber, we placed the largest stones our strength could muster, hiding as much as possible the entrance to the chamber and it's contents. On the way back to Puna, Pedro began to feel ill and collapsed unto the steering wheel. As I helped him into the passenger seat, I saw in the distance several trucks headed our way. Who are they and why are they in this deserted area? I pressed the pedal as far as possible, trying to avoid the trucks coming my way, but the jeep couldn't go fast enough to prevent being questioned or even murdered. The closer they got, the faster I drove and suddenly in the distance before me were even more trucks. I was surrounded with no escape. Realizing my predicament, I slowly came to a halt. In seconds we were surrounded by at least twenty men, rifles pointed at our heads. Now my nerves were really on edge.

While I sat there waiting for something to happen, I saw a man in a straw hat get out of the lead truck and walk over to Pedro and myself. As the sun's rays surrounded his face, it took a few seconds to see that the man was none other than Hansi. "I knew it, I just knew it," I thought. I knew Hansi was acting suspicious the other day but how is he connected to the treasure, the scrolls, and being in Peru?

As his face came into focus, I looked up and could almost read his mind. Standing before me, he uttered the words I had dreaded to hear. Hansi, peering down said, "Well, if it isn't the great Sue

Chamberlain from the New York Herald. What do we have here." I looked into his eyes and keeping a poker face said, "What do you mean. Pedro and I are just exploring the hills looking for artifacts pertaining to ancient Peruvians." I almost knew what his next statement was going to be.

With a stern face, almost reddish from anger, said, "I think you know exactly what I mean when I say what are you two up to, searching the caves of Puna." I still couldn't show any emotion, fear, or trepidation. I had to come up with a lie I was sure he would believe, but Hansi was smarter than that. Without my giving in and gaining no headway with me, Hansi replied, "I guess I'll just have to keep my eyes on you and your friend Pedro." By this time I was sure he noticed the frightened look on my face and decided to challenge me another day. As Hansi returned to his truck and had his men load up, he gave me a look I will never forget and soon I would know why.

As Hansi and his men drove off, I told Pedro, "Now we'll really have to watch ourselves. We certainly can't let Hansi know what we've discovered and perhaps kill us and steal this valuable treasure." Luckily for us, this time Hansi didn't bother searching our bags, but how long would it take before Hansi's suspicions grew to the point of ransacking my hotel room.

The whole drive back to Puna, I wondered what secrets the scrolls and chest we had discovered held for us and the world. I knew we were unto something but still I had no idea what and where it would take me.

Once I settled in my hotel room, I asked Pedro to return early tomorrow morning for the long drive to Lima to return to the Jewish temple and also pay a visit to Father Ligouri. I was very concerned about Hansi and what he could do to the both of us if he had even a small inkling to what we were up to. I could tell just by the expression on his face that he could be a huge problem and perhaps even resort to murder to get his way. As I wrapped the scroll we had retrieved from the cave and placed it back into the leather bag, I wondered what message these scrolls had and how it would affect me.

Morning came so fast I hardly had time to rest, get dressed, put on my makeup, and prepare myself for breakfast. Pedro was meeting me at a local establishment known for their sweet breakfast cakes. I can't for the life of me remember what they're called, but God are they delicious.

As Pedro and I discussed our itinerary for the day, I looked out the window and saw Hansi talking to a group of men congregating outside the local tavern. Not wanting to be seen, I took Pedro by the arm, paid our bill, and left out the side door. One thing was certain. My having this scroll on my person was dangerous, especially the fact that Hansi was suspicious and may follow us to Lima.

Once in Lima, Pedro decided that the first person we should see was Father Ligouri. I had with me one of the scrolls that was written in Latin and I was euphoric about showing the scroll to Father Ligouri. Thankfully we had a well established relationship with Father Ligouri and considered him to not only be reliable, but honest and a person that I could trust, after all, if one can't trust a priest, who can one trust.

Entering the huge foyer inside the cathedral, I began to wonder how the Latin text were coincidently related to the Jewish scrolls, but I was hopeful that soon I would have the answer. Instead, things were going to be even more bizarre than I anticipated. This was only the beginning of my journey, but somehow something told me that just as Madam Zara had predicted, danger would emerge at every turn. It would cost people their lives and put even my own family in jeopardy.

As we waited for Father Ligouri, my cell phone rang. It was my editor in New York and he informed me that I needed to return immediately to New York. Apparently there was something that concerned him and not wanting to anger, or displease him, I told him I could be back in New York in three or four days. I knew it was very important I return because I could hear it in his voice that whatever was bothering him made him sound nervous and very concerned about my safety.

As Father Ligouri showed us to his office, I asked him if he had heard anything from Rabbi Caldero. Father Ligouri said, "Funny you should ask. I learned yesterday that Rabbi Caldero was found in a back alley in a seedy part of town with his throat slashed. The culprits have yet to be caught and now the very first victim connected to this puzzle has lost their life. Who did the murder, why, and who could be next?

As we sat down, Pedro told Father Ligouri he had stumbled upon another scroll written in Latin. As Pedro handed the scroll to Father Ligouri, I asked the Father Ligouri whether Rabbi Caldero was murdered by a gang of thieves, or could he have been murdered by someone who desperately wanting these sacred scrolls, perhaps for their own profit on the black market. What Father Ligouri said next sent shivers down my spine. As he looked over the scroll, he stated that a long time ago, Nazi agents were sent searching for the scrolls and that apparently Hitler had learned about the scrolls after the Nazi's burned down the Jewish Synagogue in Warsaw,

Poland after the invasion. Father Ligouri continued saying that for at least three hundred years the scrolls were believed to have been hidden either inside the Synagogue or even perhaps underneath the building.

I asked him, "Why would Hitler want Jewish scrolls other than to destroy them?" Father Ligouri continued saying that according to the Latin scrolls, the Jewish scrolls have information that consisted not only the past, but also the future up to the end of the ages. Now it was all beginning to make sense, but Father Ligouri told me that all Pedro and I have found so far were the first of many scrolls. Hidden away long ago, perhaps by the very people associated with the prophet Abraham, thus the scrolls had mentioned his name and therefore they have been known throughout the several thousand years as the Book of Abraham. Father Ligouri said that the Book of Abraham was believed to have been accidently left out of both the Jewish Talmud and the Christian Bible. Nobody knows how, but it happened.

Continuing to read the scroll, Father Ligouri informed us that the scroll consisted of some sort of map, perhaps leading to the discovery of even more scrolls, but so far he hasn't been able to totally decipher the entire scroll.

Father Ligouri asked us if he could keep the scroll for a few more days or weeks to translate the entire document. Pedro was hesitant, but I on the other hand had enough curiosity and trust to allow Father Ligouri to keep it. I also felt that there were dangerous people who would kill to have the scrolls, one person in mind came to me and that person was Hansi. I wasn't able to connect him, but once Father Ligouri mentioned Hitler and the Nazi's, that peeked my interest.

As Pedro and I drove back to Puna, I asked Pedro if we could make a quick stop in Tarma, after all, we had to go through Tarma on the way to Puna. I had a sneaky suspicion that the town of Tarma also held some secrets. There were rolling hills around the town and I was sure we'd find something.

As we headed to the center of town, I saw Madam Zara walking briskly towards the Catholic church, and I wondered why Madam Zara was in Tarma, she always never left Puna. I told Pedro, "Hurry, I want to talk to Madam Zara." As we drove next to her, madam Zara turned her face at us and with a frightened look said, "Please, leave me alone." I got out of the jeep and began to ask her why she was so scared, but she just kept walking, and ducked into the church. I decided not to follow her even though I was concerned. I thought, "Why was she so frightened and who or what could have made her that way?"

Leaving Madam Zara, Pedro and I entered the small library a few doors away from the church. I told Pedro to look for something, perhaps a book that had information about Peru and how it was settled. Pedro went one way and I the other and after searching for half and hour I came across a book which had the title, Jewish scholars. Although my Spanish was a little rusty, I was able to take a glance at the pages as I flipped through them and at the back of the book I saw a drawing depicting Abraham and his flock of sheep. Reading over the pages, I noticed an inscription that I was unable to translate. I walked to Pedro and asked him what the words below the drawing said. As he looked at the inscription, Pedro's eyes became wide and a nervous look appeared on his face. I asked him, "What's wrong Pedro? Why do you have a frightened look just like Madam Zara?"

Taking the book from my hands, Pedro said, "Please, don't ask me any more questions about this book." Now I was really concerned. Why did this book frighten Pedro so much?" After replacing the book on the shelf, Pedro said, "Sue, let's get out of here." Running behind Pedro I yelled, "Pedro, why are you so scared?" All he would say was that the inscription gave notice to anyone searching for the lost scrolls that danger and death would follow.

After our return to Puna, I called my editor in New York and informed him that I'd be home tomorrow but that I wanted to tie a few loose ends first. I had to try to get Pedro to tell me the exact words below the inscription and drawing of Abraham and try to get information from Madam Zara before I left for home, but I wouldn't be successful. I packed my bags and left for the airport in Lima, not realizing that there was a growing threat to both Madam Zara and Pedro. Would both of them be dead before I return and what laid in store for me as well. Things were beginning to heat up and I was sure that Rabbi Caldero would be the first victim in this hunt for the secrets of the scrolls.

CHAPTER 2

As I arrived in New York, my mother telephoned me on my cell phone that my Aunt Elizabeth and Uncle Franklin had been in a serious car accident two days ago and were not expected to survive. That made my plans complicated since I was chosen to represent the family in Chicago which could delay my returning to Peru.

Having unpacked after the long taxi ride to Long Island to my parents house, I decided to return to my old high school to have a chat with my favorite teacher Mr. Harrington. He had always had faith in my abilities even when I didn't share that assumption. As I entered the hallow halls of such a fine school, I wondered whether I should reveal to him that I had discovered something that could change the course of history. I trusted Mr. Harrington, but somehow I felt that for now I should keep everything hush, at least until I wrote my article.

After I had relaxed for two days, I returned to my office at the New York Herald. My editor questioned me about why I had been gone for so long and if I was making any headway on my story. He also warned me that if I didn't come up with at least a partial outline, he would give me a rather boring assignment, and Lord knows I didn't want to be taken off this assignment.

All day I placed into my computer everything I had learned including names and places I had ventured to. The one thing that did bother me was Mansi. What was he up to and why was he so concerned about what Pedro and I were doing. I knew he didn't believe me when I told him that all we were doing was investigating the history and settlement of Peru and the towns of Tarma and Puna. There was something about Hansi that peaked my interest. Having learned of his German heritage, I decided to investigate through newspaper clippings and interviews about Hansi and his family. Why was Hansi in Peru, and what about his being nosey about what Pedro and I were doing? I would soon learn the answers to my questions which only made me shiver at the thought of what could happen to me and Pedro.

As I wrapped up at the office, my editor came up to me and asked whether I would be finished writing my story soon since he needed me for another assignment involving the military's involvement in Asia. It seems that there's the possibility that war could break out any minute. According to sources close to the military, it's believed that millions of Chinese led soldiers are massing in central China which included the North Korean's, Vietnamese, and nearly every Asian country. There were even more reports that the Indian Army was also massing troops close to Iran and Syria. I told my editor that once I wrap up my investigation I'd be more than willing to take on that task.

Having given me his approval, I then left for home, packed my bags, and headed to Chicago to see my aunt and uncle before taking the first flight possible to Peru. I really needed to get back there because I was worried that something terrible could happen to Pedro and I sure wanted to return to the caves to hopefully discover more scrolls and to take the chest out of it's hiding place and checking all the precious stones inside. I wondered why a chest laden with precious stones such as diamonds, rubies, sapphires, and garnets was hidden in a cave in Peru. Who put it there, how, and why I pondered.

Six days later and I'm back in Lima, taking time to spend a day or two in the city, meeting with Rabbi Berman as well as having a visit with Father Ligouri. I knew it would be a day or two before Pedro came to town so I unpacked my bags, had dinner, and left to see Father Ligouri before seeing the rabbi.

Father Ligouri was happy to see me and he had a glowing look on his face which made me wonder what he had to say. I knew just by looking at him that he had good news to report, but what he'd say next startled me a bit. Sitting in his massive office, I watched as Father Ligouri went to his safe, opened it, and retrieved the two scrolls that I left in his possession before leaving for New York. As he sat behind his desk, he said, "You'll never guess what I learned just from these two scrolls." Now my interest was peaked. Laying out the first scroll, Father Ligouri interpreted the writings. He stated, "According to this scroll, it was written around 576 B.C. It was mentioning that the Christ was to appear within a few hundred years and that he would be crucified, then rise again. It read like a historical novel. One question I had was if he could tell who could have written the scroll. Although he wasn't certain or even that he had the correct date, he believed that King David himself could have written the document. One thing that stood out and that was the ransacking, destroying, and the burning of the Jewish temple that yet had to be built by his successor, who incidently turned out to be King Solomon. When I told him about the chest, he became very excited. Father Ligouri felt that the chest and precious stones came from Solomon's temple during it's destruction. He felt that the Jews had retrieved as many as they could to keep for a future temple. I asked him point blank, "Are these the actual stones of King Solomon's temple or could they be from another era or something totally different?" Father Ligouri said, "I'm positive those stones came from the first or perhaps the second Jewish temple, even to the point that the well known and undiscovered arc of the covenant could have at some point in time be together. I then asked, "Could it be possible that the ark of the covenant be hidden in another cave in Peru?"

Without further investigation or proof, we may never know, he exclaimed. Good God, I thought. This could turn out to be the best discovery ever, which convinced me that there were multitudes of dangerous people wanting to get their hands on the chest, scrolls, and precious stones with the possibility of finding the ark of the covenant. This could easily become the best discovery since the dead sea scrolls were found., but perhaps danger would become something the dead sea scrolls didn't have to deal with.

The next day I returned to Saint Stevens to see Father Ligouri one last time before heading to Puna. This time, however, Pedro was with me and he seemed excited about what I had learned and even began to feel euphoria about the scrolls. I warned him though, that danger would become a factor and we could easily lose our lives. Undeterred, Pedro still was eager to learn more, no matter what the costs.

Father Ligouri took us to his office and as he closed the huge door to his office, he said, "I have very good news for you two." He had translated the second scroll and informed us that according to that scroll, there could be many more to be discovered. "Remember," he said. "These scrolls were written over many centuries, even thousands of years, so there has to be at least ten or twenty more scrolls. Question was, are they all in Peru, or could many of them be scattered throughout the world.

According to the first scroll, Father Ligouri translated the Latin text revealing that there were three scrolls buried in the land of Egypt, but where. Could they be found in the valley of the kings, or perhaps somewhere close to Cairo? I knew that now my mission was to go to Egypt and go to the main museum in Cairo to find out if the curator there could shed some light whether they had found any ancient Hebrew text buried in the valley of the kings or some other archeological digs Father Ligouri said, "These are perhaps only a small portion of text compared to what has yet to be discovered, but apparently they do have a connection to the scrolls bearing Hebrew text." The one question Father Ligouri had, as well as I, was how did these various texts make their way from the middle east to South America or elsewhere in the America's.

Leaving Father Ligouri, Pedro and I walked the streets of Lima making our way to the synagogue to see Rabbi Berman and whether he has more information for us regarding the scrolls I left with Rabbi Caldero before leaving for the states. Rabbi Berman had some degree of experience with ancient Hebrew, but Rabbi Caldero was the who had mastered the language.

As Pedro and I walked up to the door, I noticed a speeding car approaching and noticed three men, guns drawn, coming up fast. Pushing Pedro through the door, I slammed the door shut just as bullets were scattering outside. Now I was scared. Who were those men and further more how much did they know about what Pedro and I had discovered. Someone wanted us dead and grab the scrolls for whatever reason. Rabbi Berman, who had heard the gunfire, ran into the foyer asking what was going on. I said, "Rabbi, I think someone wants us dead, especially since Rabbi Caldero's body was found in a seedy part of town with his throat cut." Rabbi Berman replied, "There seems to be a group of anti-Semites in Lima who have been harassing his flock. He knew that there were many old time Nazi's living in Peru who escaped from Germany after the war. After hearing that I knew I had to investigate my adversary, Hansi.

Once safely inside, the three of us sat down as Rabbi Berman brought out the three scrolls we gave Rabbi Caldero. He said that after studying the scrolls, he discovered something very disturbing. He did say one thing and that was what he read between the lines. "First off, he said." "The first scroll mentions the historical readings of the first five books of the bible which comprise of the Hebrew texts of modern Israel. It mentions the great flood, Adam and Eve, and all the important dates right up to the time of Abraham, thus being known as the Book of Abraham." After translating the second and third scrolls, he mentioned it covered the time line of King David straight up to the beginning of the Roman Empire.

Opening the third scroll, he pointed to a paragraph that he said mentioned that a great man would soon come and he would enlighten the world. It basically had some of the writings of not only Abraham, but mentioned with pinpoint accuracy Jacob and Joseph, Moses, the falling of the walls of Jericho, Ezekiel, King David, Solomon, Daniel, and many more old testament prophets. They all had one thing in common and that was the texts were an outline of history both present and future, yet possibly having been written by Abraham himself. As for the a prediction possibly about Jesus, he says that it would happen when the seven hills dominate the world which is precisely the city of Rome. Knowing that Rome was built on the seven hills, I asked Rabbi Berman whether or not the fourth, fifth, or many have yet to be discovered in Rome.

Rabbi Berman said, "We know from history that Saint Peter had gone to Rome and was crucified, and that the Apostle Paul could also have taken some scrolls out of Jerusalem and Judea." During the Roman occupation of Israel, it was known that the Roman Emperor Tiberius had sent a special squad of men to seek out the scrolls that had been heard about by many Roman scholars throughout the ages. Emperor Tiberius knew that whoever possessed the scrolls would know the future and would have places, dates, and times of future events. Although the Romans never believed in the Jewish God or believed Jewish writings, they did however feel they had some sort of covenant with their God, perhaps giving credence.

Rabbi Berman ended our meeting by saying, "I suggest you go to Rome to find out if any other scrolls could be there or perhaps even the route from Israel to Rome bordering the coastal towns along the way." We shook hands and as Pedro and I departed, we discussed to ourselves whether to dig further in the caves of Puna, or should I fly to Rome to investigate the possibility of other scrolls having been found. One thing the rabbi said and that was it is possible that the scrolls, or Book of Abraham, were never meant to be together at one place so as to confuse anyone who may have discovered a scroll or two, mush like Pedro and I had done. Without all the scrolls together, it was virtually impossible to connect the dots, so to speak, and come up with a definitive answer.

After returning to my hotel room, I packed my bags, purchased a plane ticket from Lima to Rome via New York, while Pedro remained behind to search the caves himself to hopefully discover even more wonders. I didn't like leaving Pedro behind, especially with Hansi on the loose, but getting to Rome took precedence, and I had to take my chances. Although I did have apprehension, Pedro said, "Don't worry Sue. I'll be alright." All the drive to the airport I was consumed with fear, wondering whether Pedro would be safe, and if Hansi would follow Pedro and steal the chest containing the precious stones.

After a long journey, I finally arrived in Rome. Rabbi Berman gave me the address and name of the head rabbi in Rome so at least if I discovered anything, he would be able to help me. After unpacking I began to stroll throughout the city, first taking in the Roman Forum, then the Colosseum, then grabbing a quick bite.

After searching for several minutes, I came across the main synagogue. As I entered the sanctuary, I saw on a shelf a very large Jewish Talmud. Scanning in amazement, I couldn't help but think that perhaps someday this very book will be found by somebody researching our era. After a minute had passed, I rang the bell, notifying the rabbi that I was there. As the large door opened, in came the rabbi. He had a full beard, a Jewish prayer shawl, and a happy look on his face. He introduced himself first by saying, "I'm Rabbi Halfer, chief rabbi of Rome. How may I help you young lady?" I introduced myself then asked if we could have a discussion in private. "Certainly," he replied. Showing me to his private office, he sat behind a huge desk and waiting for him to sit down, I showed a sign of respect. I began our discussion by telling him that weeks ago I was asked by Pedro to come to Peru. He showed me a scroll he had discovered in the caves outside of Puna. Telling him about Rabbi Caldero's interpretation, I asked Rabbi Halfer if he could shed some light on why and how these scrolls we discovered ended up in Peru.

Rabbi Halfer started by telling me that centuries ago, perhaps as far back as the second century, it was a known fact that from the time of Abraham to the first century scrolls were found outside of Jerusalem. Fearing the Romans would find them, the apostles of Christ and many other loyal followers each took several scrolls and hid them away at various locations. Ten scrolls made their way to the America's, then in Europe, Asia, and even inside what is presently known as Iraq. Each are would contain ten scrolls, which according to legend was God's words to Abraham when he told him he would be the father of many nations. It was even rumored that the Ark of the Covenant had been spirited away from Judea, but there was never any record of where and if it made it's way out of Judea.

Rabbi Halfer stated that during World War 2, Hitler had heard of the scrolls and their connection to the ark and even had a special team of loyal Nazi's sent on a mission to find them. There's even a possibility that several could have been left behind in Egypt as the Jews were leaving Egypt and heading to the promised land. Hitler felt that if he obtained the scrolls, he would know the future and could arrange his battles according to what may be contained in the scrolls. Naturally, and thankfully, Hitler never found the scrolls, but it is certain that there are still Nazi agents around the world searching for the scrolls and having a blueprint of sorts to start the Fourth Reich.

I explained what I have been able to find out. The first five scrolls I discovered contained chronological information from the time of Abraham to the around 360 B.C. I did say that one mentioned King David, as well as Daniel, who according to the Christian Bible also predicted certain events.

Rabbi Halfer told me, "I must say there are at least another perhaps forty scrolls yet to be discovered, but since they could be anywhere throughout the world, the odds of finding all the scrolls is slim to none. That statement only made me think that if I managed to find all the scrolls, I would have found a form of the Holy Grail. It could even give clues to where the Ark of the covenant could be found, but Rabbi Halfer stated that is was rumored during the Second Crusade, a group of Knights found the ark, boxed it in a cedar container, and sent it either to Europe or even the area known as Scandinavia. I said, "But wouldn't it perhaps been discovered by the Vikings?" Rabbi Halfer went on to say, "If the Knights were cautious enough and kept the placement a well kept secret, it possibly was hidden so well that after those who had hidden it could have been murdered to keep the secret from ever being discovered. It's even possible the Knights Templar could even be responsible for the secret."

Knowing what Rabbi Halfer told me, I excused myself and returned to my hotel, and called Pedro to inform him that I had learned so much here in Rome and that I'd return to Peru in Five days to continue the search there, but first, I had to take the tour of the Roman catacombs. Perhaps they would also hold the mystery of the scrolls, I thought.

As the tour guide began to inform the tourists that the catacombs had actually started even before the Christian era, most of the tombs were those of the early Christians that were persecuted by the Roman authorities. I thought perhaps hidden somewhere in this underground chamber there could be a scroll or two hidden away so secretive that nobody was ever the wiser that they were there. The question was, how would I be able to retrieve such a thing even if I discovered the scrolls. I was sure that the local authorities wouldn't take kindly to my snooping around and disturbing the catacombs to search for the elusive scrolls that I couldn't prove existed underground.

As we started to finish the tour, I glanced around while the tour guide began his final moment and noticed something that appeared to be an engraving. Secretly walking toward the spot, I noticed in early script what appeared to be the tomb of a man, possibly with a connection to the Palestine area around the time of Christ, but I wasn't absolutely sure. I didn't want to ask the guide for fear I might cause suspicion about my true intentions, so I grabbed my camera, focused on the inscription, and took the picture. Once the camera flashed, the tour guide came running up and began to yell at me for taking a picture. He screamed in broken English, "I told everyone before the tour began that nobody could take any pictures because the lights from the camera could impact the survival of the walls. Remember, these walls haven't had any other light except the oil lamps which I had brought with me."

Although I had taken the picture illegally, the tour guide never asked that I delete the photo which surprised me. Usually when someone takes an illegal photograph, it must either be deleted or the film is confiscated. Luckily I had a very mild mannered tour guide.

Returning to my hotel room, I took the picture out of my purse, and began to study the photo, hoping to discover a clue that might lead to another discovery. The script appeared to either be someone's name or perhaps a Latin phrase I couldn't understand. I decided rather than risk arrest and show someone at the Vatican the photograph, I would show Father Ligouri when I return to Peru in a few days.

My last day in Rome was spent at the library inside the Vatican. I literally went through volumes of books, trying to see if any of them had photographs matching the script on the casing on the tomb. I also was wishing that the Latin writings would give me the clues necessary for further research, but I didn't read Latin, so the next best thing was to copy the text below a drawing of what appeared to look like the inscription and drawing of the tomb inside the catacombs. Seven hours later I'd be on the flight back to the states and returning to my office at the Herald to write everything into my computer at work, and catch up on some needed rest.

Today is the fifth day of January and I'm prepared to return to Peru to help Pedro continue our search for more scrolls and to determine what to do about the precious stones we found deep inside the first cave. I still had several days before I had to return to the states to get my orders from my editor regarding the meeting between President Joseph McNair and the President of the World Federation Council, Adrian. From what I had gathered it was to be a historical event. President McNair and Adrian have had their differences for about five to six years and this joint meeting was meant to repair relations between the two entities. The United States never signed a security pact with the W.F.C. but now it seems that's what's about to take place.

Upon my arrival in Peru, I learned that Father Ligouri had come down with a mysterious illness, forcing him to be hospitalized, and unable to continue his duties. From what I gathered it could be two or three weeks before Father Ligouri could return to work and that put a damper on Pedro and my determination to have more scrolls written in Latin translated by Father Ligouri should there be further discoveries made.

After checking in at the hotel in Lima, I had plenty of time to go see Rabbi Berman. Perhaps he had finished translating the second and third scrolls. I was anxious to learn more especially since the late Rabbi Caldero had translated the first scroll revealing the historical significance of the scrolls. The first scroll started with the first pages of the Book of Abraham, but it ended with the period of time concerning Jacob and Joseph. Although Rabbi Berman informed us that the first few pages of the second scroll began where the first left off, we now know that the Book of Abraham consisted of what God had supposedly revealed to Abraham. It was God's blueprint of time from Genesis through perhaps Revelation. If that's the case, there's a long way to go and many more scrolls yet to be discovered.

As I entered the Synagogue, I rang the bellpull to let Rabbi Berman know I was there. As I waited, I looked over the huge paintings portraying the first five books of the Talmud. They were very beautiful and I'd later learn that they had been spirited out of Poland when the Nazi's invaded the country, barely making it out of Warsaw without being discovered. I imagine that by sending these paintings out of Europe and hiding them here, it would prevent the Nazi's from getting their hands on them and perhaps even setting them ablaze.

In the quietness of the hall, I still didn't realize that Rabbi Berman was standing next to me until he scared me with the words, "Aren't they beautiful child." With a blushed face I nodded my head in agreement and the two of us went into Rabbi Berman's office so I could find out if he learned anything since me departure. "Yes," he said. He started out with the words I wanted to hear and they were, "Sue, you'll never believe what I have discovered from the second scroll." I listened as though I was in a college lecture hall, stunned by what Rabbi Berman was telling me. According to the second scroll, it covered the time period between Jacob and Joseph straight to the period of the Jewish flight from Egypt with Moses actually being mentioned by name, as all the others.

Rabbi Berman then said, "Sue, there must perhaps be hundreds of these scrolls hidden throughout the world." I replied, "Rabbi, are these scrolls written by Abraham himself?" As he glanced into my face, he replied, "Sue, I really believe that what you have here was actually written down by Abraham from God's own lips." I thought, my God, that means that if these scrolls were written in chronological order of time, there could be more than a few hundred, perhaps thousands even near the area where the dead sea scrolls were discovered.

After listening to Rabbi Berman for nearly three hours, I told him I'd return in a few days before returning to the states, giving him some time to read the third scroll and perhaps learn even more. I couldn't believe it myself. Imagine, having scrolls written by Abraham himself, hidden away for several millennia and Pedro and I were the lucky one's to find them, or were we lucky. I knew there was danger involved, but still the excitement surrounded me and I began to see myself in front of all the camera's of the worlds newspapers and television stations showing Pedro and I with our discoveries. As I waited in my hotel room, I decided to go to the hospital to see Father Ligouri and give him my prayers, but first I'm going to wait for Pedro, he'd love to see the priest, I'm sure.

When I finally saw Pedro, he was flushed with utter excitement. "Sue," he said. "You'll never believe what I found deep inside the cave." Now with that statement my curiosity got the best of me. "What," I replied. Pedro by this time was shaking with excitement and said, "I've discovered more scrolls and not just that, but yet another chest filled with treasures of gold and silver." I must admit that it was at this time I was beginning to shake.

Once I arrived in Puna, I placed my baggage in my hotel room, loaded up the jeep with some supplies including food, and Pedro drove us to the cave where he had discovered a treasure of gold and silver bars. Although I was apprehensive about going so deep inside the cave, I decided I had to see for myself what Pedro had discovered during my absence. As Pedro lifted the lid of the chest, my eyes grew wide, having never in my life seen so much gold and silver. I said to Pedro, "How on God's green earth are we going to take all this gold and silver away without needing some sort of lift?" Pedro suggested we take only a small amount of gold and silver bars to have them evaluated as to their value. I also wondered how safe it will be should Hansi or anyone else should find out our discovery and could kill us to get the treasure in their hands. I was sure that what we had here could be worth several million dollars worth of treasure and that thought made me nervous. I was more concerned about our safety rather than the value of this discovery.

Pedro took a few bars of gold and silver, placed them inside his knapsack, closed the lid, and started to investigate the cave even farther than before. After about a half hour had passed, we came to the back of the cave without finding any more treasure. I asked Pedro, "How are we going to hide this chest and scrolls to prevent anyone from finding them?" Pedro suggested that we return to Puna first, then return in a few days to temporarily close the cave with debris from the outside. There were mounds of dirt everywhere around the entrance and it could be used to seal off the cave for the time being, at least until we can retrieve the remaining treasure.

On our return trip to Puna, in the distance I could see what appeared to be a convoy of trucks headed our way. I thought, "Were they just military vehicles on their way to Parma, or are they trouble headed our way. It became clear once they were within several hundred yards that it was trouble. Inside the lead truck I could make out the identity of a man. It was none other than Hansi himself. Now I was sure Hansi knew what we were up to and was going to steal the loot to sell on the black market. Coming to a halt, Pedro and I waited for the trucks to come within range. As we waited, the convoy came to a halt, and out came Hansi. This time Hansi was dressed in the clothing of an archeologist rather than a businessman.

Standing before us, Hansi said, "Well, my friends. What have we here?" By this time I was beginning to fear for our lives. If Hansi was to discover what we were doing and what we found, I'm sure our lives wouldn't be worth a plug nickel, especially if Hansi decided to take us back to Puna, place us inside some sort of prison and torture us into revealing what we had found.

Hansi, standing firm, said, "Pedro, Sue, I know what you're up to. You see I had a rather interesting discussion with your Jewish rabbi. After some persuasion, he told me you two had discovered some treasures." I replied, "I guess you know what we've been doing lately?" Not wanting to show his hand, Hansi replied, "Well Sue, I know that you're a very notorious journalist from New York and that you have a reputation for using your skills to get to a story, shall I say, an important news story."

I admitted that I sometimes could be in the right place at the right time, but I told Hansi that all Pedro and I were doing was digging for whatever the ancient Peruvians had left behind over the centuries. As he started to walk towards his vehicle, Hansi said, "We will see, we will see. I must caution you. I will be watching you two with the eyes of an eagle and there is nothing you will do that I will never know."

As the convoy turned and left for Puna, Pedro decided that the small amounts of gold and silver we retrieved from the chest should be taken to Lima to be evaluated by Rabbi Berman and then perhaps we could sell the bars for some extra cash to finance or discovery. I agreed telling Pedro it was too dangerous to return to Puna with the bars for fear Hansi would find them inside my hotel or wherever we hid them. Hansi, I would learn later, had a keen way of finding things out and soon I would discover who his teacher was and that caused me to tremble.

After arriving in Lima, Pedro refilled the jeep with gasoline while I decided to recount the gold and silver just to be sure it was all there.

Finally, we arrived at the Synagogue, took the bars inside Pedro's knapsack, and went inside, ringing the bellpull to call for Rabbi Berman.

Once he saw us, Rabbi Berman breathed a sigh of relief. As he walked us to his private office, the Rabbi revealed that the man named Hansi had come to the Synagogue with a few men and had begun to question him thoroughly. Apparently, Hansi has been on the trail of this treasure for many years and has started to grow impatient. He was displaying all the attributes of a desperate man. I asked Rabbi Berman, "Why do you suppose Hansi is trying to get his hands on these treasures, I'm sure he has no interest in anything pertaining to anything Jewish." All Rabbi Berman said, "If you go to the building in Lima that houses all the census records dating back hundreds of years, you may find something out about his family roots."

As I sat there, Pedro told the Rabbi, "I have something to show you." As he gently took out the first gold bar, then another, Rabbi Berman's eyes lit up. As he took the gold bars, Rabbi Berman said, "Where did you find these gold bars?" Pedro began to tell him about the chest, loaded with these bars, and as he told him about the chest, Pedro took out the few bars of silver and showed them to the Rabbi. As he held the gold and silver bars, Rabbi Berman noticed some Hebrew text on the one side. Reading it, he stated that all the text said was, "According to the wishes of God." "What," I said, "do you suppose that means?" Rabbi Berman believes that it is some type of tithes to God and that Jewish temples around the world had always possessed treasures that they believed belonged to God and that each time there was a Jewish festival or even something as meaningful as a circumcision, when one silver bar would be donated to the Synagogue, they would be collected and be used for the operating costs of the Synagogue.

I replied, "Then what we have here is actually some sort of tax or tithe." Rabbi Berman replied, "You have found a treasure belonging to God, handed down from each generation during the centuries." Now I knew perhaps why Hansi desired these treasures, but I had to learn more about Hansi and how he is connected to the treasure. After our discussion I knew Pedro and I could never sell the bars of gold and silver and would certainly have to have Rabbi Berman decide what to do with them. I decided to leave the few bars we had with Rabbi Berman and head back to Puna to discuss our next move, but not before heading to the census office to check on Hansi and his family.

While I investigated Hansi, Pedro left to go to the hospital to meet with Father Ligouri. The first department I went to was the department of census records. As I poured through the records, it took about two hours of searching to come across Hansi's name. It seems that Hansi has been in Peru for nearly three years and that he entered Peru from Argentina. His last name is Becker and according to the records, his father moved to Argentina shortly after the second world war. Despite the record, it never mentioned anything worthwhile about Hansi other than his arrival from Argentina. Although he had a birth record from Argentine, he listed an address at 1439 Bolivar Street. That's where my next move would take me. Perhaps that address would bear fruit about Hansi and his family.

As I closed the books, Pedro came in the room. I told Pedro we have to go to 1439 Bolivar Street, that's the place where we might find out more information concerning Hansi.Pedro, enthusiastic as usual, drove us to the address listed. It was an unassuming place. It was surrounded by a thick, stone wall, with massive gates at the entrance. While Pedro waited, I walked over to the gate and rang the bell. After a minute had passed, a woman's voice asked who was here. I told her my name and that I was a journalist from the New York Herald doing a story about German immigrants. She told me that she was only the maid and that nobody was home. I asked her about Hansi and without warning, she hung up and refused to answer any questions. Now, my interest has peaked. Why wouldn't the woman answer any questions and why did she sound apprehensive? Not wanting to arouse suspicion or having the police get involved, I had Pedro drive me back to my hotel, grab my suitcases, and off we went, returning to Puna.

As Pedro and I ate our dinner, a car approached, and three men got out. They walked to our table and introduced themselves as the

Peruvian State Police. Although they were dressed in plainclothes, I was beginning to get nervous. Had the lady on Bolivar Street notify to government about my questions, I thought. The lead officer, Officer Alejandro, asked us to get in his car. I asked if we were under arrest and all he would say was that questions had to be asked and the only place to ask was at the station. Pedro began to become belligerent, causing Alejandro to become aggressive. Grabbing Pedro by the arms and shoulders, the other officers dragged him to the car and roughly threw him in. I, on the other hand, decided to go along quietly since I didn't want to display any fear or apprehension.

Once inside the station, we were escorted to interrogation room number five. After about an hour had passed, Officer Alejandro ordered Pedro out of the room and took him perhaps to another room to be interrogated. As I sat alone, I wondered if this situation had any connection to Hansi. I knew he could have had a few connections in town, but was he really up to what Pedro and I were doing, I wondered.

As I sat trembling, the door opened and there stood Officer Alejandro. He appeared angry, almost red faced. As he walked over to me, he said, "Well now dear lady. What can you tell me about Pedro and what you two are doing in my sector?" I wasn't sure about how much he knew so I played dumb and all I told him was that I was a journalist from the states doing a story about Peruvian history. "Now, you know I don't believe you, do you?" Still keeping my cover I told him over and over what I was doing in Peru and only my name and my editors. I asked him to call the states to find out the truth, but he was absolute in his suspicions.

Leaving the room, he returned to interrogation room four, that's where I learned Pedro has been for the last three hours. Suddenly all of a sudden I heard heart pounding screams wailing throughout the station. Were they torturing Pedro or was someone else being questioned?

One hour later, Alejandro returned and said, "You may go, but I'm holding on to your friend Pedro. I think he has a wealth of information to tell me." I was flabbergasted. While hold onto Pedro if he never found anything out about our relationship. I didn't like the idea of leaving Pedro behind but I had no choice and besides, I had to return to the caves to check on our discovery. I only had two days left before returning to New York to cover the story about President McNair and President Adrian. I didn't want to pass up what I was sure would be a very important assignment that my editor wanted me to cover.

Upon entering the cave, I noticed that there was a disturbance near the rear of the cave. Apparently, somebody was here and wanted to find what Pedro and I had hidden, but although they were very close to finding the chamber and the chest, they gave up and left things as they were. That is the clue I needed to know that what Pedro and I were doing was causing someone to become nervous and could murder the two of us to get to the treasure.

Once I had finished my business inside the cave, I decided to return to Puna and hopefully discover the fate of my friend Pedro. I think I'm beginning to fall in love with him; I really enjoy each other's company and I'd like to take our relationship one step further, perhaps even sexual. I never dreamed that when I first met Pedro, things would develop so fast. I am sure he may have the same feelings for me, but I better not rush things and focus on our work.

After having my afternoon dinner, I went to the police station to see how Pedro was doing. Behind his huge desk sat Alejandro, beaming with consternation. Slowly I walked toward him and when he saw me he said, "Ms. Chamberlain. Funny you should be here. Please sit down, I want to ask you a few questions that need verification, then perhaps I'll let you see Pedro." I didn't know what to make of it. What kind of questions did he have and how were they related to our business?

As I sat in front of him, the first question Alejandro asked was, "How much do you know about the man named Hansi?" I was flabbergasted. How could I tell him anything; I hardly knew the man. Fearing his question was a trap, I answered, "I hardly know him even though I must admit he's been following me and Pedro for some time now." It was then that his next question floored me. Alejandro asked, "Why were you in Lima and who did you see?" All I could say was that I was in Lima to see a sick friend, namely Father Ligouri. I could see in his eyes he wasn't buying my response, then his next question absolutely gave me a measure of panic. "Why were you in the Office of Records in Lima pouring over the census papers?" Now, I was really scared. Trying my best to keep my composure I related that all I was looking for was to find out if an old family friend had moved to Peru from Argentina. I could almost see in his eyes that he didn't believe me, but what choice did he have, he had to accept my answer because he couldn't prove otherwise.

I then asked him if I could see Pedro. As he grumbled, he told me that he would release Pedro provided that I never return to the Office of Records in Lima. Having made that statement caused me to become very suspicious. What is going on here and why am I being tailed by Hansi? As I had no choice but to say yes, he left the room and about a half hour later, in walked Pedro, appearing badly beaten. His two eyes were swollen, his neck appeared to have been chaffed, perhaps by a rope, and he stuttered his words. Hugging him, I took Pedro by the hand and left the station before Alejandro changed his mind.

Once I had returned to my hotel room, I laid Pedro on the bed, took his shirt off, and placed cold compresses on his eyes. I then asked him why he looked the way he did, but all he would say was, "I think they're onto us." I had to leave in two days but leaving Pedro in this condition seemed out of the question. I then remembered that Pedro had family near the town of Tarma. Perhaps he could convalesce there while I return to New York to prepare for my trip to Washington, D.C. to cover the event at the White House with President McNair and President Adrian.

Placing Pedro in the jeep I drove the short distance between Puna and Tarma. I remembered that Pedro had an aunt who lived at 776 Claymont Street. That's where I thought he'd be safe, rest, and wait for my return. Once I found the place, I rang the bell, introduced myself, and told her that Pedro was in the jeep and needed some rest while I'm in the states. His aunt was tickled pink over the idea of taking care of him. She always was fond of Pedro, as Pedro always told me, and she grabbed one arm and I the other, and placed him in the guest bedroom. Thanking her, I told her I'd most likely be back within a week. I paid her enough money to take care of him and although she didn't want to take it, I insisted. Now that this situation was taken care of, I could return to the hotel, pack my bags and catch the next flight from Lima to New York.

During the flight I wondered what awaited me once I returned to Peru. Would Pedro be able to continue our adventure, and what about Father Ligouri and Rabbi Berman. Would they be safe during my absence? Only a short time will tell.

CHAPTER 3

My first day back in the states made me feel good in some way, yet I missed the company of Pedro and wanted desperately to return to Puna and the caves outside town. I knew I had stumbled on the story of a lifetime, but for now my editor wanted me home to cover this historic meeting. It was no secret that President McNair and Adrian had many differences, but perhaps the world will be a better place once the nations of the world are united. Although the World Federation Council had succeeded where the United Nations had failed, there was still a lot of work to be done. There were still civil wars in Africa and there were rumors going around that the Asiatic countries were banding together as a United Front against the World Federation Council and the mistrust between Asia and the leadership of Adrian.

Having arrived at my apartment, I unpacked, took a hot bath, and spent the rest of the evening watching t.v. and gossiping on the phone with all my friends. My best friend, Joyce, was so excited to hear my voice I thought she'd have a heart attack. All she could do was ask me what I've been up to and all I could say was that I was on an adventure of a lifetime and when I had completed my task, she will be the first to know.

The next day I arrived at the office. I placed a call to Peru to check on the status of how Pedro was doing. According to his aunt, Pedro stayed just one night then decided to get back to work and I assume back to the caves. My main concern was what will he do should Hansi or Alejandro discover our secret. I still had many unanswered questions but somehow I knew that soon I'd be hot on the trail of even more scrolls to bed discovered, but I had no clue where this would all take me.

After two days of being with my parents and siblings, namely Joe and Mary, I packed for my trip to Washington, D.C. Two days from now would be a historic moment and I was euphoric that I was chosen for this assignment. I had always dreamed of being in the White House and being able to ask any question I pleased. I must admit that I am quite nervous, but God, what a chance to be there to cover the story. Adrian has been the leader of the World Federation Council ever since it was established seven years ago. Everybody who's anybody desired to have the privilege of having an audience with him. What I didn't know, or anybody for that matter, was soon Adrian would make an earth shattering announcement that would take away everyone's breath.

Being in Washington felt great and besides work, it also gave me an excuse to do some sightseeing. It's been years since I was here and I was so glad when my editor chose me for the job. While here, I decided to look up an old friend. His name is Alfred and he's been with a conservative newspaper for about five years. It must be that long since we last saw each other and I wanted to get the scoop on what's been happening lately.

With the meeting at the White House tomorrow evening at seven, it still gave me plenty of time to spend with Alfred and prepare for what my question to both leaders will be. When I arrived at

Alfred's apartment, he was very happy to see me. All he could utter was, "What a surprise. Sue where have you been all this time?" When I told him I was working on a story that took me to Peru he was excited. As we chatted and caught up with what's going on in each other's life, I received a call on my cell. It was Pedro, calling from Lima. I was shocked to learn that he had a close call with Alejandro, but he managed to give him the slip. All I was concerned about was his safety rather than what we've discovered.

Pedro informed me that Father Ligouri was out of the hospital but still very sick. According to Pedro, Father Ligouri will resume translating the two scrolls I entrusted to him soon and that we might have more clues to go on.

Although I spent a late evening with Alfred, I was able to rise from my slumber early in order to make my final preparations for tonight's event. I chose a very comfortable blue dress, and my favorite diamond earing's. I didn't want to be ostentatious but yet leaving the impression that I had some wealth to me.

I called my editor one last time for any instructions he may have for me and all he said was be ready at exactly six when my taxi would pick me up for the trip to the White House. I suddenly started to become nervous. I had never been to the White House before and I was afraid I'd make a fool of myself, yet I knew I could be professional and do a great job. As the taxi arrived, I suddenly developed a splitting headache. It was the kind that makes your eyes blur and cause dizziness. Yet I had no choice but to attend the festivities.

As we pulled into the driveway at the White House, I wondered what Pedro was up to. He had told me he was returning to the cave a few miles from Puna, and although I knew Pedro could handle himself, I still felt uneasy, perhaps something was going on. Was it just my imagination, or was it intuition. As I took my seat, I remembered that Hansi had threatened us and would stop at nothing to rob us of the treasure and the remaining scrolls. For now though, I had to focus on this meeting and the question I would pose for both leaders.

As I was seated, a severe thunderstorm presented itself. At this time of year it is unheard of to have such a severe storm and it dawned on me what my astrologer once told me. Whenever there is a severe thunderstorm, it's usually followed by something terrible. Would it happen to me, Pedro, or perhaps this meeting between the leaders would be an omen?

Finally, the meeting has started and as other journalists were asking their questions, I decided what I would ask. As I raised my hand, I began to feel sick to my stomach. I'm usually calm and cool whenever presented with anticipation, but this was something that for me was a once in a lifetime opportunity. Once the President pointed to me, I stood up, and asked my greatest concern. "Mister President, will you and Adrian sign the pact that could guarantee the Israeli's a lasting peace?" The President's response was, "I hope that now we can put our differences aside and move forward towards a lasting peace for the world and prevent conflicts from surfacing." Wow, I did it. Unbelievable it may seem that I actually had the chance to ask a question. I was so overwhelmed that I hardly heard the rest of the questions.

Once the meeting was over, I left the conference room, approached my taxi, and returned to my apartment. Just as I entered, the phone rang. It was my editor, and having watched the t.v. had called to congratulate me for asking a great question and keeping myself cool despite the pressure. I told him that as much as I enjoyed the opportunity to meet the President and Adrian, I must admit that I really didn't think I was cut out to be a White House journalist. My main goal was to return to Peru and continue the quest for the remaining scrolls.

For the next few days I caught up on preparing my article about the scrolls. As I wrote down everything that has developed thus far, the phone rang. It was Pedro and he had great news. It concerned the second scroll. According to Rabbi Berman, there could be another two or three scrolls somewhere in Rome, but where. The second scroll caught his attention because it gave a sort of clue, or roadmap, of where the additional scrolls could be found.

The Rabbi informed Pedro to have me check out an area near the Roman Forum, then another fifty feet from the main entrance to the catacombs. Somewhere between those two area's was buried two more scrolls. The problem was whether they were close to the forum or underground, inside the vast network of tunnels containing the catacombs.

Hanging up the phone, I gathered my belongings and headed for my apartment. I had some packing to do, call the airlines, make a reservation for the next available flight to Rome, and check in. Having my boarding pass in hand, I checked in my bags, went through the checkpoint, and boarded the plane. It would be along flight, and with laptop on hand, I'd at least be able to get some valuable work done. As we cruised along, I grew tired and drifted to sleep, having achieved part of my goal

Once in Rome, I went to the hotel and called Pedro to let him know that I had arrived. Luckily I did call since Pedro had something to tell me about Hansi. Apparently Hansi's grandfather had gone through Rome after the war on his way to Argentina. Pedro wanted me to check with the immigration authorities in Rome to see if they had any records about Hansi's grandfather. Did he go through here legally, or was he swept out of Europe through the underground network setup before the end of the war to help Nazi officials escape from justice. It seemed to Pedro that Hansi's grandfather had been stationed in Rome during the final Allied push through Italy towards the end of Nazi rule. Having told Pedro I'd check things out, I left for the catacombs to see if I could discover anything related to the scrolls, then perhaps I'd check the area of the Roman Forum. I was certain that the forum wasn't going to yield too much information and that if there were any more scrolls to be found here in Rome, the best chance for success would be to go underground, inside the darkened catacombs, perhaps in an area off limits to the public.

Deciding to use a tour guide, I entered with about twenty other people and once inside and down below, I peered the entire area, then asked the guide, "What's down that long, narrow tunnel?" All he would say was that it was off limits and that it's been decades since anyone's been down there. That was all I had to hear to feel that area was where I'd start my investigation. I did have one connection here in Rome. That person was Beniamino, or as in English, Benjamin. I always called him Benny even though he disliked being called that, but since we were sort of close friends, he didn't mind.

Once I left the catacombs, I returned to my hotel and called Benny. His voice mail came on so I left him my number and asked him to call me as soon as he gets my message. I really wanted to go back to the catacombs if not alone, with Benny.If anybody knew the catacombs it would be Benny. He had always had a fascination with the period of the Roman Empire and how the catacombs began to be constructed. I will say one thing and that is it was very weird to be that far underground and be surrounded with the tombs of various origins. There must be hundreds if not thousands of still undiscovered tombs and a vast network of underground chambers.

The next day Benny finally called me and explained that he had come across some great information he had retrieved from the library in the Vatican. Benny had the right connections with people that really mattered. They were not just Cardinals, but Bishops and a handful of Priests. Benny suggested we meet for lunch at his favorite restaurant, believe it or not, but it had great Italian food, not like the Italians eat but rather the Americanized versions. Suits me fine, I thought. For the next few hours I passed my time away inserting what information I had into my computer. I knew that once I had finished my investigation for this story, it would literally be volumes of information and would probably become one of the longest articles I've ever written. One thing was certain, and that was the fact that this investigation would send me to Jerusalem and a date with destiny that I'd never dream possible.

As I walked the streets of Rome making my way to meet Benny, I took in as much of the sights as possible and was amazed at how this city functioned. It was a world renown tourist destination, people from all over the world made their journey here for whatever reason they had. Some were here as tourists, but many had also come to Rome to conduct business, much as I have.

As I approached the restaurant, Benny was standing outside smoking a cigarette which was common for him. I always tried to beg him to quit but Benny was very addicted and it seems nothing or nobody could convince him otherwise.

Entering the establishment, I noticed that for a very small place, it had numerous fresco's painted on the walls. Benny told me that after the second world war ended, American soldiers had learned of this place and they mostly paid a local artists to paint the walls so they could take pictures to show the people back home. If it wasn't for the fact that this place wasn't the Vatican, I'd swear that Michelangelo himself could have painted them, that's how professional they appeared.

As we ate our meal, Benny bended over, retrieved his case, and rummaged through it. After a minute, Benny pulled out a short stack of papers. He had made copies, illegally of course, from a book, tucked away in the rear crevice of the room. He said that the book had a date of 1159 A.D. It was hand written and gave many clues about the Book of Abraham and how it's been missing for thousands of years, however, it did contain valuable information that Benny thought would interest and help me in my pursuit of finding more ancient scrolls.

According to the book, there were several scrolls buried under the city, believed to be inside the catacombs and it even gave a sort of clue. I asked Benny, "If this book had clues written down, why hasn't anybody else search for them in the catacombs?" Benny corrected me and said, "Yes, people had searched centuries ago but the area they were searching had caved in, preventing anyone from continuing the search. However, I think I know exactly where the scrolls could be hidden." As I listened, I was starting to get excited, almost to the point of yelling out my joy for the whole world to hear, but I recovered myself, and kept the secret intact.

With such exuberance I asked Benny when we could go to the catacombs to begin our search. That's when my hopes were dashed a bit. Benny said, "We can't go under the city yet. They're still open for another three days before being closed to the public for a couple months while the streets above are repaired." According to Benny, the Mayor of Rome ordered the catacombs closed to prevent anyone getting injured while the repairmen drill the pavement. I guess they were worried about a potential cave in so that would be the only opportunity to go underground to investigate the possible location of any scrolls that could be buried there. Although even I was worried about becoming trapped underground, I still had the courage to try anyway, despite any danger.

Five days later, Benny and I met each other just outside the Vatican. This was now a do or die situation and I was very anxious to enter the catacombs and hopefully retrieve some scrolls. Leading me to his secret entrance, Benny removed the wooden logs that hid the entrance, then we slowly entered the cave like area that slowly took us down, way down below to some of the deepest crevices of the catacombs. We were so deep that we had actually went passed the lit area's and began our decent into the darkness below. Having miner's caps, we both held each other's hand and continued downward until we finally came to an area that Benny was sure nobody has been to since the catacombs opened, many centuries ago. It was dark, dangerous, and smelly. Rats had taken over this entire area because it was so dark and damp. Making sure I wouldn't be bitten, I tucked my pants into my long, heavy boots. I wanted to take as many precautions as possible; I surely didn't want to catch rabies or even become entombed forever should there be a cave in. Benny and I slowly entered a chamber, off to our left. Taking his flashlight, Benny focused on a few crypts. Written in Latin and ancient Hebrew were the surnames of the people buried there. Slowly we began to walk ever more deeper until we came to another chamber. This time we hit pay dirt. I asked Benny, "How far down are we from street level?" Benny whispered, "About two hundred or so feet." "That's a lot of chambers above us," I said.

As we entered the small chamber, I focused my flashlight way in the distance. It took a few minutes to discover, but way in the back stood a small chest, much like the kind of chest Pedro and I had discovered outside of Puna, Peru. Cautiously, I made my way to the rear and the closer I got to the chest, the lower the cave became, until I was virtually on my knees, crawling towards the chest.

As I got close, I discovered that it also had the same type of seal the other chest had in Peru. That told me that whoever sealed the Peruvian chest could have also sealed this one. Bursting with excitement and anticipation, I took out my survivors knife, placing it between the chest and the lock. With all my strength I couldn't make it budge so I asked Benny to crawl over and give it a chance. The closer he got, the more claustrophobic it became. The area was so tight that we could barely move with both of us there. Taking the knife, Benny gave it a twirl, twisting the blade until finally it snapped the seal off the chest. I was so nervous and excited that I wondered to myself, dare we open it? I was shacking so bad I told Benny to open the chest. As he slowly opened the lid, the beam of light from my helmet made whatever was inside glow brightly.

With the lid fully opened, we discovered a vast wealth of gold and silver coins bearing the image of a Roman Emperor. I asked Benny, "Who do you suppose that image resembles?" As he flipped one of the gold coins between his fingers, he thought for a minute, then said, "What you have here is an image of the Roman Emperor Tiberius." God that really floored me, but my next question was, "Why do you suppose this treasure was buried here, in the catacombs?" Benny's response was that the treasure could have been hidden underground until the day came when either the Christians or the Jews could raise an army to fight the Romans but my guess is that it was most likely the Jews. Christians would never had wanted to raise an army to fight the Romans, that's for sure.

Benny believed that the coins would not only have paid an army, but could also have been used to purchase food and supplies. As he began to remove some coins, we noticed what appeared to be about two or three scrolls. Digging deeper we discovered three scrolls made of the same material as the first three. They were perhaps written during the period of 1,200B.C. to possibly around 150 B.C. I was sure they contained a wealth of information, but that would have to wait for now. As of now, the problem was what to do with the vast amount of gold and silver coins. I said, "These coins must be worth millions of dollars, who could lay claim to them?" Benny didn't sugar coat his answer. "I think the Italian authorities will confiscate this treasure, however, we must be sure that nobody finds out about the scrolls, they are more valuable than any of these coins." I had to agree. Any information contained in these scrolls were not only worth a fortune money wise, but just with the amount of information written down could perhaps change the course of history.

Opening my valise, I tucked the three scrolls inside, and as we left the catacombs I instructed Benny to keep quiet for now about our discovery of the coins. Perhaps, I thought that we might be able to use them for another purpose. Once I returned to my hotel room, I thanked Benny for all his help, then closed the door and made a quick call to Pedro, who was anxiously waiting for me to call. I was very excited that I had good news to tell him, but somehow I had the feeling that he wasn't having good news to tell me.

Once I told Pedro about my discovery, he told me that the police had followed him to the caves outside of Puna and waited for him to enter inside. Once he was inside the cave for about a minute or two, the police entered the cave, making their way towards the back where they found Pedro digging a small opening. I thought to myself, "Good God, they must have discovered our little secret." As luck would have it, Pedro knew that he was being followed and started to dig on the left corner of the cave, knowing full well nothing but dirt was there. The police captain tried to threaten Pedro with arrest if he didn't come clean so Pedro made up the story about trying to discover old relics from Peru's past history and believe it or not, the police fell for his story. I was relieved because I needed to continue our search for more scrolls and perhaps more treasure. Speaking of treasure, I told Pedro about the coins Benny and I discovered. Pedro felt that we should keep the secret to ourselves until he and I see Rabbi Berman. Perhaps he would know what to do.

If the coins were hidden by the Jews during the first century, Rabbi Berman will most likely suggest that the head Rabbi in Rome should be the one to have knowledge of that treasure. If anybody would know what to do, it would be him.

Two days have passed since Benny and I left the catacombs and as I was packing my bags to return to New York, Benny came knocking at the door. I was stunned to see him, but he had bad news to tell me. Apparently somebody saw Benny and I entered the catacombs late the other night and followed us inside. The man's name was Carlino and he was very threatening. He said that unless Benny lets him take some of the treasure, he would go to the police and inform them of our discovery. Carlino knew he couldn't retrieve the entire treasure by himself, so he wanted Benny to help him steal the coins. Benny had to make a decision so he told Carlino that he would take him into the catacombs the next night and help him carry the treasure from the catacombs. I said, "Are you mad. We can't let him take any of the coins that would be shear suicide." Benny agreed, but what he said next shook me to the core. Benny's reply was, "I'll take him down there, but only one of us will come to the surface." I thought, my God Benny, are you mad to think you can murder that man and get away with it? When I pleaded with Benny to reconsider, he still thought his idea was better so all I said was, "Make sure nobody else follows you and make it quick and hide the body deep into the catacombs where nobody will find it."

As I left for the airport, all I could think about was Benny showing Carlino the treasure and perhaps Carlino had the same idea as Benny. Would Carlino kill Benny or would he need him to help carry the chest full of coins and then kill Benny. As I boarded my flight, all I could think of was about Pedro and Benny's safety. The flight home was long and exhausting and as I entered my apartment all I wanted to do was hop into a hot bath and soak. I'll deal with those issues tomorrow after a good night's sleep, something I haven't had in a long time.

Morning brought sunshine, but bitter cold. It was January and the weather was the least of my problems. As I sat at my desk at The Herald, my editor walked towards me and with the look that could kill, he began a tirade about how much time I was taking to finish my story, but I told him once again that this story was something that would make not just us an award, but also The New York Herald. His response was, "Just don't take too much more of our precious time. I expect a finished story by the end of the month." Knowing I probably couldn't guaranty that, I entered the information I acquired in Rome, then spent the rest of the day relaxing and taking in the sights and sounds of the city. Tomorrow

I'd catch a flight and return to Peru with the three scrolls I found in the catacombs, and hope that Rabbi Berman could translate them as quick as possible. I needed more information and fast. I was sure that the police and perhaps Hansi were on to us and I wanted to wrap things up before my boss takes me off the case and assigns me somewhere unpleasant.

My arrival in Peru brought me back to my childhood. The air was warm, since it is summer here, and the fresh flowers being sold in the city made the air even more refreshing. I checked into the hotel, called Pedro to inform him of my arrival, then walked the few city blocks to the city's only Synagogue. As I entered the foyer, I pulled the rope tied to a bell letting Rabbi Berman know I was here.

As he approached me, Rabbi Berman's face showed he was very happy to see me. As we walked to his private office, he informed me that he had great news.

Rabbi Berman had finished translating the second scroll and it had substantially more information than the first scroll. Whereas the first scroll contained basically the same information as the first five books of the bible, the second scroll revealed just how accurate the scrolls have been so far. The second scroll gave what is now historical fact, the names of people and places that the bible contained during the second few centuries after the first scroll. It named the prophets Daniel, Ezekial, Job, as well as King David, and many others. It did end with the name of the prophet Samuel. Rabbi Berman told me that if these two scrolls contained this much information, then perhaps the rest of the scrolls yet to be discovered would bear more information.

Rabbi Berman then told me quite excitedly, "If I'm correct, then it seems that each scroll will contain information from the beginning of time around the book of Genesis all the way through the Book of Revelation in the Christian Bible. Do you know what that means, Sue. We could actually have the message from God revealing his intentions right through the end." By this time I was beginning to become as excited as Rabbi Berman. Perhaps, I thought, the scrolls would reveal the names of very important people in various governments ruling the world in the last days, but I still needed to continue searching the caves near Puna as well as other areas around the globe as I was sure the scrolls would give clues to their location.

Having heard Rabbi Berman's assumption, I bent over the chair, retrieved my valise, and brought out the three scrolls I had discovered in the Roman catacombs. Needless to say he was dumbfounded at what I had discovered. Taking one of them, he showed me the mark bearing the Hebrew word for number three. This scroll, he said, will uncover even more information and perhaps by then we will have uncovered something that either was never meant to be discovered or that our ancestors had hidden away to protect them from evil people.

Silently I sat, waiting with anticipation for Rabbi Berman to say something about the scroll. Just as I grew impatient, Rabbi Berman translated the first paragraph. "According to this, it deals with the time period from the year 366 B.C. through the beginning of the Roman Empire, even naming Julius Caesar by name. He was sure the third scroll contained a treasure trove of information, perhaps even things never mentioned in any Holy Bible or Talmud.

I then asked him, "Why did the people throughout history keep such precise records? For what purpose, I asked. We have already read that the scrolls were the hidden Book of Abraham, but why were they hidden away so long ago? Rabbi Berman believed that perhaps the Jewish Rabbi's during the Roman Empire had them placed in the holy of holies in the Jewish Temple but that they feared the Roman's would find out they were there and that they contained information about the future that they could use for their own benefit.

I must say that I had to agree. If Hansi was interested in my discovery, I'm sure empires throughout the ages were just as interested.

The one scroll that made a believer out of me was the fourth scroll. According to Rabbi Berman, it mentioned the name of Jesus, the twelve apostles, and what their works were. The rest of the scroll had things that we knew as historical facts such as the names of Tiberius, Caligula, Nero, and many other Roman Emperors during the first century. Where the fourth scroll ended, the fifth scroll started. That scroll had very little to say except that it did mention the crucifixion of Jesus Christ, and what would become of his apostles. Without reading the entire monologue, Rabbi Berman skipped towards the end of the fifth scroll.

With bated breath he translated the text as saying that there was another scroll, hidden somewhere in Judea. Apparently whomever hid these scrolls was well aware that the previous four were hidden and that a sixth scroll was hidden by a young Jewish man named Joseph. It didn't have any other information about Joseph or the exact location of the scroll, but only that it was well hidden in Judea. I then said to Rabbi Berman, "I guess I'll be going to the land of Judea in Israel." Once I said that, Rabbi Berman was wishing he could come along, but I had to do this journey alone. Anyone with me would take the risk of someone spying on what we were up to. I was sure that even today, and in Israel also, there were unscrupulous people that would stop at nothing to steal the scrolls and perhaps murder each of us. I couldn't take the chance of putting someone else's life in jeopardy.

Closing the scrolls, Rabbi Berman thanked me for letting him see the scrolls and he was just as anxious as I was to discover the remaining scrolls, but most of all, we might learn something about our world and what to expect.

As I took the train from Lima to Puna to meet with Pedro, my mind wandered with the feeling of complete peace. No matter what happens to me, hopefully the scrolls will survive and that the Israeli's might discover what's on God's agenda for them. Perhaps the scrolls will bring peace to the world and that mankind will put away their weapons of war and lasting peace will be assured. That is what I was hoping for, but somehow I felt that once the final scroll was translated, it would only bring disaster.

As the train pulled into the station in Puna, I peered out the window and was happy to see the beautiful city, adorned with the warmth of summer. It was good to be back and I am looking forward to seeing Pedro and tell him what all I had learned while in Lima.

Unpacking once more only made me feel as if I'd never be at one spot again. If I'm not here in Peru, I'm either back in New York City or somewhere else in the world. As I prepared myself with the proper attire to investigate the caves one more time, Pedro came knocking at my door. To my amazement he was dressed in a suit. I asked him, "Why are you dressed like that? Aren't we going to the caves?" With an amusement, Pedro invited me to a gala celebration at the Jewish Synagogue in Lima. Rabbi Berman was being replaced soon with another Rabbi and it's his going away celebration and besides I was told that Rabbi Berman had some rather interesting information regarding the last two scrolls. I thought, "What could that mean?"

While I changed into a formal dress with my favorite earing's, Pedro relaxed on the sofa watching t.v. to pass the time. As I presented myself to Pedro wanting to get his reaction to my evening gown, I knew I was beginning to have a romantic connection to Pedro. He is quite handsome and has been a Godsend to me in my search for the scrolls.

Once back in Lima, it was nearly sunset and the bright neon lights of the city glared through my glasses. Lima is such a beautiful cities with everything a major city could offer. As we pulled up to the synagogue, we were surrounded by a large crowd of people, all specially chosen by the secretary to Rabbi Berman. I was dazzled to say the least. I had never been to quite an event as this one and I knew once I started making the rounds, introducing myself, I'd probably connect with someone from New York City.

As I mingled with the people, Rabbi Berman approached saying, "Follow me to my office. I have great news to share with you and bring Pedro as well, he'll want to hear what I have to say." I must admit that I was extremely anxious and started to get that feeling of butterflies in my stomach. Taking Pedro by the arm I explained that Rabbi Berman wanted us in his office immediately. Even Pedro was starting to come unwind. Entering the office, Pedro and I sat down in the huge sofa, waiting to hear what Rabbi Berman had to say.

As we sat in front of his massive desk, Rabbi Berman took one of the scrolls and began to open it. It was scroll number four and there was a ton of information inside. According to the Rabbi, scroll four contained basically the same information concerning the period from roughly 1255 B.C. through to 847 B.C. It was actually a road map of sorts about the prophet Samuel and Job, even mentioning the prophet Amos, a native of Judea who preached during the reign of Jeroboam II. The scroll mostly consisted of very little information with one exception. At the end of the scroll, it mentions there will be another five scrolls, all written in ancient Hebrew. It even went as far to say that there would be texts written in Latin, perhaps by one of the Apostles of Jesus. At the very end it gave information concerning a great man, yet to be born, who would become a great man, perhaps even going as far as to state that he would be the Messiah, the man the Jews have been waiting forever since their bondage in Egypt centuries ago.

Rabbi Berman ended saying, and this last sentence gives a vital clue to the location of perhaps two or three other scrolls. One area is near Alexandria, Egypt, then one buried in Babylon, meaning Iraq, and the third scroll perhaps somewhere in Persia, meaning I'd have to travel to Iran, a place that presented danger all of itself.

As the evening progressed and the wine was taking it's toll on my senses, I came to realize that what I had stumbled upon since Pedro made that first telephone call to me, would change me forever.

The dawn of a new day has emerged and I'm very anxious to return to the cave outside of Puna. Today, Pedro and I will load the chest of jewels into the jeep and drive to Lima to give to Rabbi Berman for safe keeping. It would be a dangerous journey I'm sure, but it was a chance we'd have to take. Once the jeep was loaded with provisions, Pedro drove the road out of town towards our destination when out of nowhere a convoy of vehicles raced towards us. It was the same type of convoy that we had engaged once before and as they drew closer, I saw through my windshield the face of none other than Hansi himself. He had his men with him and as we started to get closer, I asked Pedro whether we should make a run for it, or stop to find out what Hansi wants.

It didn't take long for Hansi to get out of his truck and run towards us. Screaming at the top of his lungs, Hansi yelled out, "Well, Miss Chamberlain, where are you going in such a hurry?" Dumbstruck, I had no idea what to say when Pedro said, "We are only going on a picnic." Hansi wasn't buying that at all. Now he was agitated and once agin asked, "Where are you two going in such a hurry? Don't try to convince me you're going on a picnic." As I sat there speechless, Pedro started to explain why, when Hansi broke in and said, "I think you two are headed for the caves far from town." Now I was really getting scared. I knew if we told him exactly where we were headed, he'd discover the chest of jewels and they'd be lost forever, and not only that, but Hansi would have no choice but to kill us, make it look like an accident, and keep the jewels for himself to perhaps sell on the black market. For such a treasure, it had the potential for bringing in millions of dollars and that was something I didn't want Hansi to have. Besides, I still had some investigating to do about why Hansi had come from Argentina to Peru and what his families background consisted of.

As I kept my silence, Hansi said, "Well, I guess you two are keeping quiet. Ok, I'll buy that excuse, but remember, I'm keeping my eyes on the both of you." Walking towards his vehicle, Hansi turned his face and had a grin. I was sure he knew what we were doing and perhaps he even suspected that we had discovered a treasure, but Pedro reminded me that if Hansi knew anything, he would have retrieved the treasure already so for now he was in the dark, but very suspicious.

As the convoy drove out of sight, Pedro decided it was too dangerous to return to the caves for now so we turned, headed back to town, and unloaded the jeep.

By late afternoon, Pedro and I were deciding what to do next so Pedro felt we should return to Lima to have a chat with Rabbi Berman about what to do next, let him know about Hansi, and perhaps have a light discussion with Father Ligouri as well.

As the conversation began with Rabbi Berman, he instructed me to go to Egypt, snoop around, and try to discover something about the next scroll. According to the third scroll, another one was placed somewhere near the valley of the kings, perhaps near one of the pyramids. It would be a very dangerous journey but somebody had to do it and I knew Pedro would stick out like a sore thumb if he went either alone or with me. Even I was beginning to feel that something bad might happen to me, yet, Pedro was in more danger than I was, having to stay in Puna where Hansi would be watching his every move.

As we approached the Catholic church, I decided to go to the library to check their records on everybody whoever lived in Peru. Perhaps they could shed more light concerning Hansi and his family.

Father Ligouri was happy to see us. He said, "It's been so long since we last chatted I almost forgot whet I wanted to tell you." I felt as though my ears had perked when Father Ligouri said that the second Latin scroll stated that the disciples of Jesus had taken the Jewish scrolls and placed them at various locations around the earth. The scroll even mentioned the name of the scrolls for being the lost Book of Abraham. Now I knew that I had to find every scroll that was written and that once they were discovered, I'd take the entire manuscript to Israel and place them in the confines of the Hebrew University for safekeeping. The one question I had was how were we going to get the chest of precious stones to Israel without having to register them with the Peruvian authorities. Father Ligouri said, "Sue, let me worry about that. You just go and find the other scrolls."

As dusk settled in the city, Pedro and I spent the night at my favorite hotel to discuss our plans for retrieving the jewels, spirit them to Lima, and get them to Israel, unnoticed. By midnight I was exhausted and slept like no other time in my life.

The time had come to check for any information concerning Hansi and his family. As Pedro and I poured over as much information as possible, it still took three hours for us to come across a document, written in German. Why was a German document laying among other documents about the people of Peru, I wondered. There must have been twenty pages of documentation so the only thing we could do was make copies and take them to Rabbi Berman for translation. Rabbi Berman spoke German as well as English and Spanish so he was perhaps the only German speaking person in all of Peru we could trust.

Taking the copies in hand, Pedro and I made our way to see Rabbi Berman. As happy as I was, I still wondered whether or not to grasp information about Hansi and his family.

Rabbi Berman was more than cordial to say the least. As we sat before him, Rabbi Berman began to translate the documents and as he read, we discovered something very disturbing. Apparently, Hansi's father was an escaped Nazi official that not only involved him with the dreaded S.S. but also the document stated that Hansi's father was with a special unit, personally ordered by Adolf Hitler to seek out the long lost scrolls that made up the Book Of Abraham. It was well known for centuries that the Book Of Abraham was actually Abraham's writings portrayed by God himself, even more valuable than the Ten Commandments or even perhaps the long lost Ark of the Covenant. The Book Of Abraham was a chronological order of world events from the time of Abraham to what many scholars believe contain names of events in the modern world. Whoever possessed the book, could potentially rule the world, that's why Hitler and the Nazi's desperately wanted to find the book and they were willing to kill for it. That's the reason Hansi has been trailing Pedro and I everywhere. I began to think that Hansi knows we have discovered at least partially the Book Of Abraham.

Hansi's father was the person in charge of the search, but thankfully, he never found the scrolls and died virtually penniless in a small village in Peru. My greatest concern was that if Hansi's father failed in his search, perhaps Hansi swore to him on his deathbed to continue the search and possibly use the scrolls to finance another Nazi government in Germany or anywhere else they could thrive. Rabbi Berman cautioned us that Hansi is very dangerous and must never have possession of any scroll, much less the entire volume. Thanking Rabbi Berman, Pedro and I left for the town of Puna. There was more searching to be done and hopefully more scrolls to be discovered.

CHAPTER 4

The time had come for Pedro and I to return to the caves outside of the town of Puna and perhaps even more danger. As drove the jeep towards the caves, suddenly Pedro saw in his rear view mirror a convoy of trucks chasing us down. I was sure it was Hansi trying to get us to reveal what we were up to, but Pedro had an idea, It seems that Pedro had discovered another site where he began an archeological dig while I was in Rome. He had only started to dig but as yet found nothing. Pedro decided to have Hansi on a wild goose chase, at least for now. Pedro was sure there could be more scrolls hidden at that site but he knew there were other objects that were believed to have been buried there a couple centuries ago. At least it would make Hansi believe that it was the place where the scrolls could be found, and hopefully we could discover another scroll or two, keep them hidden from Hansi, and leave him with empty pockets.

Once the convoy caught up with us, I saw Hansi looking through the windshield with a stern look on his face. As we all came to a stop, Hansi ran towards us, pistol drawn, and came beside me. Pointing the pistol in my face, Hansi said, "Ok, Miss Chamberlain, where are you headed and don't tell me you're going on a picnic with your friend Pedro?" Stunned, I replied, "Pedro and I are headed to a cave where he believes ancient Peruvian artifacts are buried." As he shook his head, Hansi replied, "Well, perhaps Pedro wouldn't mind if we all have a look." Pedro's hands were practically glued to the steering wheel, too upset to move or utter a word. I could tell that Hansi could feel the fear in Pedro's eyes.

I looked at Pedro and said, "Come on Pedro, let's show Hansi your discovery." Nodding yes with his head, Pedro began to slowly drive ahead with Hansi and his men behind us. As we drove, Pedro said to me, "Are you mad. Letting him follow us to where I began to dig. Suppose we find something and Hansi steals it from us?" I assured Pedro I knew what I was doing and to alleviate his fears. I wanted to have Hansi believe that we had found nothing so far and send him on his way feeling we found nothing. Hansi was a very dangerous man, but I could be just as dangerous as he.

Once at the site, Hansi said, "Ok you two, start digging. Let's just see if you found anything or not." Pedro knew there would be some Peruvian pottery and other utensils scattered about and it could be enough for Hansi to lose interest and go on his way. In my heart I believed Pedro and I could fool Hansi, but we were in for a rude awakening. Hansi wasn't easily fooled and we would find out just how cruel and desperate he'd become.

After a couple of hours had passed and nothing was found, Hansi grew impatient and began to have a tantrum just as though he was a child. He was very determined to get his hands on any scroll, just to be able to say he found something. After waiting for another hour, Hansi finally gave up on discovering anything and headed back to town with his men in tow. Now, finally Pedro and I could search for what we had come to find, question was, would we find anything pertaining to the scrolls?

As evening approached, Pedro and I finally gave up, packed our things, and headed back to Puna. I was sure we were being watched by Hansi's men so we took our backpacks out of the jeep, headed to my hotel room, and prepared for a night on the town, at least that's what I thought we'd be doing. Pedro had other idea's. He insisted we have dinner as planned, then around two or three in the morning when it was dark and very quiet, we'd return to the caves outside of Puna where the chest laden with precious stones was sitting, retrieve the chest, pack it up, then head straight for Lima to hand the chest over to Rabbi Berman. It was the only way to prevent Hansi from getting his hands on the treasure and perhaps making him think there was nothing to discover.

As dawn approached, we arrived in Lima and drove to the best hotel in the city. The chest wasn't very large but it was quite heavy since the stones made the weight of the chest heavier than it would be otherwise. Pedro grabbed the golden chest and placed it inside a cardboard box so not to have any curious eyes take note. I checked us into the hotel, grabbed my room key and went straight to the fifth floor, room 564 to be exact. It was in the rear of the building, hidden from wondering eyes. Within two hours I placed a call to the Synagogue to let Rabbi Berman know we were back, and with a surprise.

It didn't take long for the rabbi to get to the hotel; his curiosity had the best of him. Once seated, Rabbi Berman asked, "So, what have you got to show me. Perhaps another scroll?" I then silently said, "No, I have something more valuable, I think." Turning towards Pedro, I said, "Pedro, show the good Rabbi what we have for him." It was so quiet one could hear a pin drop, but once Pedro came from the bathroom holding the golden chest, Rabbi Berman's eyes lit up and he was almost speechless. Taking hold of himself, Rabbi Berman took the chest from Pedro and just sat there admiring the golden chest in his hands.

I said, "Rabbi, open the chest." Nervously taking the lid, not knowing what he was about to see, gently lifted the lid and immediately before him was the chest containing a trove of diamonds, rubies, sapphires, and many other stones, too many to mention. His favorite stone was the garnet and he was dumbfounded at first. As he spread his hands over the precious stones, all Rabbi Berman could say was, "Where in God's name did you find these?" I could tell he was very excited about our discovery but did warn us of the danger of having the chest. If anybody, much less Hansi, learns we possess the golden chest and it's valuable contents, our lives would be in grave danger so we had to act quickly to make sure the proper people get the chest. The main problem was that the place where it belonged was in Jerusalem, where it had originated from centuries ago and how would we be able to smuggle the chest out of Peru without any suspicion.

Rabbi Berman came up with a beautiful idea. He suggested that Pedro and I catch a flight out of Lima, headed to New York, then on to Israel. He would mark the crate as containing Jewish Talmud's, discovered in South America and being transferred to the antiquities department in Jerusalem. That way, nobody would question what was inside since it was Jewish custom that only a Rabbi had the authority to open the crate and retrieve the Jewish Talmud's inside. Perfect, I thought. This was the only way to have them taken back to Israel without any red lights beaming in someone's mind, besides, I thought, I have to return to Israel anyway to prepare for my journey to Egypt in search of more scrolls and then journey to Iraq in search of any remaining scrolls taken by the Babylonians centuries ago during their occupation of Jerusalem.

As Pedro and I left Peru on the way to New York, I asked Pedro, "Would you mind coming with me to Egypt" Pedro was dumbstruck. That was one question he never saw coming. "Of course, I'd be delighted," was his response. Besides, I thought having a man of Pedro's size with me would make me feel secure and safe. I never suspected that we were being followed all the way to Israel. As Pedro and I sat in coach on the direct flight from New York to Tel Aviv, Hansi and three of his men were in first class, keeping as good a distance as possible. Never realizing the danger, once we arrived at the airport in Tel Aviv, Pedro and I grabbed our luggage, rented a car, went to the airports freight department, retrieved the crate containing the golden chest, and drove straight to Jerusalem.

As we entered the city, I wondered what we would discover in Egypt and could we return any more scrolls to the Synagogue in Jerusalem for safekeeping. Driving up to the front of the King David Hotel, I went inside to check in while Pedro drove to the parking deck. Once checked in, I went back outside, expecting to see Pedro standing there with the small crate, but instead, he was nowhere to be seen. Now I was getting nervous, not realizing that Pedro had been taken by Hansi and his men to a small souvenir shop located a block away from the Dome of the Rock. There is where Pedro was being held as I would soon learn.

Leaving my suitcases behind, I started walking down the street when a car drove up, two men got out, grabbed me, and threw me inside the car. It was at this time I knew I'd see Pedro and somebody I really didn't want to see, namely Hansi himself. As we pulled up to the shop, I saw the sign that read, Saleem's Gift

Shop. Quickly taken inside, I was placed into a darkened room, waiting for something bad to happen. What seemed like forever, the door to the room opened, and standing with the light from outside the room enveloping him, stood none other than Hansi himself. It was at this moment I realized was in extreme danger and even Pedro couldn't be of any help.

As I stood there in the darkened room, Hansi entered and sarcastically said, "Well, Miss Chamberlain. We meet again. I have many questions to ask you and it would be wise to cooperate or your friend Pedro will experience extreme pain. Grabbing me by my left arm, Hansi forced me to another room, this one marked, storage room. Once inside I focused my eyes to a chair with someone sitting there, covered with a bed sheet. Hansi, standing next to the chair told me, "I have someone I want you to meet. He should be very familiar to you." As he swiped the sheet away, I saw who was sitting in the chair, bound, gagged, and very bloody. Although his face was badly bruised, I knew it was Pedro. Hansi had begun to torture him to obtain information about the scrolls, and what is most important, the chest, laden with precious stones.

I started to run over to Pedro when Hansi grabbed me by the arm and said, "Not so fast Miss Chamberlain. We have only started our little session." That statement scared the heck out of me. I knew Hansi was cruel, but I also remembered that he was most likely responsible for the beating and death of Rabbi Caldero back in Lima, Peru.

Staring Hansi in the eyes, I yelled loudly, "Let him go. You have no reason to beat him." Laughing loudly, Hansi replied, "I must disagree, I think Pedro has a lot of information that I need answers to. Please have a seat." As he pushed me into an old armchair, Hansi prepared to begin another question and answer session with Pedro. I couldn't help but feel pity for Pedro as I saw the terror in his eyes, especially once we both saw what Hansi held in his right hand. As I watched in horror, Hansi turned on an electric drill. Strolling towards Pedro, Hansi said, "let's see how much information I get once I begin to drill in Pedro's knee caps."

Knowing myself what kind of pain he was about to inflict on Pedro, I screamed in horror and pleaded with Hansi not to torture Pedro. I tried to explain that we were hiding nothing, but I knew Hansi could tell I was lying. As he grabbed Pedro's left leg, Hansi began to drill a hole into his kneecap causing Pedro to scream in agony. As he pushed and pulled the drill bit through his kneecap, Hansi asked, "Where are the Jewish scrolls. Tell me or else you'll experience more pain than this." Pedro's knee was spurting blood and all he could do was scream and try to yell out that he knew nothing.

As Hansi pulled out the drill bit, he laiughed said, "Enough for now. We have plenty of time left to get the information I need." As Hansi opened the door, he said, "I'll give both of you time to think for yourself what is coming next," as he left the room, slamming the door shut and locking it.

I ran towards Pedro and tried to unloosen the bindings holding him down. Although Pedro was a bloody mess and in extreme agony, he told me that Hansi questioned him about not only the scrolls, but also about the treasure from the cave outside of the city of Puna. I asked Pedro, "How does he know about the treasure and did you tell him anything" Pedro told me that Hansi told him that his father had searched for the treasure chest for most of the second world war but never found the chest. Hansi felt it was his duty to find it and finance another Nazi army to take on the world. Hansi told Pedro, "Why should these Jewish people have that treasure. Let their wealth finance our revolution, how fitting." Pedro assured me he never told Hansi where the treasure was, in fact, Pedro even kept me in the dark about where he hid the treasure. Pedro told me his little secret saying that he had made a false bottom in the trunk of the car which if someone opened the truck they would never notice it was below the bottom mat.

Once I had Pedro freed from his bindings, I started to question him about how we could escape without being caught and certainly tortured until dead at the hands of Hansi. There were no windows and the only door to the storeroom was locked and certainly guarded by one of Hansi's men.

After several minutes thinking to myself, I came up with a possible solution. I would try to get the attention of the guard and once he opened the door I'd stab him with an iron bar left standing in the corner of the room. I could only imagine what Hansi had planned to do with that bar, but I was determined to escape before finding out. Pedro was in such pain that it was very difficult for him to stand, much less walk. I assured Pedro my plan would work, as long as Hansi doesn't return to resume the torture session. I had Pedro stand about six feet from the door clutching a wooden rod I found in the rear of the room while I started to scream for the guard. The more I screamed the guard would yell for me to be quite but I was determined to have that door open come what may. Finally, after screaming for a few minutes, the guard opened the door and yelled out, "What's going on here?" As he turned to face Pedro six feet away, I held tightly on the metal rod and plunged it into the guards back, actually through his body. As the guard collapsed to the ground, I took Pedro by the hand and slowly started to walk towards the only way out, through the front door.

As I peeked through the curtain, I saw three women standing at a display counter looking over the items on display and I noticed the young lady working there was busy behind the counter, unable to see who was inside the shop. As I whispered to Pedro to muster enough courage to keep silent, we slowly walked to the front door and slipped away. Once we were safely outside, I hailed a taxi and took Pedro to the nearest hospital for treatment for his wounds. Once inside the emergency room, two nurses and a doctor began to treat Pedro but did have a question concerning the deep wound on his knee. I didn't want to draw attention so I came up with the story that he fell on top of a fence causing the metal rod to puncture his leg. I couldn't tell the doctor about Hansi and draw even more attention to myself and Pedro.

As the doctor ordered x-rays, I told Pedro I'd return to the hotel, get the car, return to the hospital, then we could drive to the Synagogue and give the Rabbi that golden treasure chest before something really bad happens to it, not to mention ourselves. Pedro pleaded with me not to go without him but I assured him that it was safer if I went while he was being treated. Leaving Pedro behind, I began my trek through the city until I finally arrived at the hotel. Luckily my suitcases were still where I had left them when Hansi kidnaped me. I went to my room, changed clothes in case Hansi remembered what I was wearing, and returned to the hospital.

I arrived in time to hear the doctor tell me he wanted Pedro admitted for a few days to rest and be sure his wound wouldn't become infected, then in a few days he'd release him. Pedro was more concerned than I was. He knew I wanted to take the chest to the Rabbi, then leave for Egypt in search of more scrolls, supposedly hidden somewhere in the Valley of the Kings. I was sure danger could follow, but I needed to take the chance. I only had a few days before I had to leave for Iraq hopefully to discover another scroll or two.

Leaving Pedro in the qualified hands of the hospital staff, I was assured by his doctor that he wouldn't release Pedro until I returned in a few days. That assurance made me comfortable since I was concerned that with Hansi on the loose, danger would surround Pedro's every move, not that I'm a valuable asset in protecting him, but at least if something were to happen, I'd be with him and Pedro stood a chance that I could persuade Hansi that we were only here in Israel on vacation. Funny thing was that I knew that was a pile of baloney and I knew deep in my heart that Hansi would never believe that.

The next morning I packed a suitcase, left for the airport, and took the next flight from Tel Aviv to Cairo. Once I arrived in Cairo, I was to meet a man named Hakim. Hakim was a professor of antiquities in Egypt who's expertise pertained to the period when the Israelites were held captive in Egypt and shortly after the exodus of the Jews under Moses's guidance. If anyone could trace the possibilities of another scroll or two, Hakim was the man.

As the hot sun beat down from above, I waited at the entrance of the airport for Hakim. All I knew was a description that he was tall, hairy, and a very pleasant man to deal with. After a few moments, the car arrived with Hakim at the wheel. As expected, he was very cordial and placed my bag in the trunk. All during the drive to the hotel, Hakim told me that he understood that there was a possibility that somewhere in the vastness of the desert, there could be scrolls, buried since the second half of the first century A.D. He began to explain that there were always rumors that ancient Jewish texts were smuggled out of Palestine shortly after the crucifixion of Jesus, but they never had any solid proof. According to Hakim, several scrolls were taken to Rome for protection by the Apostle Peter himself because the Romans had learned about the scrolls and were searching for them. He said that the belief at the time was that if Saint Peter took a few scrolls with him to Rome, hide them there, that the Romans would never think to look anywhere in Rome for the sacred scrolls.

After hours of driving towards the Valley of the Kings, I was beginning to wonder whether or not I was on a wild goose chase or perhaps I'd get lucky and find something, anything to prove their existence.

Scanning my surroundings, I noticed way in the distance were the famous pyramids, higher than I ever imagined them to be. Could a few scrolls be nearby, I wondered. Hakim suggested we begin our search a few miles away at a spot that was rumored to have been a campground during the time of Moses. It was only local legend, but what the heck, anything was possible. Stopping at an area that all I could see was desert and scorpions, I unpacked my bag with all the tools I'd need for an excavation, at least a partial excavation until I either discovered something or gave up trying. Hakim had a very special tool to help. It was a type of metal detector that could pick up anything buried very deep in the sand, deeper than anything else.

At first I didn't think he'd find anything, but after several minutes he was able to find metal utensils and a few other metal items that had been buried for many decades. At one point, his detector picked up an anomaly, buried deep down under the sand. Hakim thought it was something very large and was deep enough that centuries could have passed without it's discovery. By this time my hopes were getting the best of me, but I was still a little leery about finding anything so soon. Taking his shovel, Hakim began to dig and it seemed that the more he dug, the more sand he produced. Hakim said, "Don't give up. I'm sure something is buried way below."

I don't know how Hakim did it, but after spending another hour digging, he struck something with his shovel. In anticipation, I stood there shaking with excitement. Have I truly found something so soon or was it nothing.

Scooping more sand away, Hakim discovered an old wooden box, practically falling apart. As he picked up what was left, he reluctantly said, "Sue, it's nothing more than an old wooden box with nothing inside." I was speechless. I desperately wanted to find something but I also realized that it was going to take much more time and many visits to hopefully find another scroll. The question that came to my mind was whether there actually is a scroll or scrolls buried somewhere in this vast desert. Perhaps it is all a ruse, trying to have me look here when in reality, it could be closer to Israel or even could it be possible that it could be somewhere else in northern Africa? With evening approaching, Hakim and I returned to Cairo, feeling quite depressed that we failed to find anything or even a clue to where the treasured scrolls could be. I didn't want to spend too much time in Egypt since I still had to go to Iraq and the most dangerous place yet, Iran.

As I returned to Tel Aviv, I was concerned that Hansi might find me and I had to get Pedro discharged from the hospital to aid me in our search in Iraq.

Pedro's first question once we were together was whether Hakim was of any help. It was disturbing to tell him I came to a dead end, but I was hopeful that we'd find something in Iraq. I had one connection in Baghdad and that man was a British archeologist named Bill Butler. Bill has been in Iraq for several years digging around the town of Nineveh, searching for artifacts dating to the time of Jonah. If anyone knew Iraq, it was Bill.

As Pedro and I left the hotel, in the distance I saw Hansi talking to a couple men. I immediately shoved Pedro in the car and said, "Let's get out of here now. I just saw Hansi." I surely didn't want him to find us and return us to that storeroom for further questioning. I knew Pedro couldn't take much more punishment and I was certain of my own limitations. Making tracks, we drove out of town, straight to the airport for first Jordan then Iraq.

As the plane landed in Baghdad, I asked Pedro whether he wanted to stay with me for three days, then head back to Egypt, as I was hopeful that Hakim found anything useful. Pedro at first insisted he stay with me since Iraq is a very dangerous place these days, ever since the U.S. invasion many years ago. As usual, I won and Pedro agreed to return to Egypt only once he was sure I was safe and that my contact had met me.

Unpacking in the hotel, I called my contact, Dijloti. Dijloti was a man roughly sixty years old and had been the curator of Baghdad's Museum of History. If anyone would know where to look, it would be Dijloti.

Pedro and I took a taxi to the museum to meet my contact. Dijloti was very happy to see me after we had talked for hours on the phone, having never met each other. As Pedro and I shook hands, Dijloti ordered coffee for the three of us while we discussed our plans to investigate an area about four miles south from the ancient city of Nineveh. My other contact, Bill Butler, was out of town for a few days so all I could depend on was whether Dijloti actually knew anything about the scrolls or was he taking us on a wild ride. Dijloti assured me that he had heard many years ago about the existence of the Book Of Abraham, but over the course of many centuries, nobody has ever had proof of it's location or even if it did exist. I told Dijloti that Pedro and I have found several scrolls and that we had also stumbled upon scrolls written in Latin.

Dijloti asked me, "Sue, where do you think any scrolls could be buried or hidden somewhere in the desert?" I had no idea, but I was determined to search, besides, Rabbi Berman had read the Jewish scrolls and Father Ligouri read the Latin texts and they both gave clues to the whereabouts of three scrolls that were taken by the Babylonians centuries ago when they occupied Palestine. Dijloti knew the history of the Babylonians but had never connected them with scrolls pertaining to the Book Of Abraham. I informed Dijloti that according to the third Jewish scroll, three had been taken to Nineveh by Jonah himself, but after his journey, ordered by God, to the city, Jonah apparently gave them to a Priestess, and after that they disappeared.

Dijloti was curious yet at the same time very cautious. He only had heard rumors throughout history, but there never was any substantial proof. I told Dijloti that there was written proof that Jonah had taken three scrolls and even supposedly held them tightly when God had the large fish swallow Jonah until he relented and told God he would go to Nineveh. Dijloti replied, "How could Jonah hold unto three scrolls while at the same time swimming in the water, then swallowed by a fish, them puked up, still holding unto the scrolls?" All I could say was I had no idea how, but if God was involved in having Jonah go to Nineveh with the scrolls, it could have been done.

I could see the apprehension in Dijloti's eyes, yet he still agreed to help me in my investigation. Thanking him and leaving for the hotel, Pedro wondered if we could trust Dijloti or would he kill me rather than see the scrolls be taken to Israel for further analysis. I wasn't quite sure, but I told Pedro that I would not begin my search until my other contact, Bill Butler had returned. Bill knew the country quite well and he had his own team of men and women that would be vital in my search. Having assured Pedro I'd be very cautious, Pedro agreed to return to Egypt to search for the possibility that two scrolls were hidden in the Valley of the Kings, however, I warned Pedro to be careful since I knew that Hansi was in Egypt and would think of nothing in the way of harming Pedro for information.

After waiting another day for Bill Butler to return, Pedro and I decided to go to the museum to see for ourselves the numerous items that were there. Perhaps those items could give me a clue to whether or not I would discover the location of the three scrolls that had been taken to Nineveh long ago.

Once Bill had returned to Iraq, I was prepared to begin my search. Pedro, on the other hand, left for Egypt, leaving me with two men I had never met before today, and hopeful that something tangible would result in my investigation.

It was a cold rainy day when Bill and his team, along with Dijloti and his team drove with me to the ancient city of Nineveh. What would I find, or was this going to be a bust. Despite my reservations, I was still determined to find all twelve scrolls that would reveal God's plan from the beginning to the end of time. The thought of gaining the hidden knowledge frightened me. Would Hansi find Pedro, torture him for information that would result in my own death. I tried not to dwell on that thought. I was too excited to continue this journey, the same journey that many people before me had taken so long ago.

Finally arriving at Nineveh, or what was left of it, I unpacked my gear, and asked Dijloti and Bill Butler where we should begin our digging. According to Dijloti, most items found over the years were discovered along the northern and eastern walls that were now ruins, leaving very little evidence of where they could possibly be. I decided my investigation should begin near the southern wall then if nothing else we could always dig close to what was left of the western wall. Ancient Nineveh was a known fortress and should yield a wealth of information including everyday items used by it's inhabitants.

With so many men digging, I never realized how much it was raining. The ground became soaked, making mud out of everything. Before I knew it, two hours had passed and we had only scratched the surface. We were about three feet below the surface and all we found were old stones, buried long ago, not yielding any clues to what I was searching for. Giving up, I told everybody we will return tomorrow and resume the excavation of the southern wall.

As evening approached, I sat at the desk in my hotel room, inserting my information into the file I had started since I began my quest. I had tons of information to pour over once I returned to New York City and my office at the New York Herald. My editor has been getting harder to deal with since this investigation has taken longer than I thought it would. I never thought in my wildest dreams that when Pedro contacted me several months ago, I'd be sitting here in Iraq and digging at the ancient ruins of Nineveh.

The next morning I packed my bags and took a taxi over to the museum to connect with Dijloti and Bill Butler. Bill was concerned that we could be wasting our time at the location, but I implored him to continue the digging at least for another day or two, and if nothing was discovered, I'd leave Iraq and travel to Iran or perhaps I'd be served best by going to Damascus, Syria. It was historically known that Saint Paul had taken the road to Damascus in the first century and he could have taken one or perhaps two scrolls with him. The one question that perplexed me the most was how did several scrolls in both ancient Hebrew and Latin end up in South America? I was curious about who could have taken them there and for what reason.

As we continued the search, Bill may have struck gold. Buried several feet below the surface was a metal box that was unlocked and appearing to have been made during the first or second centuries. Why hasn't anybody found this box before, I wondered. Hundreds of people had excavated this area over time, but lo and behold, there it was. I was smaller than I had imagined it to be, but still, it was a great discovery.

As bill retrieved the box, I stood there, shaking uncontrollably. Had we discovered something of value? Taking his time opening the box, he revealed that it held two ancient scrolls. As he held them up, I became overcome with joy. Just as I was about to give up and leave the city, there it was, right in front of me. I took one of the scrolls, unfolded it's pages, and saw the Hebrew inscriptions. I told everybody, "I can't wait to show these scrolls to Rabbi Berman." Suddenly, without thinking twice, Bill stated that it would be illegal to remover them from the country under severe penalty. I could see anger in the eyes of Dijloti. He desperately wanted them on view in his museum, but I tried to convince everybody that I needed to have a Jewish Rabbi translate the documents first, then perhaps they could be returned to Iraq.

Dijloti became irate at the suggestion. "Never," he shouted. Now I was in a pickle of sorts. The scrolls belonged to the Iraqi Republic since they were discovered in Nineveh, but I needed to have a Rabbi see them first since I had already discovered six scrolls in Peru. How desperate could I get. I wished Pedro was here and then it dawned on me. Pedro was in Egypt and was he in any danger there. I had spotted Hansi in Cairo when we left the country, but did he find Pedro and torture him for valuable information?

As we left the ruins of Nineveh, I told Bill Butler that neo-Nazi's were attempting to grab the scrolls for their own benefit and they would stop at nothing to achieve their goals. It was at this moment that Bill's next statement shocked me. Bill said, "Sue, I know the Nazi's had attempted to find them during the war and there was money to be made here. That's why I contacted Hansi while you were digging in Peru." I was dumbfounded. I said to Bill, "How could you do this. Don't you know the valuable information these scrolls contain and that Hansi will use them to finance another Nazi revolution either in Germany itself, or perhaps in South America." Bill didn't seem to care. All he saw were dollar signs waving before his eyes. Now I was in a quagmire. Not only did I have to deal with Dijloti, but I also had to prevent Bill Butler from selling the scrolls to Hansi. I now realized that Hansi's tentacles stretched over the globe and that danger was finding it's way to me.

For the next three days I tried to persuade Dijloti to let me take the scrolls to South America, or even to the head Rabbi in New York for translation and safety. I now had discovered eight scrolls and from the first Latin scroll, I had determined that there were twelve scrolls in all, perhaps believing that all twelve of Jesus's Apostles had each possessed one at some time and scattered them around the world for safe keeping, especially since the whole Book Of Abraham detailed with pinpoint accuracy the events with names and places that stretched from the time of Abraham to the end of time. It was a book that would give anyone the knowledge necessary to become God like, and I was determined to have them gathered and hidden away at one place for all time.

After a couple days had passed, I finally convinced Dijloti that it was best for me to take the scrolls to New York City, however there was one thing I had to promise. Dijloti insisted I take them to Jerusalem instead of New York City. Dijloti stated that he had connections with the Israeli Mossad, and if anyone could protect them and prevent Hansi from grabbing them, it was the Mossad. I had no choice but to agree, so as Dijloti took them from his safe, he handed me the scrolls and warned me that if I didn't take them to Israel, I'd have to fear him more then Hansi. Although I really wanted to take them to Lima, Peru for translation, I had to agree with Dijloti that Israel was the best place to translate, hide, and protect them from any evil person such as Hansi and Bill Butler from using them for their own reasons.

As I left the museum, I took a taxi back to the hotel, placed the scrolls beneath my clothing in the suitcase, and left for the airport. As I went through Iraqi customs, I was afraid that they would discover the scrolls hidden in my suitcase, but luckily they never bothered scanning them. I was overcome with joy, but I still wasn't out of it yet. I still had to go through Israeli customs upon my arrival in Tel Aviv, and take them to Jerusalem without anyone taking notice.

After the adventure of going through Israeli customs, I caught a ride to Jerusalem and kept to myself at the King David Hotel. I thought I'd call the chief Rabbi in Jerusalem the next day and make an appointment to see him and hand over the two scrolls I discovered at Nineveh.

As I rested on the bed, the phone rang. It was Pedro, and he informed me that he had discovered a scroll, written in Latin buried in the sands of Egypt near Alexandria. Wondering how he knew I was at the hotel, he explained that he had a tail on me the whole time. It was his way of protecting me, but I let him know that there was danger and deceit the entire time and that nobody could be trusted except a Rabbi, Father Ligouri, and Cardinal Catelli. Speaking of Cardinal Catelli, Pedro told me that tomorrow he was going to take a flight from Cairo to Rome to see the Cardinal at the Vatican. All I could say was, "Be very careful, Pedro. You know as well as I that Hansi is unto us and will stop at nothing to grab any scroll." Assuring me he'd keep a close eye out for Hansi, Pedro thanked me for going to Iraq and discovering another two scrolls.

As I continued my research in Jerusalem, my editor called to order me to leave immediately for New York. I was told I had to cover a very important event. It seems that the leader of the World Federation Council, President Adrian, was to give a speech at the last session of the United Nations. He was to announce that a new world body was to replace the United Nations and he was the keynote speaker at the event. All the worlds leaders were to be in attendance including President McNair. I knew it had to be a very important event to cover and that's why my editor wanted me to attend and cover the event for the New York Herald. Perhaps, I thought, this coverage could get me the promotion I so desired, and that was to be the chief foreign reporter for the newspaper. It not only paid well, but also would give me the notoriety I craved.

Taking the next flight from Tel Aviv to New York, I called Pedro to let him know that I'd contact him in another three or four days and that he should stay near the Vatican and continue his part in the investigation, especially with Cardinal Catelli. If anyone could give us a hint, it would be Cardinal Catelli. He had a doctorate in Latin history and a master of the language. I also thought of the possibility that Hansi was hot on his trail and figured that Pedro was in grave danger since I knew Hansi wouldn't take the risk of following me to New York, but rather tail Pedro.

After being back in New York for two days, I spent most of my time at the Herald, downloading all the information I had gathered over the previous two months, guaranteeing that as long as the information was here in New York, Hansi or anyone else couldn't steal the information. I had no idea that the amount of danger was to become even worse, perhaps costing people their lives.

The evening of the event I was to cover had come. I decided to wear a blue outfit that always made me look younger than my age. I took a taxi to the United Nations, taking my designated seat. The very first thing we were told was that we were not permitted to ask any questions, just take notes. Darn it, I thought. I really wanted to ask Adrian about his upcoming trip to Israel during Easter. All I knew was that it was to be the most important event in the history of the world. Confused, I wondered what was going to be that important that all that was said was it was going to possibly herald in a new age, and everybody wanted to be a part of it.

As I nervously sat waiting, my cell phone vibrated, letting me know I was receiving a text message. I didn't have the time to check it, but I did notice it was from Pedro. What could his message consist of? Had he learned more to the puzzle or was he requesting I come to Rome as soon as possible, I wondered.

Finally, the President of the United States arrived followed within minutes by President Adrian of the W.F.C. As the two men sat at their places, a hush permeated the room. One could almost hear a pin drop and as everybody waited anxiously, the Chairman of the United Nations walked to the podium. Chairman Bosby began to announce that President McNair would speak first, followed by President Adrian. As I listened to President McNair speak about how the nations of the world had come together for decades at the United Nations, he reminded everyone that at times the U.N. was incapable of achieving unity and preventing nations from going to war, but now, a new world order was needed to achieve the same goals but that it was to be led by President Adrian of the World Federation Council. The world was to be divided into ten divisions, first the North American Division which includes the United States and Canada, the second division, the Central American Division which included Mexico, the third division, the South American Division, the fourth would be the North Asian Division which included Japan, Korea, and China. The fifth division would be the Southern Pacific rim, including Australia, New Zealand, Indonesia, the Philippines, and the entire Southern Pacific Islands. The sixth Division be Southern Asia, consisting of Southeast Asia and India and Pakistan. The seventh division would include the nations in the Middle East with the exception of Israel. The eighth division would include Southern Africa, the ninth division, Northern Africa, followed by the tenth division, Europe and Russia. Each of the ten divisions would be ruled by one leader each with all ten leaders answering to President Adrian of the World Federation Council. Only Adrian had the final say in any discussions, also the three major religions would be combined into one sanctioned religion, led by Pope Peter.

As I sat listening to President McNair inform everyone what was agreed, I couldn't believe my ears, but what I was about to hear from President Adrian floored me completely. When it was President Adrian's turn to speak, the chamber became so quiet one could almost hear everybody's breathing.

President Adrian spoke for close to two hours saying what his goals were and that there was to be one currency for the world, one set of laws covering every nation, one government, and one sanctioned religion. It was to be a one world government with Adrian in control. The only thing missing was what he wanted to announce in Israel on Easter Sunday. The announcement would come outside the newly rebuilt Jewish Temple in Jerusalem. Televison camera's would dot every inch of the grand plaza and I certainly wanted to be a part of it.

As I returned to the Herald, I nervously wrote my article, worried that my editor would be displeased, but when he gave it his critique, he was flabbergasted. All he could say was, "Great job, Sue. I'll see to it you get a raise and perhaps something more." I was so exited I forgot to read the text message Pedro had sent me the night before.

The next morning I read my e-mail from Pedro while eating my breakfast. In his message, he stated that he had spoken to Cardinal Catelli concerning the scrolls he had taken for translation. According to the one scroll, one Hebrew scroll had been spirited out of Palestine by a man named Hylori back in the third century

A.D. The scroll went on to mention the fact that Hylori had taken the scroll to a very remote place in Asia, perhaps China itself. The question was, where in China would we start to look and would we not only have difficulty finding the scroll, but would the Chinese authorities even permit us to take the scroll outside of China? As I finished reading his message, it dawned on me that I had a connection with a Chinese journalist stationed in Beijing. If anyone could help, perhaps he could.

I immediately contacted Pedro informing him that I'd see him back in Peru in a few days, but first I had to catch a flight to Beijing and meet my contact, Gou Fe Jong. Packing my bags, I left for the airport, but not before advising my editor where I was going. He wasn't so keen on the fact that I was spending so much time with my research, but I managed to calm his concern with the possibility of gaining a Pulitzer Prize and even gaining notoriety for the newspaper. It sure would put the New York Herald on the map.

As I left for the airport, I made a quick call to my contact, letting him know that after a very long flight from New York, to Los Angeles, then onto Beijing, Id meet him at the very exclusive, The Forbidden City Hotel. I could hardly contain myself at the prospect of discovering another scroll, making a total of ten scrolls with only two others to find to complete the picture. I didn't realize at the time that not only would the scroll somewhere in China prove difficult to find, but that the last two scrolls would be almost impossible to discover. Meanwhile, while I was on my adventure in China, I was sure there was more to be discovered in Peru, but somehow I also felt that I still hadn't escaped the clutches of Hansi.

China was always one of my favorite places to visit. I loved the culture, the food, and all the archeological places to search. China was a treasure trove of undiscovered wealth. It's history goes back centuries, perhaps beyond the period pre-dating the great flood.

As I arrived, I checked through customs, gathered my suitcases and took a taxi to the hotel. Once settled in, I called my friend, Gou Fe Jong, or as I always just called him Fe. Fe and I go back about ten years, ever since he had come to the states to study at one of our fine universities. Ever since then we have practically been inseparable whenever we were together. We would even share articles, and most times cover the same stories either in New York or Beijing.

As the sun began to fall, Fe had arrived to take me to dinner at my favorite place. I always felt at ease there and the ambience was as one would expect in China.

As we ate, I discussed my project with Fe, asking if he could help in any way. Fe had never heard of the scrolls, but there was an old Chinese saying that many centuries ago, a man had come to China bearing many treasures and that he had supposedly buried some of the treasure somewhere in Southeast China, perhaps close to the border between China and Vietnam. There was even a rumor that treasure was in the vicinity between China and North Korea, but if that were true, it would be almost impossible to retrieve, especially if it was across the border somewhere in North Korea. Fe assured me that he would help discover the treasures and if we were lucky, perhaps another scroll.

My one concern was, if it was in North Korea, how could we lay our hands on it. I certainly couldn't go across the border, much less dig there. Fe had a very good idea. Fe knew a man who often crossed the border, trading with the Koreans. He always spent lots of time there and even knew most of the North Korean border guards. He would lavish the guards with western goods in order to have them turn their faces to what he was actually doing. Hey, if it worked, only the better. Once I knew that, I asked Fe if there was any chance that he could sneak me across the border as well. Fe as well as I knew the dangers, but all he said was that he would go over first, check with his Korean contacts, then return with an answer. He did warn me that if the North Korean officers discovered that I as an American had illegally crossed the border, I would probably end up spending many years in a North Korean prison, and that could be a death sentence of itself.

Knowing the dangers, I still wanted to cross over, but my suggestion was to travel towards the Vietnamese border first and if unsuccessful, I'd take my chances and go into North Korea. I was determined to find all twelve scrolls no matter where they were hidden. At this juncture I hadn't realized the fact that there was even more danger in China then I dealt with in Peru and Jerusalem. In fact, even Fe had no idea what was about to happen.

The next day, Fe and I drove south, towards the Vietnamese border. We would only spend about one week searching in the south and if nothing was found, then we'd travel back to Beijing and Fe would make his contact with the North Korean that could possibly be of assistance.

Our journey began in Beijing, then to Changsha to spend the night. It was a long, arduous journey, but my determination had the best of me. The next day, we drove to the city of Nanning where we'd unload the truck and spend the next night. According to Fe, the only possible place to search was an area outside of the town of Jingxi, near the border.

Once morning arrived, we packed our bags and prepared to drive the short distance to the Vietnamese border. Before leaving, I wanted to make a phone call to Pedro to find out what he's been doing the last few days. After several attempts, Pedro finally answered his cell phone. He was still in Rome but was preparing to return to Peru. He had told me that he had nearly been seen by Hansi and his crony's, but had managed to dodge the bullet, so to speak. Cardinal Catelli was finishing the scroll and Pedro had to return to the Vatican to retrieve the scroll and pack it inside the false bottom of his valise. That was the only way Pedro and I decided to hide any scrolls we had found. I t would prevent Hansi or anyone else from discovering the scrolls and stealing them. The scrolls were too important to have them fall into the wrong hands, especially since we were finally coming to the end of our journey.

My one concern, of course, was the danger involved in crossing the Chinese and Vietnamese border without being discovered. Fe knew most of the border guards on both sides, but there was always a chance that we could be sold out by someone wanting to make a name for themselves. Fe told me that any Vietnamese border guard who arrests anyone crossing illegally, was given extra rations of food and a few extra dong, the Vietnamese currency.

With the border within site, Fe used his binoculars to see if the coast was clear. In the far distance he saw two Vietnamese border guards sitting under a shade tree eating their lunch. Although I felt we'd have to cross over, Fe decided that we'd first begin the treasure hunt here in China, then perhaps cross the border into Vietnam.

As I placed my bags down, I noticed someone coming in the distance. I whispered to Fe that someone was coming, but Fe assured me there was nothing to worry about. The man approaching us was his nephew, Bo. Bo appeared to be quite tall for a Chinese lad, but he certainly didn't run from any danger as I was about to find out.

Fe began digging near a rock formation while Bo helped me search an area around a thicket of bushes. The hot sun scorched my back and sweat began to pour from my brow. It was a backbreaking chore but it had to be done and my desire to find the last two scrolls made me determined to continue no matter what I had to endure. As time clicked by, it seemed like an eternity had passed and after four hours of searching, I decided to call off the search, at least for today. Fe wanted to continue but I was exhausted and needed rest, and besides, how do I know we're on the right track. This was only a hunch that Fe had regarding the possible location of one scroll. Even his nephew, Bo, wanted to stop for the night, so Fe reluctantly agreed. This night we'd share a few drinks of Chinese beer at the local establishment in the town of Jingxi. I had to admit that I was exhausted myself but I felt that I was nearing the end of my journey and desperately wanted to return to New York City and the Herald.

After five more days of digging, I decided it was time to search near the Chinese and North Korean border, but the question that ran through my mind was whether the treasure was in China or was it buried somewhere in North Korea.

The next several days we drove throughout China, making our way towards the border. Fe told me that he had cousins in the town of Dandong, close to the border. According to Fe, if we weren't successful near Dandong, then the only possible place could be outside the North Korean town of Oiju. Fe and Bo appeared to me to feel comfortable despite the danger, but I, on the other hand, began to have butterflies in my stomach. I knew full well that if caught, I'd be taken to the main prison in Pyongyang, possibly to rot in a vile North Korean prison camp somewhere that I'd have no hope of escaping. Day after day and night after night being on the road made me even more exhausted than ever, but I had to do whatever necessary to achieve my goal. I had even promised Rabbi Berman that I would find the final two scrolls that I was sure would contain a wealth of information.

As we approached a small village on the Chinese side of the border, I began to have second thoughts. Perhaps this wasn't a very good idea after all. Fe tried to assure me that if we were cautious enough, we might just pull this off. Fe, taking his field glasses out, scanned the border, hoping to see anybody he could recognize. He had a cache of goods to trade with the proper North Korean border guards, sort of a bribery. Bo and I would stay behind until Fe gave us the signal that it was safe to cross.

As we watched Fe approach the first border station, I wondered whether there could be one or two scrolls buried somewhere near here, but I kept my fingers crossed, hoping that this time I might have hit pay dirt. With the rising sun giving us a better view, Bo and I saw Fe talking to one of the border guards. With seconds clicking away, I was relieved when I saw Fe hand a package to the guard. In a few seconds, Fe started the walk back to our position. When Fe returned, he told me that the guard only promised us two hours since his replacement would arrive. Fe never dealt with the other guard so we had to act quick or lose this opportunity.

As we crossed the border, I took a quick look at the North Korean guard, standing in the side of the small road, busying himself opening the package that Fe had given him. The package only obtained some Chinese cigarettes, soap, other toiletries, and a small portable radio. At least it was enough to satisfy the guard for now, but I was certain that if we had to return the next day, he'd most likely would be expecting more than a few toiletries.

As we neared the small village of Oiju, there was an open field, blossoming with flowers and consisting of a rocky hill. As I looked toward the village, I saw several people working a small patch of potatoes hoping we wouldn't be noticed. Fe asked me to keep a low profile so as not to raise any suspicion from the locals. Fe said, "One never knows who to trust here in North Korea. People will turn anyone into the authorities for a few extra rations." All I knew was that I wanted to do my investigation and get back over the border in China before something very bad happens.

Once we found a spot that had possibilities, Fe, Bo, and I began to shovel some soil to try to determine if the soil had ever been disturbed over the last few decades. Fe told me that this area was a hotbed of activity during the Korean War when American bombers flew missions overhead to take out North Korean fortifications. Upon hearing that, I knew that the possibility of finding anything was remote. If this ground had been disturbed in any way, searching any further was fruitless.

After we had dug for nearly an hour, without success, Fe decided we had better return to the Chinese side of the border soon since the guard he bribed was being replaced. Gathering our equipment, we raced beck towards the border when Fe saw something that terrified me. The guard had been replaced by not one, but two guards, Fe once again took out his field glasses and saw that the two guards were men he had never dealt with before. I began to think, "Are we trapped here in North Korea, and would Fe be able to keep the guards busy while Bo and I slipped back over the border?" Fe was the type of person that could practically talk his way through anything but I wasn't certain that this was a situation that he'd have any luck.

Bo and I squatted down, low on the ground, while Fe walked to the border. My nerves were on edge so it was, but something happened that gave our position away. Suddenly my cell phone rang, alarming the two border guards. As I looked at my phone, I saw it was Pedro's number, but there was nothing I could do for now. All I could think of was avoiding the two guards and making a dash across the border.

I told Bo that we had to run as fast as possible, and in a second, we were making tracks. Just as we got to the marked border, there was a volley of gunfire heading our way. By this time I think my legs were moving faster than my body and then a terrible scream rang out. It was Bo. He had been hit by two bullets. One in his right leg, the other closer to his chest. I was now presented with a dilemma. Do I run or do I stay to help Bo? I decided that I had to help Bo so I knelt by his side, took a towel I had brought to wipe my face from the brutal heat, and wrapped it above the wound in his leg. As I began to unbutton his shirt, blood poured out so fast I didn't know whether it was too late or not, but I still felt I had to stay by his side.

Just as I took off my shirt to put some pressure on his chest, one of the border guards approached and using the butt of his rifle, shoved me aside, took aim, and fired at Bo's head, killing him instantly. Seeing that happen caused me to have a panic attack. Nevertheless, the North Korean guard shoved me to the ground and threatened me with death. Trying to see his face that was surrounded by the sun, I pleaded for my life and all the while wondering what happened to Fe. As the guard stood over me, I was relieved to see Fe walk towards us. Fe began to speak and although I didn't understand anything he was saying, I knew Fe was trying his best to get the border guard to let us cross, but it seemed that the man wasn't listening, he was yelling something to me in Korean and as I just lay there on the ground, he became even for upset. By this time, four more North Korean guards had arrived. Now it was getting serious. Even Fe was being treated roughly. The officer in charge walked over, took one look at me, and in broken English said, "What is a vile American doing in my country?" I didn't know how to respond. Seeing my situation, Fe remarked that we had accidently crossed the border during the night when it was pitch black and all we wanted to do was return to China. At first the officer had a stare that could pierce your face, but as Fe continued to discuss the situation, I could see the officer began to relent. At the time I didn't realize what was going on, but later Fe told me he had promised the officer several items he could get in Beijing that would be in his best interest. I could see that Fe even had a look of trepidation at first, but within a few minutes, the officer allowed us to cross over. I thought, "What a relief. All I could ponder was being in some torture chamber pleading for mercy.

Once we were back across the border, I asked Fe, "What in heck did you promise that man?" I was stunned at Fe's response. "I promised him that tomorrow he could have you for sex in exchange for the opportunity to continue our quest." I replied, "What did you just say?" I was floored by what he had just told me. His response was, "Don't worry Sue. He doesn't know when we'll return." I must say I was somewhat relieved but just the idea of what he told the officer made my skin crawl.

Once we returned to the truck, I placed a call to Pedro to find out whether he had any good news. I asked Pedro, "Did you have any good news for me?" All Pedro could say was that I had to return to Rome immediately, he had some good news to tell me but he didn't want to say it over the phone, just for safety sake. I was curious and couldn't wait to return to Beijing to take the first flight from China to Italy via Turkey. The good news is that I wouldn't have to return to North Korea because Fe felt that there were no scrolls to be found there, especially after Pedro told me I didn't have to return to North Korea, he'd explain when I returned to Rome.

As we arrived in Beijing, I felt sorry for Fe. His nephew was killed and left at the border. How could I ever repay him for his help and sacrifice, I wondered.

As I boarded the flight out of China, I gave Fe one last hug and promised him that once my quest was finished, I'd return and we could celebrate together.

As the flight to Rome began, I thought to myself, "What if this was all a wild goose chase and there were no more scrolls to be found. Besides, how did several scrolls make their way to South America?" In time that question would soon be discovered.

My arrival in Rome was met with a vicious snow storm. Winter was nearly over, but it sure didn't look or feel like it. I took a taxi to the hotel, unpacked and placed a call to Pedro to let him know I had arrived. Waiting for Pedro was one thing, but wondering if the jig is up as far as Hansi is concerned is another thing. As I sprawled on the bed, I soaked up the warmth of the room, never realizing the harsh winter outside.

The knock at the door was the one I had been anticipating for some time. It was none other than my friend and associate, Pedro. The look of sheer excitement glistened from his face. No sooner was he in the room when he said, "Sue, you'll never guess what I had found out." Wondering to myself why the sudden excitement radiating from Pedro's face, he began with the words, "Sue, I've discovered very important information concerning the scrolls."

According to Cardinal Catelli, the fifth scroll written in Latin stated that in the fourth century A.D. a young man living in Palestine had retrieved several Hebrew scrolls and spirited them out of the country. His name was Joseppa, and he was a merchant that often traveled the world. Joseppa had traded in merchandise in Rome, Egypt, Syria, and numerous countries in the Middle East, however, it was recorded that he had taken his fleet of three ships, sailed westward, and was never seen again. It was possible that Joseppa had made his way to the America's and had hidden those sacred scrolls throughout Central and South America. The question was, which countries had he visited and buried the scrolls. Pedro and I knew that Peru was one place, but where were the other ones scattered? Feeling quite frustrated, I told Pedro that it seems that just when I felt that things were nearly at an end, this information pops up. I said, "How in God's name are we going to find out which countries the other scrolls could be buried?" Pedro had the answer I didn't want to hear. He whispered, "Let's have Hansi take us there. Besides, he's been searching for the scrolls for years and perhaps he has some idea where we could find some of them." I was so nervous I began to crack my knuckles. I always did that whenever I was upset and nervous. In fact, my mother always yelled at me for having such an irritating habit, but I could never help myself.

Settling down for the night, the two of us drifted off to sleep, unaware of the danger that would come the next day.

CHAPTER 5

With the morning sun shining on my face, I stretched and strolled to the shower while Pedro slept. Pedro was always a sound sleeper and it took a lot of nudging to awaken him. I had at least a few minutes to shower and call down to the hotel's kitchen for a quick breakfast.

As I thought about how far we had come to solving the mystery and now we knew there was more to the story than what we had discovered. I imagined the young man, Joseppa, and how he sailed away from his homeland never to see his family again. With his three ships and a crew of perhaps two hundred men, Joseppa would never realize the importance his journey would become. I imagined Joseppa finally reaching the shores of a new world. Just the language barrier alone was something he had to deal with, not to mention having to hide the scrolls from bandits and any other undesirables.

As I dressed in a warm, soothing outfit to ward off the bitter cold outside, Pedro was waking up. Yawning, he asked, "How long are you up and where will we be headed today?" I explained that I wanted to have a conversation with Cardinal Catelli to find out what the last Latin scroll we had found contained. Would it yield further clues to where more scrolls were buried, or would it only give more information about Joseppa?

Arriving at the Vatican, we strolled through Saint Peter's Square, unaware we were being followed. Knocking on Cardinal Catelli's door, it only took a few seconds for four men to drive up, get out of their car, and grab us, forcing us into their car and speeding away. As we were blindfolded and bound, one man angrily stated that we were becoming a nuisance. As I struggled with the rope binding my wrists, I was slapped across the face with such force that a tooth began to quiver. I was afraid I'd lose a tooth. The man warned me not to try anything or else he'd be forced to shoot me, besides, there was someone waiting to see us. Who could that person be, I wondered. I didn't think it was Hansi because he would never send anyone to do his dirty work; he always did that himself.

After winding through the streets of Rome, we were driving along a highway, far out of town. It must have taken a good two hours before the car seemed to slow down and come to a stop. I heard the driver tell someone that we were there and I then heard what sounded like a large gate opening up. As the car continued, I began to feel like this was the end of the journey and my parents would never see me again.

Once out of the car, I struggled to walk, being blindfolded and bound at the wrists. Someone grabbed my arm and led me towards the door. As I was roughed up and thrown into a chair, I could hear Pedro screaming in agony. What were they doing to Pedro, I wondered. As I began to ask the question where were we at, a hand came slapping across my face. Hurting as much as expected, I once again asked the question, almost to the point of demanding to be told.

After sitting for what seemed to be forever, a door opened and I could hear that three people had entered the room, two men and one woman. The woman sounded as though she was wearing stiletto high heels as they always made a special sound. In Italian, a man gave an order and suddenly my blindfold was off, but I was still left bound at the wrists behind my back.

In front of me was a huge desk and sitting there was a man, wearing a dark blue suit and rather handsome. Taking a cigar from a box, he lit the smoke, gently puffed it at me, and then began the questioning. The aroma of the cigar surrounded me, making me choke from it's smoky scent. I pleaded with him to blow his smoke the other way, but he just laughed and loudly said, "I make the decisions around here." By the tone of his voice I knew he demanded the attention of other people and he certainly wasn't a friendly type of person.

I started by asking him where I was and what he wanted. Slamming his fists on the table, he once again said, "I'll ask the questions. You supply the answers, or else." Taking my eyes away from him, I saw two men standing guard at the door. They appeared to be muscular and apparently aggressive and I was sure they wouldn't give it a second thought to roughing me up somewhat.

The man behind the desk began by saying, "Let's begin the questioning with why are you in Rome and what does the Vatican have to do with what you're searching for?" That statement made me realize that he must certainly know or have a suspicion about what Pedro and I are doing.

As I didn't want to tell the truth, I told him that Cardinal Catelli is an old friend of my family. He didn't buy that one. Growing increasingly angry, the man demanded I tell him the truth. After about an hour going back and forth and getting nowhere, he suddenly stood, flicked his right index finger, and the two guards opened the door. Focusing my eyes, I saw three men, holding a battered and beaten Pedro, dragging him across the floor. Despite having my wrists bound, I rose to my feet and rushed over to Pedro. He was a bloody mess, had a swollen right eye, and his chest was bloody.

The man behind the desk asked me, "Perhaps your friend here doesn't want to cooperate, but maybe you will, unless you want to see your friend die right in front of you?" Gazing at the man, I said, "You can kill us if you want, but I assure you I'll never tell you anything." The man's only response was, "Well, I guess you have me, don't you?" Snapping his fingers again, the door opened and in came a short, skinny man. He was Oriental and gave me an angry glance. The man introduced him to me saying, "Here's a good friend of mine. May I introduce you to Xia Ping." Now, I wondered, who could this man be and how is he involved.

It then dawned on me that perhaps this man called Xia Ping, may have followed Pedro, our friend, and myself to the Chinese Korean border. He may even be aware that the location of numerous scrolls could be found, even in the border town on the North Korean side. I was to discover his real intentions. As I pondered my predicament, I realized that the man behind the desk could be an intelligence agent from either China or even Russia, because he did have an accent. Finally, after waiting for half an hour, the man behind the desk rose from his chair, and slowly walked toward me, the shadow that concealed his face began to fade away. As he approached, I saw he was wearing a uniform, but I hadn't a clue from which country. It wasn't until he introduced himself by saying, "Let me introduce myself Miss Chamberlain. I am Major Krykovsky. I am in Russian intelligence. I know you and your friend are searching for something very valuable and I want you to tell me what it is and where I might find it." My response was simple. I said in an angry voice, "I don't know what you're talking about." With a glare in his eyes, he responded, "Very well. Perhaps you'll tell me when I bring in your friend, Pedro." Snapping his fingers, he yelled out, "Bring the man Pedro to me. Perhaps Miss Sue Chamberlain will talk once her friends life is at risk." In the darkness I saw the door open and with the blinding light surrounding the room, three men entered, holding up Pedro. His arms were shacked behind his back, a metal rod shoved between his arms and back. Once he entered the light, I saw his face was badly beaten. His eyes were blackened, his cheeks puffy, and he could hardly stand on his own two feet.

Major Krykovsky ordered the three men to tie Pedro to what he referred to as, the punishment chair. As I nervously watched them place Pedro into the chair, I began to tremble, wondering what was going to happen to Pedro or even myself. How could we ever escape from this mad Russian who seemed to be going to great lengths to get to the truth.

With the snap of his fingers, Major Krykovsky ordered the three men to strip Pedro's shirt from his body. Next, he had Pedro tied to the chair, not with ropes, but with a string of barbed wire. As they tightened the wire, Pedro screamed out in sheer agony. Next, his ankles were also tied to the chair in the same manner. With his head lowered, Pedro yelled out, "Don't tell them anything Sue" That statement only perked the Russian officer's interest. Now he knew there was something we were hiding, but could I keep my composure and prevent myself from revealing our true intentions.

The Russian officer then began his questioning. He started out by asking me, "Miss Chamberlain, what are you searching for, answer me or your friend Pedro will suffer even more than he has already." As I paused in my response, the officer snapped his fingers and then the real torture began. The barbed wire surrounding Pedro's arms and hands began to be tightened, so much so that his blood began to squirt from his body. As Pedro writhed in pain, I still refused to answer the question, remembering what Pedro had told me, never to reveal our intentions. As Pedro screamed in agony, the Russian officer screamed out, "Tell me what I want to know or else your friend will find out what pain is really like."

Clutching my fists, I refused to answer the question. That's when the Russian officer slammed his hands on the desk and said, "Ok, still don't want to talk. Perhaps our next torture will give you reason to talk." Snapping his fingers again, the officer ordered the three men standing guard over Pedro, to attach electrodes to his nipples. Turning my head away, I heard the officer say, "Well, Miss Chamberlain. Perhaps our next torture will give you reason to talk." As the stillness and silence permeated the room, it was broken only by the sound of electricity entering Pedro's chest. I heard the most chilling scream I ever heard in my life. Pedro was in sheer agony, yet I still had to refuse to answer the questions.

After several seconds had passed, I began to wonder if I was to be the next victim of this madman. Suddenly, silence. Pedro was holding back, but the sheer torture of his wrists and hands being torn apart by the barbed wire only made his agony all the more excruciating. Walking towards me, the Russian started more of his interrogation, but this time, he warned me that I could be next to feel the sting of the electricity. I had a funny feeling that he was bluffing and that his goal was to frighten me and give me a reason to talk.

Finally, the officer said, "Perhaps I'll let the both of you rest and think about answering my questions. I'll be back in a moment." Having said that, the officer, the three guards, and the silent one, Xia Ping, left the room, thankfully with the lights on. I heard them turn the key to lock the door, preventing any hope of escape. I rose to my feet and gently walked over to Pedro, still wrapped in barbed wire. I stroked his bloody head and as he looked up, I saw the results from the beating he endured. I whispered, "Do you want me to tell him our investigation. It would help alleviate the pain and torture?" Softly trying to speak, Pedro whispered, "Don't tell them a thing. They know nothing and besides, if you talk and reveal anything, they'll likely kill us anyway."

I knew Pedro was correct. I had to come up with a very convincing story to lead them off track from our real objective and the possibility of another one or two scrolls somewhere in China or North Korea. I was sure either country held the secrets to the other scrolls, but the question I had to answer to myself was, "Will we get out of this situation alive and continue our search without being trailed by the Russians?" If there was someway of contacting Gou Fe Jong and his uncle Bo from here, I was sure the situation would change and perhaps I might even have help from of all people, Hansi. Question was, "Could I actually depend on Hansi freeing us, and could I trust him despite everything that he has already tried against Pedro and me?" I knew Hansi was in Rome, but exactly where in the city could I find him. Then it dawned on me. I remembered the small shop three blocks from the Vatican. That's the place Hansi had us held against our will. I'm more afraid of the Russian than the German, Hansi.

After perhaps an hour had passed, Major Krykofsky, the three guards, and Xia Ping entered the room. Major Krykofsky then said, "Well Miss Chamberlain. Are you ready to tell me what you've been doing here in Rome and in China. Or are you stubborn enough to watch your friend suffer some more?" As I just stood there in sheer terror, the Major then asked me, "By the way Sue. How's your sex life been lately?" At that moment the three guards ripped Pedro's pants from him and attached another set of wires to his testicles. Once secured, the officer repeated his question but this time he asked me, "Miss Chamberlain. If you don't answer my question, I will fry his testicles making them useless for any more sex. Do you understand me?"

As I stood, shaking and sweating profusely, the officer said, "I'm waiting Miss Chamberlain. Are you ready to talk or shall Pedro suffer more pain?" Seconds passed as though they were minutes. Snapping his fingers again, the man next to Pedro threw the switch, causing electricity to flow through Pedro's groin. This time the torture lasted a couple minutes and when the Major thought Pedro had enough, the switch was turned off and Pedro slumped in the chair, and by the look on his face I could tell Pedro was at the breaking point and most likely couldn't endure any more pain.

I finally relented and told the Russian officer that I would tell him what he wanted to know. I just couldn't stand to see Pedro suffer anymore. "Good," the Russian said. "See how it only took your cooperation to prevent your friend from enduring any more pain. If you had just answered from the beginning, all that could have been prevented." In my heart I knew he was right, but now I had to make up a story as I went along, hopeful that he'd be gullible enough to believe the lie I was about to say.

Although he kept Pedro tied to the chair, still suffering from the barbed wire attached to his hands and arms, I began by saying, "Sir, Please release my friend and I will tell you anything you want to know." Hesitant at first, the Russian Major agreed, but only if he truly believed what I was telling him was actually factual.

I started explaining that I received a telephone call at my desk at the New York Herald. It was a message revealing to me that somewhere in Asia or North Korea was a golden statue buried somewhere that supposedly came from the Ming dynasty, or even earlier. I told him the statue was laden not only with gold, but also with precious stones, worth a Kings ransom.

After giving him a line of crap for nearly one hour, he stood to his feet, and said, "See, you do know something. We'll just have to see how honest you really are. All of us are going on a journey to China then North Korea. Let's just see if there truly is a statue buried somewhere that's worth millions of dollars. Then, perhaps, I'll let you and your friend here, live." I was relieved that for the time being I had spared our lives, but what will happen once we enter China, and more important, North Korea, and nothing is found.

As the three men loosened Pedro's bindings, his agony projected throughout the small, darkened room. His arms and hands had been twisted into bare, bloody, flesh. The Russian told me he had a jet on standby just for this occasion. My thought was how would he be able to spirit us out of Rome without raising any suspicions. Come to learn that his uncle is the Russian Ambassador to Italy, making it possible to use diplomatic cover to pull this off.

As the three men shoved Pedro and I into their car, two vehicles came racing towards us. In a matter of a few seconds, all heck broke loose. Machine guns blazing, two men in each car began firing on the three men and the Russian Major. Once the four were killed, two men left their cars, approached us, and practically threw Pedro and I in one of the vehicles. Racing from the scene of the crime, we traveled for nearly an hour before approaching a massive gate that was guarded by gun toting men. By this time I began to question the driver where we were, but he kept totally quiet. I was so relieved to have been rescued from the Russian, that I was so relieved I never gave it much thought about who could have rescued us and why.

Driving through the gate once we were given clearance, the two cars drove up the long, winding driveway and stopped at one of the most beautiful houses I had ever seen. A man, dressed in a business suit, approached, opened the car door, and asked Pedro and I to follow him. I had no idea who these men were or where we were for that matter.

As we entered the foyer, all I saw surrounding the walls was granite. Chandeliers hung from the ceiling, and Asian rugs were everywhere. Once inside, the gentleman asked us to have a seat and wait. Pedro was in such agony he never wondered what was going on and I must admit that neither did I. I was sure that whoever rescued us also had a reason, but what. After waiting for about fifteen minutes, I heard footsteps coming towards us, sounding just like shoes walking over granite. As the man approached, I nearly fainted when I laid eyes upon his face.

"Welcome," he said. It was none other than Hansi himself. My first response was, "How in God's name did you know where we were?" Pausing a while, Hansi replied, "Miss Chamberlain, I know everything, except why the Russian Major kidnaped you and your friend." I was flabbergasted. I started to explain that the Russian wanted to know about a golden statue, buried somewhere in China or North Korea, worth a handsome amount of money. Hansi shook his head and replied, "Now, Miss Chamberlain. You know as well as I that there is no statue." Now I was beginning to become very scared. I knew Hansi's methods were just as cruel as the Russian's, but yet this time Hansi didn't seem so harmless.

Hansi began to explain that he knew all the time that Pedro and I were searching for the long, lost Jewish scrolls, considered being the long lost Book Of Abraham. Suddenly, my stomach began to tremble. How did Hansi know about the lost scrolls. My answer became apparent. Walking over to a magnificent desk, Hansi opened the middle drawer, reached inside, and brought out what appeared to be a lost scroll. I nearly fainted. How did Hansi manage to discover one of the scrolls, I thought to myself. Visibly shaken, I asked Hansi what he was holding and his response was, "Sue, I'm holding in my hand one of the scrolls written in Latin and you're going to go to the Vatican with me and my men and get it translated by your friend, Cardinal Catelli." I couldn't believe the amount of knowledge Hansi possessed about our discovery and what we've been doing all this time in Peru, Europe, and Asia, not to mention the Middle East, especially Israel.

The next thing out of Hansi's mouth was unexpected. He began by reminding me, "Sue. You and your friend would probably be dead by now once the Russian discovered your little secret. You and Pedro owe me your lives and now it's payback time." I couldn't believe what I was hearing. I actually owed Hansi my life and now it was time to give something in return. How could I live with myself if I allowed Hansi to know the truth? I was informed by Rabbi Goldstein that Hansi was involved in neo-Nazi organizations around the world, taking after his grandfather. Hansi needed the scrolls for the knowledge they possessed and would be able to ignite another worldwide Reich. I just couldn't allow that to happen, but how will I be able to prevent that from happening. These people were just as diabolical and dangerous as the Russian Major. A while back I even prayed for Hansi to rescue us. There was something about him that always made me think that perhaps he wasn't as bad as I had assumed. Having Hansi rescue us also made me wonder if he really wanted to rescue us from the mad Russian, or was he saving us for his own purpose?

As Hansi and his men drove us towards the airport, I realized that it has been some time since my last communication with my editor. Luckily, I still had my cell phone, neatly tucked away in one of the rather large pockets of my pants. When, I thought, would be the best time to discuss my whereabouts with my editor. I had no clue of where Hansi was taking us, only that we were headed for the airport. After we had driven a few more miles, I asked Hansi to make a quick stop. "Why," he asked. I really needed to go to the bathroom, but Hansi wouldn't stop until we were at the airport and taking off for God knows where. I really wanted to contact my editor before leaving the country and I had to think of a way of making the call without alarming Hansi or his men.

Once at the airport, we drove towards a private jet, on the tarmac a short way from building G-7. I had to somehow make my call before boarding the aircraft because once on board, I didn't know whether I'd be able to make the call, and besides, I wanted to keep my call as private as possible, leaving Hansi in the dark of what I was really up to.

Finally, I was permitted to go to the ladies room. As I struggled to get the best reception, I made like I was really busy and flushed the toilet so Hansi's men, who were waiting outside the door, wouldn't be suspicious. Time was swiftly passing. The longer it took, the more impatient Hansi's goons became. All I could say was, "Wait a minute, I'm washing my face." Finally after three attempts, the call went through. Once my editor answered the phone, I relayed to him what's been going on and that I was being taken, against my will, to God knows where and as soon as I could call back, I'd be try to call again. By this time Hansi's men pushed the ladies room open and quickly hiding my phone, I walked towards them and muttered, "How impatient can you be."

As we walked through customs, I was thinking, should I take Pedro by the hand and run away as fast as possible. Just as that thought raced through my mind, Hansi grabbed my arm and led me through customs. I was worried that Hansi could be taking Pedro and I to a place we couldn't escape from. As the plane took off, it was only then that Hansi revealed to me where we were going. When he said, China, I almost did a double flip. How did he know that there was a possibility that one or more scrolls could be in China, and how was he able to come across that information? Apparently, Hansi did something I never thought he'd be capable of doing. Hansi turned to me and said, "It's funny how much information a Roman Catholic Cardinal knows when you prod him>" Stunned, I looked into his eyes and remarked, "What did you do to Cardinal Catelli?" His response shook me to the core. "Funny, but when I began to threaten to gouge out his eyes, Catelli began to sing like a canary." I told Hansi there was no proof that any scrolls were in China, but he interrupted me saying, "My dear, dear Sue Chamberlain. I know everything now and you're going to help me gather the scrolls, all of them."

I tried to explain that I didn't know how many scrolls there were. Hansi responded by saying that it would take as long as it took, he was in no hurry. One thing Hansi let slip was a name. He uttered to one of his accomplices, "Take our guests down below. I must call Colonel Krip." Now who could this Colonel Krip be, I thought. Now I was beginning to really become concerned. If

Hansi isn't the head master, who is this Krip character and what is he capable of? I was about to find out and believe me, I wish I hadn't.

After flying for several hours, we landed and I took a glance through the window to try to find out where we were. Hansi, noticing my attempt to discover my whereabouts, calmly suggested, "Sue, trust me. We are only making a short pit stop." I was puzzled. Where was I and where were we headed. As I sat quietly in my seat, I looked around and noticed four men embarking on the airplane. Who are these guys and what do they want. How are they connected. All these questions raced through my head and I wasn't too sure I wanted to know the answer. Although Hansi had rescued Pedro and I from the Russian, I was sure he was saving my death for himself. Who could be trusted and how am I going to get Pedro and I out of this dilemma?

Taking off once more, we flew for what seemed like an eternity before once again we were back on the ground, but where was I. As the plane came to a stop, the door opened, and Hansi in the tone of a drill sergeant yelled, "Ok, everybody off the plane." Once escaping the confines of the aircraft, I scanned the area, trying to discover where I was taken to. It didn't take long to find out. A black limo drove to our exact spot, and when the back door was opened by an aide, I got my first look at who it was. It was none other than Xia Ping, the man who was with the Russian officer. All that ran through my mind was being tortured, or worse yet, watch Pedro being tortured. I knew Hansi wanted me alive and not in pain, but as for Pedro, that was a different story. As we were shoved inside the limo, I pondered the big question. Do I reveal the scrolls once I found them, or do I send Hansi and Xia Ping on a wild goose chase. If I deceived them, they'll likely kill Pedro, leaving me even more vulnerable to Xia Ping. I thought that

Hansi really didn't want me dead, he seemed to have a fascination about me, but when it came to Xia Ping, who knows what he is capable of. I saw him witness the Russian officer torture Pedro and I was sure he wanted us in his country where he could do whatever he wished. I started to twitch from my nerves, especially when Xia Ping asked that we be searched. As one of his goons started to grab me and run his hands around my body, I thrust my knee into his crotch, causing him to experience a lot of pain. I demanded not to be treated as though I was a criminal. That's when Xia Ping displayed his temper. He walked to me, took his left arm, and gave me such a terrible slap across my face I thought he had loosened one of my teeth. His response was brutal and swift. He screamed, "You pig. You'll do whatever I want done. Continue searching her." This time a young, beautiful woman approached and said, "Raise your arms. I promise not to hurt you." Once she had checked my chest, she began with my legs, discovering the cell phone I had hidden in my pants.

As she lifted the phone high into the air for all to see, I did something I'd soon regret. Trying to reach above to grab the cell phone, I was kicked in the stomach by the woman holding tightly unto my phone. Hansi, very angry at my attempt, took the phone and went through my list of numbers, hoping he'd see one that he would recognize. Not seeing any, he continued by placing one call, just to see if it was someone I could call for help. Placing it on speaker phone, he had dialed my editor. Snapping his fingers as if to let me know to answer, I spoke to my editor, reassuring him that everything was fine and that it might be a long time before I could return to New York. As Hansi placed the phone in his pants pocket, he said, "Now that is settled, we won't be interrupted, now, will we." I began to be frightened wondering how I'd be able to place a call to summon help, but having no ability to grab the phone, all I could do was trust that Hansi wouldn't do anything to either Pedro or me.

As we drove farther east, I was thinking about the time Hansi nearly killed is back in Peru. Even wanting to return to Peru or the United States seemed unlikely. As we continued the drive through the hot, dirty landscape, Hansi decided to turn to me and began with a series of questions, one of which was, who was our Chinese connection. I told him that I didn't know his real name, just an alias he went by. Well, spill it, Hansi commanded. Sitting there wondering what to say, I blurted out the name Pia, that's all I knew I told Hansi. Realizing the name Pia was of no use to him, he decided that if I didn't come up with a real name he'd see to it that I'd regret not being up front and honest with him.

Finally reaching our destination, Hansi ordered us out of the car. The warm breeze and the amount of bugs flying around made me realize that we were somewhere in China, but where. Hansi walked over to chat with Xia Ping, probably to discuss where we were going and arranging for our entry into North Korea. Hansi knew we had been to the north and were searching an area only a mile from the border. Hansi returned to the car and told his men the North Korean border was only three miles away and that we'd have to use mules to get us there. The spot Pedro and I entered didn't resemble the area we were presently located. I wondered, how far are we away and how will Hansi slip us across the border. Did he have any connections with the border guards or were we just taking a chance.

After loading supplies from the jeeps and transferred them to the mules, we began our trek towards the North Korean border. According to Xia Ping, this area was rarely patrolled since it was a desolate and dangerous place. There were all sorts of vicious animals, snakes, and God knows what else lurking about. I must admit I was starting to become concerned. Suppose we were bitten or worse yet, attacked by something that would chew us apart. If the North Koreans rarely entered this area, or even the Chinese border guards, it had to be a very dangerous place. Even those wanting to escape from North Korea didn't even venture into this area.

After about two hours, we had approached a vastly wooded area separating China from North Korea. Peering through his field glasses, Hansi watched for any sign of activity, even through the trees the Korean border guards would stick out like a sore thumb. Having the coast clear, Pedro struggled to his feet while Hansi, Xia Ping, and two of Hansi's men besides myself unloaded our supplies, strapped them to our backs, and made the long walk through the thicket of trees and tall weeds, all the while looking for snakes. The darkness of night had already began to fade away and the smell of the pine trees permeated the air.

Finally, after getting to the border, we were halted by a vast amount of barbed wire separating us from North Korea. Wire cutters in hand, Hansi and Xia Ping made a large opening. Sneaking through the wire, keeping our bodies lowered, we entered the forbidden land. If we were caught, it was certain death, even for Xia Ping.

Walking for several miles, we came to a deserted village. The North Korean government had evacuated the citizens years ago to prevent further escapes. Racing to the first building we saw, the six of us rested inside one of the abandoned buildings. Hansi had no clue to where we were, instead relying on Xia Ping for answers. According to Xia Ping, he had heard there was a vast amount of treasure that had been buried in the vicinity centuries ago, still untouched. The question was whether the treasure was more scrolls, or was it just gold, silver, and precious stones. It was known that during the Han dynasty, Han's army had buried treasure in this part of the country, but the question was would we find it and what is more important, would we discover the treasure. Unpacking our load, Xia Ping decided the best place to look was southeast of the village. It was he choice since he was more familiar with the terrain, and had some knowledge about the rumors of buried treasure somewhere close to where we were located.

Having his map, Xia Ping felt that we'd have a better chance heading southwest, then turn south towards an area that a great battle was fought seven centuries ago. If any place could have buried treasure, it would possibly be there. Starting our journey, my main concern more than the animals and snakes was being spotted by any North Korean border guards. I didn't know whether to trust Xia Ping or not. Would he talk his way out of arrest and have the guards believe we had forced him into the country. Hansi, on the other hand, wasn't trustworthy either, but at least he would fight the guards rather than have us taken captive.

After treading another couple miles, we came to an abandoned farm house. Taking a break, Xia Ping and Hansi strolled the area, talking, and turning to Pedro and I often, just to be sure we weren't trying anything stupid. I thought, "How could Pedro and I escape. We had no idea where we were and besides, the baggage was extremely heavy making it impossible to run away.

As Xia Ping took out his metal detector, Hansi approached Pedro and I and explained that I had to reveal exactly what I was searching for. That made me realize that Hansi might have no clue about the remaining scrolls, but then I realized he had given me a small hint that he knew something about our adventure. Hansi might not know everything but he also wasn't stupid.

Xia Ping yelled out, "I've found something buried below and it seems very large, perhaps a chest of some kind. It was known that the Chinese would bury chests laden with diamonds, sapphire, rubies, garnets, and other valuable gems, but did Xia Ping actually discovery something. Hansi ordered Pedro and I to retrieve the shovels and start digging while Xia Ping and Hansi's men watched over us. In the meantime, Hansi took out a two way radio, called somebody, and speaking in German so nobody knew what he was saying, apparently was making contact with someone, perhaps a person higher up giving the orders to Hansi. Was a vast international criminal organization behind all of this and what would happen to Pedro and myself if they actually were able to retrieve what I had been searching for all this time. Suddenly a creepy feeling flowed through my spine. Would Hansi and Xia Ping take any treasure found, tie Pedro and me up, and leave us there to either die or eventually be captured by any North Korean patrol? Leaving us behind was one thing. Cutting our throats was another thing.

Continuing digging, Pedro's shovel made a noise. He had perhaps found something. Now all we had to do was somehow mark the area, keep some dirt above, and somehow be able to return to this place to retrieve whatever Pedro had discovered. I told Hansi we had been digging forever. There can't be anything of value here. "Perhaps," I said. "We may be totally off course since there are few records surviving that would give us some sort of clue other than what Xia Ping thought. "Ok, let's move on," Hansi yelled out. Pedro and I gathered a few rocks, placed them over the filled up hole to mark the spot, then loaded up our supplies and continued walking for another mile or two. Once again, Xia Ping took out his map, scanned the area, and decided to dig at this place, an area crawling with venomous snakes and spiders. I had heard that the spiders in Korea were so huge that during the Korean War, loads of American soldiers actually caught them, marked their back ends, and held races, hoping their spider would win the race. The one who bet the most and the one who was most likely to win, won the jackpot.

As we approached a small town, we spotted several North Korean soldiers, strolling about, watching over the citizens working in the industrial complex. The place was crawling with guards and it didn't take long for us to be spotted by an alert guard. Firing his rifle into the air, it was a warning shot that caused a loud alarm to sound off. Within few seconds, there were scores of North Korean soldiers firing at us. Xia Ping said, "Let's get the heck out of here, now." It didn't take a brick to hit me on the head to convince me to run as fast as possible. Suddenly, one of Hansi's men was hit, falling to the ground. I wanted to help, but Hansi yelled out, "Let him be. We have to make our way back to the border area we crossed over.

Moving on, it only took another three minutes to hear the Korean guards shooting Hansi's man. By this time my nerves were stretched, my heart beating ever so fast, and my legs almost giving out. Just as we approached the small farm house we had earlier rested, another rifle shot rang out. This time Xia Ping had been hit. Falling to the ground mortally wounded, Xia Ping's last words were, "Run." Now it was one of Hansi's men, Hansi, Pedro, and myself, running so fast we all thought we couldn't make it.

Just as we made it to the border, two North Korean soldiers, drew their weapons, pointed them at us, and barked orders at us. Since none of us spoke Korean, we literally stood still, not making any kind of move that could provoke the guards into killing us on the spot. Hansi quietly said, "When I make my move, fall to the ground." What was he thinking. Fall to the ground. In a sudden move, Hansi took his pistol out of his holster and shot the two guards dead, but not before one of them managed to shoot Hansi's man, killing him instantly. Now it was just the three of us and we still had to crawl through the opening in the barbed wire fence before the remaining guards approached. Leaving everything behind, we crossed the border, just in time. There were about ten North Korean guards that came racing towards the fence line. It was against the law for them to shoot anyone on the Chinese side of the fence which gave me a sigh of relief.

Abandoning one of the jeeps, the three of us made our way back to town. We'd rest up at the hotel before deciding what our next move was.

I asked Hansi who he was speaking to when we were on the other side. At first he didn't respond, but after several minutes of me harping at him, Hansi began to tell what I believed was the truth. He went on to explain that in the closing days of World War 2, the Nazi's ordered his grandfather and fifty other men to make their way to South America hoping that American forces wouldn't capture them. As they made their way through Switzerland, the men split up into four groups, leaving eleven others to make their way. They had fake passports, American currency, and maps showing them the place they were to meet. Once the fifty one men were together again at the docks, they boarded a ferry, then caught a German U-boat, making their way to Argentina and Brazil. Once there, they would scatter all over the South American countries, making it impossible for all of them to be captured together should word get out about their daring escape.

Hansi even said there were rumors that Adolf Hitler himself had escaped by U-boat and had made his way to Argentina, but after several months went by, they discovered there was no truth to the rumors. The organization that helped them escape is still in business, but is presently running guns and historical artifacts. There are numerous individuals all over the world who would buy stolen artifacts and gun smuggling was how terrorist organizations are able to wreak havoc.

I never would have believed in my wildest dreams that Hansi would be the one person to come to my aid. Pedro still didn't trust Hansi, but I felt that he may have been honest enough to thwart any attempt by the Chinese to exploit our expedition. There was still one person to worry about and that was a Chinese Intelligence officer, a man known as Han Li. He was nobody one would want to mess with and soon I found out why, but for now my only concern was returning to Rome and have a chat with Cardinal Catelli. I was curious whether he had finished translating the Latin scroll I had entrusted with him. It might hold the clue to this entire investigation.

The journey was long and tiresome, but I had to move forward and not look back. As I arrived at the hotel in Rome, I turned the T.V. on and watched with absolute horror that there was an attempt on the life of the President of the World Federation Council, President Adrian. I called my editor to inform him and he ordered me to go to Spain and get as much information as I could retrieve. The attempt happened at the railroad station in southern Madrid. A man only known as Juan, was the gunman and the Spanish authorities began their investigation as to how the would be assassin managed to get within a few feet of Adrian and shoot him.

Having to leave Rome without seeing Cardinal Catelli first, made me very un happy, but orders were orders and this was an earth shattering story. Pedro and I took a taxi to the airport as fast as we could, bought two tickets to Madrid, and raced towards the aircraft. Time was of the essence and I wanted to be there to get the full story. The New York Herald was depending on me and I realized that combined with this story and my expedition to retrieve the scrolls containing the Book Of Abraham was very important. Somehow, I began to think that the scrolls would contain some very important texts concerning this attempt. Everything that ever happened in history was revealed to Abraham and was in the Jewish scrolls.

Arriving in Madrid, Pedro and I drove a few miles to the city, trying to find a hotel room, but none were available. Now what, I thought. How in God's name are we going to have a place to stay while we were in Madrid. Pedro had a thought. He said to me, "Sue, I have a cousin that lives in a small town about thirty miles north of Madrid, perhaps he will let us stay at his house?" Thirty miles was a long distance from town, but what choice did we have. We had to have a place to stay and I had to cover this story for my editor, otherwise, I'd be in a heap of trouble and could quite possibly be ordered back to New York, never returning to Peru or searching the globe for more scrolls.

At the airport in Madrid I rented a car, packed our belongings in the trunk and raced towards the hospital. The place was crawling with news reporters from across the world, all anxious to get the full story first. We managed to squeeze close to the front entrance and luckily for us because no sooner were we in a good position when a hospital spokesperson came outside to hold a press conference. Apparently President Adrian had taken a bullet to the head, causing extreme damage. For the time being the spokesperson from the hospital could only say that the doctors were working feverishly trying to save his life. There were reports that some world leaders were headed to Madrid to see Adrian. One other American newspaper reporter announced that he had received word that President McNair was on his way to Madrid to find out for himself what had happened.

For the next five days all I did was report back to the Herald everything I had learned, but on day six, there was a stunning report from the hospital. Apparently, President Adrian survived the attempt on his life and was reported to be walking, talking to the staff at the hospital. Even the spot where the bullet entered was beginning to heal at a very fast, complete rate. Unbelievable, was what everybody was thinking. "How could Adrian be shot in the head, survive the attempt, and be walking within four days afterwards?" There were reports that Adrian even seemed to possess supernatural powers. Something had happened to make Adrian survive and even reportedly have some sort of unworldly power.

Once I reported on President McNair's arrival, I told Pedro we had to return to Rome, then make our way back to the states. I had to install all my information into my computer, then think about returning to Peru. Pedro went without me but I warned him to be careful. I had no idea where Hansi was and could I trust him anyway. There was something about him that gave me chills, but for now my main concern was making my report on the attempt to kill Adrian and install the latest information about the scrolls into my computer.

After two weeks had passed and I was well rested, I decided it was time to return to Peru. Although my editor was frustrated with me he still didn't give me much grief about being gone so long, just to cover a story, but I assured him that his patience would pay off, and soon.

As my flight approached Lima, I wondered whether Pedro had investigated the caves again. Something told me that if Pedro and I furthered our investigation, we would finally discover the last clue that could hold the future of the world in it's writings. The long lost Book of Abraham was a treasure trove of information and I was determined to find each and every scroll and turn them over to the museum in Jerusalem. I thought that was the proper place for them to be, after all, I was sure that is what Abraham would have wanted, but there still danger lurking around every corner and could Hansi be one of those dangers. He explained his reason for finding the scrolls but somehow, even though he told me he was only concerned about my welfare, I had a sneaky suspicion that Hansi was up to no good.

Finally arriving at the hotel, the first thing I did before unpacking was to call Pedro to let him know I had finally arrived after being gone for such a long time. Pedro told me he had begun to search another cave about two miles from where he and I had searched. According to the last Latin scroll, there was possibly two or three more scrolls to be found and they would be the last scrolls to be discovered in South America. The Latin scrolls had given the name Joseppa, and I couldn't help but wonder why Joseppa brought the scrolls here and how did he manage to leave Palestine and make the journey here?

Before I met up with Pedro, I went to the local library to see if I could find any information about Joseppa and how he got here. There were volumes and volumes of information written about the history of Peru as well as Argentina, Brazil, and finally Chile. The second volume I examined contained some information pertaining to a voyage that had arrived first in Chile. It stated that three vessels arrived with twenty men on each and that they had brought many artifacts from Jerusalem, including various amounts of scrolls. The witnesses to this arrival had written down their version of events, such as that the Hebrews had brought a total of fifteen scrolls, each vessel containing five scrolls. They were the first generation of Jews that had settled in Chile and eventually Argentina, Peru, and Brazil.

The third volume was written around one hundred years after the Hebrews arrival and only gave a few lines about their wives and offspring. The one thing that caught my attention was the fact that Joseppa had returned to Jerusalem, and returned on a five ship journey back to Chile, then began to spread to other countries in the region. Joseppa would settle in Peru with his three wives and twenty children. According to the fourth volume stated that Joseppa lived to the ripe old age of 174 years, dying of a disease that had spread throughout the region. The volume said that possibly as many as five thousand people perished before the disease finally was wiped out with a concoction of herbs and spices.

After researching further, I had to quit, my eyes were darkened from the amount of time I had read them. I wrote down the volume number I had seen, placed them back on their shelves, and walked the few blocks to Pedro's apartment.

Once we were together, Pedro and I discussed what we were about to achieve. If Pedro's calculations were correct, we'd find more scrolls further south of our last dig. I was all goose bumps, filled with excitement at the possibility of discovering the last scrolls. As we filled the jeep with our suitcases, a car sped towards us and stopped a few feet from where we were standing. It was Father

Ligouri. I could tell just by the look in his eyes that he had good news for me.

According to Father Ligouri, Cardinal Catelli had finished translating the final Latin scroll and he said it contained a wealth of information and I was to return to Rome as fast as possible. I explained to Father Ligouri that it would have to wait until I completed my search. I just had to go to the place Pedro had started to dig and I was determined to find something. Father Ligouri was somewhat disappointed, but he understood and told me he would contact Cardinal Catelli once he returned to Lima.

I knew in my heart that Cardinal Catelli had found something in the last Latin scroll that would give the final answer to the question I had. That question was, "How would the final age of man come to be and who would cause it?" I knew the Christian Bible had a wealth of information in the Books of Daniel, Ezekiel, and Revelation, just to name the three I could remember, but the Book of Abraham was not only a book inspired by God, but God had revealed to Abraham a wealth of information that covered the time of the great flood during the time of Noah, but even giving names to those in the future as well. Would the Book of Abraham reveal to me the name of the anti-Christ and the false prophet as well? That thought alone gave me the inspiration I needed to continue my search.

Accompanying Pedro, we made the long journey to a new site that Pedro had begun to excavate. The place was miles from where we had begun to dig and I wondered to myself whether Pedro was taking us on a wild goose chase, especially since Pedro had found nothing so far and what made Pedro think that there would be more scrolls. I had researched during the few days I was in Lima and discovered the possibility that perhaps a scroll or two could be found in Argentina or perhaps Brazil. So far the only name I had found during my research was the man named Joseppa and other than the fact he had settled in Peru, I found no evidence of Joseppa being any place else, but what the heck, I believed that anything was possible

As we arrived at the place Pedro had preselected, I was amazed that he even found this place. It was in the middle of nowhere and although mountains were abundant, there were also flat lands and that's where Pedro said we'd have to dig. As I unpacked my gear, Pedro took out a special instrument capable of scanning for any underground objects, the best money could buy.

Pedro began to scan while I decided I'd rather follow, then dig a few inches to check whether we were close to a discovery. After nearly three hours of scanning, Pedro and I decided to call it a day and return to town, rest for the night, then drive to Lima to see Father Ligouri and Rabbi Berman. I wanted to discuss our next move and rather than try to decide myself, I'd let either the Rabbi or Priest decide what to do next.

Lima is an active city. Besides the great cathedral and Jewish temple, there were various sites to see, one of them the newly built Lima library. I had been there before but each time I see the building, I'm fascinated with it's architectural radiance. It was a part of the new, modern Lima.

I decided to check numerous records in the library before walking the short distance to Father Ligouri. One of the oldest records on disc contained information about early Jewish life in Peru. The disc was a wealth of information dating back as far as one thousand years before Christ. As I continued reading, I came across a paragraph that mentioned the name, Joseppa. I wondered whether it was the same man I had researched before and as my eyes poured through the massive amount of information, I found another paragraph that mentioned the name Joseppa, but this time it mentioned that Joseppa had taken a Peruvian woman named, Shedaiya as his wife. Shedaiya, according to the records, was a beautiful Jewish woman whose father was very wealthy. He had taken a friendship with Joseppa and after several months had passed, Joseppa married Shedaiya. The couple eventually had eight children, three boys and five girls. The one boy named, Jonathan, would become the senior Rabbi in Peru and even had connections to the Jewish community in Argentina. That, I thought, made the proper connection between Peru and Argentina. That's why Hansi was very interested about my work. Hansi knew there was a large Jewish community in Argentina, and besides, his grandfather left Nazi Germany for Argentina in search of the Book of Abraham.

Even though I couldn't trust Hansi totally, I still felt that perhaps he was really trying to help me. Was Hansi a new breed of Nazi, or was he a grandson of a Nazi who felt compelled to make amends and prevent the Book of Abraham falling into the hands of unscrupulous people trying to achieve a fourth Reich?

Now that I discovered that Joseppa had a wife named Shedaiya, and Jonathan was perhaps the first senior Rabbi in South America, my next objective was to research whether there were others who had left Palestine during the first century, and scattered throughout the world, hiding this very valuable book, making sure that the Roman's and future Kings would never find it to use to the own advantage. People sacrificed their lives hiding this holy book, believed to have been written by God himself, much like the tablets that contained the ten commandments.

With the amount of scrolls discovered so far, I had a record of everything and everyone from the time of Abraham through to the third century. It was clear to me that there had to be a lot more scrolls to find, not just the Jewish texts, but also perhaps those scrolls written in Latin that were hidden beneath the earth for all time. My excitement was overshadowed by the fact that there was a very good possibility that danger lurked ahead, even more than what I had already suffered.

After I left, I went straight to see Father Ligouri. I was excited by the fact that the priest would have tons of information for me, after all, I had given him three scrolls to decipher. I was just wishing the Latin scrolls would reveal a hiding place, hopefully around South America. One place I didn't want to travel was back in North Korea. Those North Koreans didn't fool around and would never hesitate taking one before a firing squad or just as bad, a long prison sentence.

Once I arrived to see Father Ligouri, I sat on the huge, comfortable sofa in the waiting room. I rang the bell and with excitement I waited for several minutes before Father Ligouri greeted me. The very first thing he said was, "Sue, I have great tidings for you. You have hit pay dirt, that's all I'll say for now." Now I was certain I had stumbled unto some good information, but I was not prepared for what Father Ligouri was about to tell me.

Before he could tell me anything, I requested that Pedro be present as well. If anybody deserved to know, it was Pedro. Taking my cell phone in hand, I dialed, counting the ringing. It took some time before his answering machine came on so all I did was inform his where I was and if it was possible for him to the cathedral. Father Ligouri said, "Sue, you'll never believe what I had discovered." Sitting as still as I could, I waited for Father Ligouri to explain.

Father Ligouri began, saying, "Sue, the third Latin scroll contains information about the location of five Jewish scrolls. They had been taken from Palestine shortly after the crucifixion of Jesus."

According to Father Ligouri, the five scrolls are located on the Island of Patmos. They were taken there by Saint John personally to safeguard them from the Roman's. It was the same place where Saint John had written the Book of Revelation, the last book of the Christian bible. Perhaps the Book of Revelation contained some of the information yet to be found in the Book of Abraham? Then it dawned on me. The Book of Abraham contained to much information that I was sure Saint John may have been told by God himself to keep out of the Book of Revelation. John's book only gave hints without mentioning anything that would reveal people and places except where the last battle would be fought.

Father then revealed what the next scroll revealed. That scroll revealed that some scrolls were scattered about in what is now the Turkish State, and also in what was once called the Persian Empire. That would mean returning to Iraq and onward to Iran. Iran is one place I shivered about. The Iranians never tolerated anything that would reveal information pertaining to the history of mankind, although I was sure that the scrolls would peek their interest, nonetheless.

The last Latin scroll revealed that the last scroll was taken to what we know today as Siberia, Mother Russia. Another dangerous place since it was learned that the Russians were massing a huge military war machine east of Moscow. Tensions have been very high lately since the attempt assassination of Adrian, the leader of the powerful World Federation Council. Speaking of Adrian, I recently learned that Adrian had special powers of persuasion since the attempt on his life. It was reported that Adrian had caused what appeared to be something angelic to appear in Rome. I didn't know if that was true or just a rumor.

Concluding our conversation, Father Ligouri said, "Sue, be very careful and always remember there are people our there that would cause you much harm, perhaps even death, to obtain what you are about to discover." I assured Father Ligouri I would be ver cautious, especially in Russia.

As I left Father Ligouri, I began the long walk to see Rabbi Berman. Perhaps the Rabbi had great news for me, but first I needed to call Pedro to meet me at the Synagogue for my discussions with Rabbi Berman. Once I had my conversation with the Rabbi, I wanted to return to the states to submit my information in the secure computer then go on a long vacation. I needed to see my parents and relax, especially since I was to travel to three countries, then return back to New York City.

As I arrived at the Synagogue, Pedro pulled up in his dusty, dirty jeep. When I saw the condition of that vehicle, I knew Pedro had been digging somewhere. Before we opened the massive door leading to the waiting area, I had Pedro dust himself off. I said, "How can you come here looking like this?" Pedro could only say that it is my fault. Apparently he took what I told him as meaning come right away and not change clothing.

Once Rabbi Berman entered the room I was filled with anticipation. I thought to myself, "What is so urgent that he wanted us to come here as fast as possible?" Sitting behind the desk, Rabbi Berman pulled out a drawer, revealing the first of three scrolls we had entrusted to him. Upon opening the scroll, he showed us what appeared to be a map. Pointing to the center of the map, Rabbi Berman said, "Here Sue, is where you will find the scroll preceding the final scroll." As I looked closely at the page, I noticed what appeared to be a road map that read in ancient Hebrew, Damascus. But the question I had was where in Damascus would I find that scroll. Rabbi Berman responded, "That my dear is what you must do. Find exactly where in Damascus this scroll is hidden. I told the Rabbi that before I could return to the Middle East I first had to return to New York City for my parents wedding anniversary. After I spent one week back home, my next journey would take me to the Island of Patmos. I had to try to find three or four scrolls buried wherever it's assumed Saint John wrote the Book of Revelation. Question was whether he buried them along the rocky coast or farther inland?

The next scroll Rabbi Berman took out described mostly information about the Middle Ages which we learned in school anyway, but still contained a valuable amount of information. It even described events covering the years 851 through 1127, even mentioning the names of the Popes that would be in control of the Catholic Church. Quite a good source of documentation.

Finally the third scroll. Although it was a wealth of information, all it contained were names and places already known, however, it did give one clue to where another scroll could be found, however, Rabbi Berman said, "That's where the message ends. It doesn't give an exact location like some of the others." Having poured over the scrolls, Pedro and I left the Rabbi, returned to the hotel, and prepared for tomorrow's meeting with Father Ligouri. I was hopeful that the last Latin scroll discovered would reveal more than previously. The Latin scrolls were a vital part of this very difficult discovery. By this time my editor was beginning to get upset on the fact that I've been away from New York City so long, but as always, I assured him that it would be worth the wait.

When I saw Father Ligouri, I could see the excitement in his face. Once I was seated, I was uncontrollable. Filled with anticipation, I said, "Father Ligouri, what is so great that you had us come before I left for home?" "Wait, you'll see." Rising from his chair, Father Ligouri walked toward a filing cabinet in the corner of the room, unlocked the drawers and reached in for the scroll. As he placed the document on the desk, he said to me, "Sue, you'll never believe what I've learned from this scroll." As he read the Latin text, then translated into English, I started to quiver with the feeling of nervousness. Finally getting to the bottom of the scroll, Father Ligouri read the best sentence I think any of the scrolls revealed. It read, "As the Father prepares his return, there cometh a man who will claim himself God and Abraham was shown his face and name by God himself and once the final scroll is discovered, the name will be revealed."

With that said, I was now more determined than ever to find the final scroll and return the scroll to the Synagogue in Jerusalem, near the very spot where the scrolls were supposedly written then distributed to be spread throughout the world. It even went as far as to say which disciple had what part of the entire volume, even mentioning the man called, Joseppa. As I gathered the scrolls, I left Father Ligouri and Pedro behind and returned to New York City, to my office, and secured the scrolls before leaving for my apartment to prepare the festivities for my parents anniversary party. As I sat in the aircraft returning home, all I could think about was what the final Latin scroll revealed and how I would discover the information that would reveal to me the final outcome of mankind. But first, there were the festivities ahead.

CHAPTER 6

The cold air in New York City was fresh but with a little sting to my face. Christmas is in four days, the day after my parents wedding anniversary. The festivities would be noted as a who's sort of thing. Practically everybody that had high offices would be attending. My parents were friends with the mayor of the city as well as knowing the Governor of New York. My father was a well known artist who painted fresco's for the city and state. I sure was looking forward to attending the party since I might be able to meet a very well known archeologist named Robert Calisi. I believe I may have been introduced to him many years ago but perhaps he'll remember me.

As I sat at my desk at the Herald, I inserted the disk, saved the information into the computer so to have another copy of all I had achieved so far. At least my computer is secure since I and I alone have access to the computer. I couldn't believe how much I have discovered so far, but I had no idea that there was so much yet to discover. The journey ahead would take me to places unknown and even places I could almost predict. Once I left New York City, I'd first travel to Jerusalem to hand over the scrolls I have in my possession. The one thing that bothered me was that although I placed them inside my parents safe, I was still concerned that someone may enter their home and steal the scrolls, but I had to leave them there because my apartment isn't as secure.

Just as I was about to leave the office for the day, in comes my editor, and he has the meanest look on his face that I ever saw. I knew he wasn't very pleased that I have been gone for so long but I just had to continue my quest. Before he began to scream at me, I interjected saying, "I know you're angry with me but believe me you'll understand once I reveal what I've been doing." Standing firmly in front of me, he said, "Sue, you told me that all you needed was one month, then you'd be back at your desk." I told him once again that after I've completed my assignment, he'd be more than pleased. Quietly standing in front of my desk, he said, "Well Sue. I have another assignment for you and I want you there in three days. I want you to fly to Belgium to cover a story. Adrian and President McNair are having a meeting and there may be an announcement once the meeting is over and I want you to cover the story." I must admit that put a damper on my plans, but he is my editor and I must do what I'm assigned to cover. The one problem I had was that I had to attend the party for my parents, then quickly get to the airport, fly to Belgium in time to cover the story. That wouldn't leave me to much breathing room to arrive at my hotel room, unpack, and make my way to the palace to cover the story. At times I'd like to kill my editor for being so determined to make my life a living hell, but I had to obey whatever I was told to do.

As the gathering began for the party, I had worn a beautiful blue gown and lot's of glistening silver jewelry. I wanted to look my best and perhaps I'd meet a guy I could latch onto. As I walked through the very large room that could be described as an auditorium, I met Mayor Cooper and Governor Hankins. Besides, there were movie stars, major newspaper people, t.v. big wigs and an assortment of very high and powerful people. On display were numerous paintings my father had completed. Many were going to be auctioned off in a few days for charity but unfortunately I wouldn't be able to attend that auction.

The evening was magnificent, but now it was time for me to pack my bags, get to the airport, and catch the next flight from New York to Brussels. It would be a long flight so I had plenty of opportunity to prepare my coverage of the event. I had never seen Adrian in person and this was at least my chance to get a close look at him. I've been told he was handsome, and had the most fascinating blue eyes anyone could have. Furthermore, I knew Adrian could charm the pants off anybody, especially women.

As the plane landed in Brussels, I had finished writing down my schedule while in Belgium. The first thing I had to do was cover the story, but I also wanted to meet an old friend of the family. His name is Harvey and he practically raised me whenever my parents were away, which was quite often. Harvey retired here and knew many well to do people, not just here in Belgium, but also all over Europe. I learned he might even have a person with access to Adrian. Wouldn't it be great if I could do an interview with Adrian, I wondered. Hardly anyone gets the chance to interview Adrian. He generally avoids any personal contact other than with world leaders. In fact only one other journalist had been given the chance and he was the highest paid journalist in the United States.

When the first day arrived for the meeting, I took my place outside the grand entrance to the palace, hopeful I'd have an opportunity to ask a question to Adrian and President McNair. There were thousands of people everywhere and the crowds were jubilant at the prospect of seeing Adrian himself. As the world's greatest leader and well liked, people went to any lengths to have a chance to look at his face. Adrian was the only person in the world who had the ability to have other leaders around the world do exactly what he wanted without question.

After what seemed liked forever, the darkened figures of the two men emerged from the palace. President McNair approached the podium and began to say a few words. President McNair only said a few words saying, "Ladies and gentlemen. Tonight a historic agreement has been reached between the United States and the World Federation Council. Adrian and I have agreed to combine our military forces in the event aggression rears it's ugly head anywhere in the world, our forces will be lead by a General Officer under the military office of the World Federation Council. Our military commanders will obey the orders of the World Federation Council without question.. I have agreed to this protocol. Thank you."

With that statement, it meant that the American military leaders will only play a secondary part in any military operation conducted by the W.F.C. That can only mean that the United States has relinquished it's independence to the World Federation Council, placing Adrian as the one calling the shots.

Once the American President had finished his brief statement, Adrian took the podium but only confirmed what President McNair had stated. Adrian was a man of few words and getting anything from his was always difficult.

After the announcement, the two leaders began to take questions. After several questions, I raised my hand and with awe I was chosen. I asked Adrian, "Adrian, what are your plans if President McNair decides to use American military power without the consent of the W.F.C.?" Adrian answered saying, "President McNair has signed the agreement that the United States will never take any action without first consulting the World Federation Council and my personal decision." I was shocked that the President would even sign such an agreement. That meant that America can never use military action independently without first consulting the world body.

The next day I left Belgium, making my way back to New York to write the article about my attendance at the W.F.C. My article was front page news at the Herald which made my editor very happy to say the least. Once I was finished with that assignment, I returned to my parents house to share some quality time with them. I hardly ever get to see them, especially since I've been preoccupied with this business concerning the scrolls. I assured my editor that soon I would be finished and be able to spend more time at the Herald and thankfully assignments closer to home. I was travel weary but I had to see this thing through.

The time had come to return to Peru but something came up that cautioned me about returning to Peru. The telephone rang and it was none other than Hansi. He had kidnaped Pedro, Father Ligouri, and Rabbi Berman. His demand was that I return to Peru with the scrolls I had found so far or he'd kill all three of them beginning with Rabbi Berman. I was in shock. I thought from my last meeting with Hansi that he was beginning to be our friend, not adversary, but I was wrong. Hansi was the grandson of the Nazi officer who was searching for the scrolls to deliver to Adolf Hitler shortly before the end of the war. I knew I couldn't trust Hansi but now I had a big dilemma. How can I rescue the three from Hansi's clutches without turning over the scrolls we have already discovered, and besides, several are in Jerusalem and Rome.

I pleaded with Hansi not to hurt my three friends and I agreed I'd return to Peru with the scrolls just so he wouldn't kill the three hostages he has held. This was the first time I was being blackmailed and I wasn't certain I knew how to handle this. Should I go to the authorities? After what I heard come from Adrian's mouth, I was apprehensive, feeling that the W.F.C. would grab the scrolls to use for it's own benefit. After knowing how much energy was given in human history by many dictators and kings to grab them, I was certain that Adrian would benefit from possessing them for his personal grab for supreme power. If Adrian could get the American government to hand our power over to him, anything was possible.

As I pleaded with Hansi to release his hostages, I knew I had to come up with a plan and quick to free the hostages, avoid Hansi forever, and get the scrolls we've already collected to stay in Jerusalem. As I was thinking what I was going to do, I got a call from an old friend, Alfredo Ortega. Alfredo is from my college days and while I pursued a career in journalism, Alfredo continued his studies to also be an archeologist. His call came from Mexico and he told me that while he was excavating near an ancient temple, he discovered two scrolls, written in ancient Hebrew. He told me that through the grapevine, he had heard of the exploits of Pedro and me. I was afraid to ask, but I said, "Alfredo, who told you what I was doing?" It was then that he revealed that he was friends with the man I met in Egypt, Hakim. In one way I was disturbed that Hakim would divulge what I was doing to someone I had no idea of telling, but Alfredo is an old friend and I know I can trust him.

As Alfredo and I talked about old times, I brought up the subject of Hansi. Alfredo told me he had heard of Hansi through an old friend of his, but he had no idea Hansi was in Peru or anywhere in South America. When I asked him what he meant by that statement, Alfredo told me, "Sue, he's wanted by the authorities in Peru, Argentina, and Brazil for exporting illegally ancient artifacts to collectors around the world." As he explained that the three countries could never track him down, Alfredo insisted I contact one of his old friends, a police official named Jose Fasmios. Jose has been trying for years to grab Hansi and nothing would make Jose feel better than to finally grab Hansi and hold him for trial.

As I thanked Alfredo for that piece of information, I then asked where I could contact him and hand the two scrolls he found to me so I could take them to Rome to have Cardinal Catelli read them, since my friend Rabbi Berman is one of the hostages Hansi has grabbed.

I immediately grabbed a suitcase and flew to Mexico City to meet Alfredo. All the while my thoughts were about Pedro and the others. Would I be able to rescue them by going to the police? Question was, would I have enough time, could I stall Hansi long enough to get to Mexico City, have Alfredo give me the two scrolls, return them to my apartment for safekeeping, and return to Peru before Hansi did something drastic?

As the plane landed, I decided to have Alfredo keep them safe until I was finished with business in Peru, I just wanted to stay long enough to have a glance at them and marvel about the appearance of the two scrolls.

Standing along the curb, I was waiting for a taxi when along comes Alfredo in his dilapidated pick-up truck. Unbelievable to me was that Alfredo owned that old, rusty truck way back in college and to think it's lasted this long is incredible. I was never so glad to see Alfredo. He was like a brother to me ever since we met. We would go to parties and generally hang around with each other. There were times that I even considered marrying Alfredo should he propose, but he never did so we went our separate ways after college, although Alfredo kept my phone number. I was glad he did otherwise how would he have ever been able to find me to hand over the scrolls? Suddenly, I realized that how did two scrolls make it to Mexico? Did Joseppa and Shedaiya bring them here?

After riding for two hours, we came to a small village somewhere in Mexico. As we stopped, there in front of me was the worse looking shack I ever laid eyes on. When Alfredo said, "We're home," I was floored. How could he live in such a place, but I must admit, I've been to worse places on earth.

As I sat on a chair, Alfredo walked over to a small, locked chest, opened it's lid, and there they were, the two scrolls. I was so excited. I nearly jumped out of my skin. What, I thought, will they reveal? In the beginning of my investigation, I couldn't tell the difference between ancient Hebrew and Latin, but these scrolls sure looked like all the rest, written in ancient Hebrew. As I cuddled the scrolls, I was careful not to drop them. As delicate as they were, they somehow survived all the thousands of years, lost it seemed forever. It hit me that the Book of Abraham was perhaps the longest book of what should have been the Christian Bible, the Torah, the Talmud, and perhaps other holy writings throughout the ages.

By this time I had learned a few words of Hebrew and a few words I was able to decipher. Apparently, these scrolls might cover the period of 1277 through perhaps 1358. At least those numbers I could read, but yet I wasn't sure.

I could only spend a few hours here in Mexico before going back to Peru to have the police rescue my friends. While I was here, Alfredo showed me the many items he had discovered. There was pottery, jewels, and other ancient artifacts.

Hours flew by and suddenly it was time to leave. Alfredo assured me he would keep the scrolls hidden until I return. I was relieved and very anxious to have them translated and have them reveal even more information that God told Abraham.

During the flight from Mexico City to Lima, I pondered to myself why God chose me to discover these ancient writings. I couldn't explain it to myself, but I was sure there was a purpose. Despite all the ups and downs, I was happy and determined to see this investigation through.

As I checked into the hotel in Lima, I picked up the telephone and called the main police station. After two rings, an officer answered saying, "Sergeant Hoppes, how may I help you?" I asked to speak with Officer Jose Fasmios. "Hold on, one minute please," the man answered. Waiting for what seemed to take forever, Jose Fasmios finally answered. I informed him that a friend of mine by the name of Alfredo Ortega gave me his name and that I had very important information for him regarding Hansi. When Officer Fasmios heard the name Hansi, that really got his attention. Officer Fasmios asked me to come to the station to answer questions relating to Hansi. I agreed and said that I'd be there in an hour. Hanging up the phone, I realized that I had no idea where Hansi was or the hostages.

Arriving at the police station, I waited several minutes before Officer Fasmios entered the waiting room. Officer Fasmios was a heavyset guy with bushy eyebrows and unshaven. When he called out my name, I answered, "Here I am." Guiding me to his office, I sat in the chair in front of his desk and explained to him what Alfredo told me. I told the officer about Hansi and how he's been following me for months but this time he has taken hostages. Then the thousand dollar question came from his lips. "Where is this Hansi fellow?" When I told him that I Didn't know his exact location but that Hansi was going to call me in aa day or two to find out whether I had any of the scrolls with me.

It was then that I realized the trouble I was in. Officer Fasmios told me that it was illegal to go digging for buried treasure in Peru, even if you're an archeologist. When I told him I was a journalist, he became very agitated and asked me where I have been digging. I tried to explain that I meant no harm and that the scrolls were ancient texts that were sent to Peru for safekeeping. I discovered the scrolls buried near the town of Puna, not far from Tarma. "Even still, you shouldn't have removed them and taken them out of the country." I tried to tell him that Hansi has been trying to find them to help set up another Nazi Reich.

After hearing my pleas, Officer Fasmios then told me why he's been trying to find Hansi himself. According to the officer, Hansi is suspected of not only exported stolen goods, but also may have been involved in three bank robberies over a nine month period. When I heard that I knew Hansi was trying to finance another Nazi empire. I said, "He has to be stopped or else something very bad is going to happen, not only to Peru, but also Europe, not to mention the hostages. Once I had his agreement, he told me that when Hansi calls, try to find out his location. The one thing I knew was that Hansi was clever and that it could prove impossible to find him ever again, especially once he has his hands on what he truly wants, the scrolls.

It would take another five days before I heard from Hansi. When I asked him where he was, he scolded me saying, "I know what you've been up to Sue Chamberlain." When I asked him what he meant by that statement, he angrily replied, "You've been to the police, haven't you?" I made up a story that I was only reporting to the police that one of my travel bags was stolen at the airport in Lima. Naturally, he didn't believe me, but I said, "Believe what you want. I'm telling you the truth." Finally, he bought the story. When I asked about the hostages, he replied, "Don't worry yourself yet, they're ok."

Although I knew Hansi couldn't be trusted, I still had to believe that Pedro and the other two were still alive. I just had to play Hansi and find out exactly where he is and the hostages, then report back to Officer Fasmios. I knew I was in a dangerous cat and mouse game with Hansi but I had no choice. I had returned to Peru with one of the scrolls that only mentioned briefly the years 896 through 1047. There wasn't much information but perhaps Hansi would buy the fact that I was cooperating.

Once the conversation turned to the scrolls, I asked Hansi where I could meet him to hand over the scroll. Hansi replied, "I'll tell you when and where in three days. Until then, I want you to stay away from the police or else the first person to die will be Father Ligouri." I knew Hansi meant business and would do precisely what he threatened to do. All I could do for now was wait and hope I could set him up for Officer Fasmios to grab.

For the next few days all I could do was stay in my hotel room and wait for a call from Hansi. After what seemed to take forever, Hansi finally called. The first thing he said was, "Miss Chamberlain, do you have the scrolls?" Dumbfounded at the very thought that Hansi would even begin to think that I would hand any scrolls to him without knowing whether or not the hostages were alive, I answered rather sarcastically, "Yes, I have a scroll." When I said scroll rather than scrolls, Hansi became violent through the phone. His answer was, "I told you to bring me all of the scrolls." My reply was simple. I would hand over a scroll, then I'd want to talk to the hostages before I release any more scrolls.

Hansi was agitated, I could tell by his response. It was then that I knew I was in deep trouble. Apparently, Hansi has taken the hostages to three different locations. That was his way of guaranteeing that if I turned over only a couple scrolls, I would never be able to find the hostages and only after several scrolls were handed to him would he even consider releasing one hostage. His response when I asked about the hostages was, "Don't worry, the hostages are fine, but, if you don't do exactly as I say, it will be your fault that a hostage has been killed, starting with Father Ligouri, then Rabbi Berman, then finally Pedro, who I know you have a special bond to."

By this time my nerves were on edge. I couldn't be seen by any of Hansi's men going to the police, I didn't have all the scrolls with me, and the hostages lives were hanging in the balance. My reaction to what Hansi had said was nothing short of perpetual fear. I knew what Hansi was capable of, but would he really kill all three hostages and not be able to assure himself a victory and possess all the scrolls that made up the most important book ever written besides the Bible, the Book of Abraham. He knew that whoever possessed the Book of Abraham would have powers unimaginable. It would be the absolute power over the masses.

Hansi then instructed me to go to the Reiman's Bar, at the outskirts of town and wait there. When I asked if he would personally see me, he hung up the phone, making me feel uncomfortable not knowing who I was to meet. I had to be there in one hour, with the scroll. If I was late or didn't show up, one hostage would be tortured until I handed over the scroll. I saw what type of torture Hansi could do and I had to prevent any harm coming to the hostages or even myself. Somehow I had to make contact with Officer Fasmios.

An hour later I found myself sitting in a lounge chair in the lobby of the hotel. The warmth of the sun shined throughout the lobby from the afternoon sun. As I scanned the area trying to find someone who may stand out, all I was able to achieve was watching tourists arrive and later leave. After seven hours had passed, I was ready to leave when a tall, dark skinned man approached me. He introduced himself as the hotel security guard. He handed me a piece of paper and said that a young man left it with him to give to me. I thanked him and opened the paper and read this note. "Sue, sorry nobody could make it but be ready for further instructions tomorrow." I was so angry at the idea that Hansi kept me waiting for more than seven hours for nothing, but it then dawned on me he was testing me to see if I was setting him up. Thankfully, Officer Fasmios knew nothing about this or someone was to pay the price.

I waited another two days before a letter arrived with further instructions. This time I was to meet one of his associates at the train station, track three. There I was to hand over the scroll, wait several minutes before leaving the station, then return to my hotel room to wait for Hansi's next call. Once at the train station, I waited at track three not knowing what this person looked like or anything. After about a half hour had passed, a man walked up to me and said, "Are you Sue Chamberlain?" Nodding my head affirming I was the person he was looking for, I stood there as still as I could. His next question was, "Do you have my package?"

I opened my bag, took out the fake scroll, handed it to him and watched him leave. I was too petrified to even think of following him so I waited and after what seemed to feel like an eternity, turned around and returned to the hotel.

As I walked, I was thinking, "What if Hansi knows the scroll is a fake. What would be his next move?" As the seconds felt like minutes and the minutes like hours, all I could do was pace the hotel room, wondering what was next. Five hours later the phone rang. As I slowly picked up the receiver, I said hello and waited anxiously for a response. Thankfully it was Hansi and not the police. I asked Hansi if the hostages were ok but all Hansi wanted to know was when I would hand over more scrolls. I told him that until I get to talk to a hostage there would be no more scrolls to turn over. His anger could be felt over the phone line. He angrily screamed, "Who are you to make demands. Just for that outburst one of the hostages will lose a finger." Realizing my mistake I begged Hansi not to hurt any of the hostages and that all I wanted to know was how they are and where they are. When he answered he said, "The hostages were in three different locations. That way if you try anything heroic, there will still be two other hostages for me to kill."

It was then that he instructed me to hand over more scrolls in two days but this time I was to meet a man outside the main Synagogue. There I was to hand over at least three more scrolls then return to my hotel room to wait for further instructions.

The time dragged on and I only had five more fake scrolls and Hansi wanted more scrolls. Soon I was going to run out of scrolls, then what will I do. I somehow had to find a way to contact Officer Fasmios to let him know what's been going on. As luck would have it, the next day there was a knock at the door. When

I peeked through the peep hole, there stood two policemen and Officer Fasmios. Opening the door with trepidation, Officer Fasmios said, "Good afternoon Miss Chamberlain. May I come in for a chat?" Slowly opening the door I was hesitant at first but I didn't want to raise any suspicion.

Officer Fasmios asked whether I heard from Hansi and at first I didn't want to say anything, but within a minute I told him what's been going on and that there are three hostages at three different locations, insuring Hansi that I would follow every demand and not jeopardize the lives of the hostages. Officer Fasmios realizing my dilemma said, "I will put a trace on every phone call coming to this room and have several of my best undercover officers follow you wherever you go." That was all well and good, but what if Hansi is in a secure location where he would never be found, I asked. Officer Fasmios assured me that Hansi is trapped. He'll never be able to leave Peru without raising any suspicions. Trying to assure me, Officer Fasmios left the room, leaving me to ponder what was going to happen next.

After the police left, I had to wait for word from Hansi on what my next move should be. I felt I was playing cat and mouse with him, but I had to go along with whatever Hansi asked of me.

Several days passed and still no word from Hansi. I must admit that I'm started to get concerned. What if Hansi had already killed the hostages and would catch me and force me to turn over everything I had? Finally, on the sixth day, the phone rang and it was Hansi. He requested I bring one scroll to the House of the Divine Mary. There a man would meet me, take the scroll, and leave. If I tried to follow the man, Hansi said he would kill Father Ligouri immediately. I didn't want to endanger Father Ligouri so I decided not to tell Officer Fasmios about my rendezvous with one of Hansi's men. I had to keep a low profile at least until one of the hostages could be set free. I knew Officer Fasmios might have one of his men tail me, but I had to meet with the man and hand over a scroll. Hansi told me he wanted one scroll to have someone look it over to see if it was real or not. Once Hansi said that, butterflies seemed to enter my stomach. I knew they were fakes because Rabbi Caldero gave them to me shortly before Hansi had him murdered. Rabbi Caldero was a master of deception and purposely made the fakes just in case someone would do this very thing. I was just hoping that they were of good quality to fool Hansi and his men.

As I waited outside the tabernacle, I tried to think of a way to find out where the hostages and Hansi were. If I could just get someone to give a hint without realizing it, it may be beneficial.

After waiting for about a half hour, a man in dark shirt approached. The first thing he said was, "Do you have the package?" I replied, "Yes, but where are the hostages?" The man took the package and told me that if everything was all right, one hostage would be set free, but if I tried to deceive them, one hostage would be killed and I'd have myself to blame. I stayed at the church as instructed until the man was out of sight. Once I was alone, I went as fast as I could back to my hotel room to wait for Hansi's next call. Did I deceive Hansi enough that he bought the whole deal?

Four days went by and not a word. Finally, on the fifth day the phone rang and it was Hansi. He started the conversation by saying, "Good girl Sue Chamberlain. My buyer is satisfied. Now for another scroll." I asked Hansi about the hostages and that's when he replied. "Sue, I will release one hostage once I have assurance that all the scrolls are real. Until then just wait." I was beginning to become alarmed. What if Hansi has already killed one or all the hostages and is there a way I can find out where they are and have Officer Fasmios rescue them and catch Hansi and his men?

After three days had passed, I took a walk to the police station. By this time I was ready to risk anything to help my friends. Hopefully Hansi will never know I was here. Officer Fasmios was delighted to see me and once I was seated he asked me whether I was ready to cooperate with the investigation. Once I said yes, Officer Fasmios began asking a slew of questions. When I told him that I had already handed Hansi one of the scrolls, he became upset. He replied, Miss Chamberlain, do you realize how dangerous it was to do such a thing without telling me." I assured him that I wouldn't make a move without notifying him and that although one scroll has been handed over, I told the police that the scrolls I was turning over to Hansi were fakes. Officer Fasmios asked, "What do you mean they are fakes?" I told him that before Rabbi Caldero was murdered, he had made several fake scrolls just in case something like this eventuated. Rabbi Caldero knew about Hansi and he even knew that Hansi was on the trail of finding the scrolls to finance another Reich in Germany and throughout the world.

Officer Fasmios instructed me to return to my hotel room and wait for the next call from Hansi, then to advise him of the next meeting. Officer Fasmios wanted to have his men surround the area whenever my next rendezvous took place. He didn't want to arrest my contact but rather follow him and surround the place. I said, what if Hansi and the hostages aren't there?. Officer Fasmios said that if my contact took the package, he would return to Hansi and chances are that the hostages would be there. I wasn't so sure. I had a funny feeling that the hostages are some place else and even if he catches Hansi, perhaps Hansi has already given instructions to his men to kill the hostages in case he is caught or killed, Just that idea alone gave me the shivers.

The next day Hansi called and said that I was to meet his contact at the local cemetery. He would be waiting at the grave of Agnes Floures, in the center of the cemetery. I was to hand him two more scrolls, then return to my hotel for the next phone call. I called Officer Fasmios to inform him of the phone call and where I was to meet the contact. The one problem was that if any of Officer Fasmios's men were in the cemetery, Hansi's man will know something's up and leave to return to a secondary location to fool the cops. The cemetery was wisely chosen by Hansi. It would give his men a wide view in case anyone was hiding behind a headstone.

As I approached the cemetery, I looked around and after a few minutes had passed, I saw a man standing next to a headstone, appearing as though he was visiting a family plot, but as I got closer, I noticed he was carrying a pistol and had a large envelope under his sleeve. When I asked him who he was, he replied, "I'm the person you're looking for. Hand over the scrolls." I looked at the headstone to double check that it was indeed the right headstone and once I saw the name Agnes Floures, I took out the scrolls and handed them to him. When I asked him about the hostages, all he said was, "Hansi will contact you. Wait for his telephone call and no tricks otherwise a hostage will die." As I knelt at the grave as instructed, the man walked away and once out of view, I rose to my feet and left for the hotel.

Every minute seemed like hours and every hour as though a day had passed, and still no word from Hansi. I was beginning to get concerned. What if Hansi discovered the scrolls were fakes and are the hostages still alive.

Two days later, Officer Fasmios knocked on my door having some enlightening news. Officer Fasmios had followed the man from the cemetery. He had followed him to an old warehouse that he believed that one hostage is being held. When I asked him why he didn't rescue the hostage, he replied, "Miss Chamberlain. If I had entered the building, I could have endangered the remaining two hostages. We must first discover where all three hostages are being held before we make our move." I must admit he made perfect sense. It's just that I wanted Pedro alive as well as Father Ligouri and Rabbi Berman.

Four days passed before another call came through by Hansi. Apparently, the fake scrolls were being thought of as real by whoever Hansi was taking them to have them analyzed. If they were buying what I was doing, perhaps I could talk Hansi into releasing at least one hostage, but which one did I want most to see, I wondered.

Hansi stated that he wanted another scroll but this time he would personally arrive to retrieve them. Hansi instructed me to meet him at the Del a Rosa Restaurant at exactly eight tomorrow night. I was to be alone and to be sure I wasn't followed. As I agreed to his demand, I hung up the phone, left the hotel, and walked directly to the police station to tell Officer Fasmios that Hansi was going to personally pick up the next scroll and that he even agreed to release one hostage in three days as a show of appreciation and goodwill. I wondered which hostage would Hansi free first.

Officer Fasmios decided to make his move tomorrow night even though he didn't know where the three hostages were being held. It could be his only chance at grabbing Hansi and turning him over to the International Court as well as try him here in Peru.

I was starting to get nervous. What if Hansi had given instructions that if something happened to him, the hostages were to be killed. Officer Fasmios had thought about the same thing but still wanted to catch the elusive Hansi anyway.

The next day I had a telephone call from my editor. He wanted me to go to Belgium to cover a story that concerned President McNair and Adrian. The two men were to sign an agreement that would create a western alliance that would counter the alliance recently signed between Russia and China as well as several Asiatic countries. Adrian had guaranteed Israel that the World Federation Council had voted to protect the Jewish state from attack by the eastern alliance. President McNair reluctantly agreed to the proposal made by Adrian but succumbed to his demand.

I agreed with my editor and prepared myself for the long plane ride from Lima, Peru to New York, then onto Belgium. While I got ready, the phone rang and it was Hansi. When I explained to him where my editor wanted me to go, he became upset and threatened to kill the hostages. I pleaded with Hansi and after several minutes of pleading, Hansi agreed to wait a few days for more scrolls to be delivered to him. Thanking him, I finished packing and took a taxi to the airport. Luckily for me there were four seats still unassigned for. As the plane lifted off, my prayers were for the hostages and I wondered if Hansi would keep his word.

During my flight to Belgium, I considered going to the World Federation Protective Services. It is the newly formed International Police, successor to Interpol. I though perhaps they would want to know about what Hansi was up to and maybe I'd discover Hansi is a wanted man on the international stage. Hansi is involved, if not one of the heads of the organization, in various criminal enterprises. It would sure do me good to know that Hansi is wanted and I knew where he was hiding.

The day before the big meeting between the American President and Adrian, President of the World Federation Council. The WFC is perhaps more powerful than the former United Nations ever was. Adrian was it's leader and what he said goes. Never in the history of mankind did one man possess such power. Many have tried, but failed. There was something about Adrian that puzzled me. He was handsome, gentle at times, yet could be overheard saying terrible things, frightening things.

I spent the day before the meeting taking in the sights and preparing my question should any journalists be able to ask a question to either leader. I'm thinking, which leader do I ask, or yet, what should the question be. I was more nervous thinking about the prospect of asking Adrian the question rather than President McNair. Once the meeting between the two leaders was completed, tomorrow would be the official signing of the pact. All the council members which consist of every world leader must be in attendance. Adrian had the chair of the President of the council. He would then read the agreement and every member would vote yes or no, but almost always they voted yes for fear they would anger Adrian. It was just a matter of formality, that's all.

As I stood in the crowd, the two men came out the door and stood at their respective podiums. President McNair was the first to speak and take questions. This was my opportunity to ask the question that raised some eyebrows.

I raised my hand to be recognized and shockingly, President McNair chose me. My knees shaking, I asked possibly the worse question one could ask, and a very dangerous one at that. I asked President McNair, "Were you pressured by Adrian to sign this historical agreement, giving Adrian the only vote" What my question amounted to was that Adrian is nothing more than a world dictator. Refusing to answer, President McNair would only reply, "That question is inappropriate, then turned to another reporter. In seconds I was whisked away by International Security Agents. They had considered my question radical and perhaps boarding on antisocial activities which is against the law.

Once they returned me to my hotel, I was given twenty four hours to leave the country or be arrested to being a threat to the council. Brother, tell me about a dictatorship.

As I left the hotel to walk the seven blocks to the security agency, I noticed I was being followed. Agents were told to keep tabs on me until I left the country tomorrow but to me I was no threat. I had simply asked a question, nothing more. As soon as I entered the building, two agents approached, asking me what my business was. I explained that I needed to find out whether Hansi was a wanted criminal. Having me take a seat, the two men walked into an office, picked up the telephone and spent about three minutes discussing me with someone on the other end, perhaps their superior.

When they returned, the one said quite nasty in my opinion, "Follow me." Up the elevator to the fifteenth floor we entered an office. I was told to take a seat and wait and wait I did. Somehow I felt that the mirror on the wall was a two way so I kept my composure so not to raise any further suspicion and sat quietly with my thoughts.

Ten minutes later, a man with thick black curly hair and quite short came in the room. He introduced himself as Agent Myers. "What do you want to tell me?" I started out by mentioning Hansi and as soon as I mentioned the name Hansi, I could tell Mr. Myers became furious. He asked, "Are you connected with that son of a bitch?" I assured him that I wanted to let him know where they could find Hansi. He replied telling me that he had heard about the incident between me and Adrian. I explained that it was only a simple question and that if I insulted either President McNair or Adrian I was very sorry. Once I apologized, things settled down.

It took me five hours to tell Myers all of what's been going on. That Hansi is following me everywhere and now he has taken hostages to get his hands on my discoveries. I did keep it secret what I had discovered but only told the man I was doing a very important assignment for my editor at the Herald.

By the time I had finished, Myers agreed to help and said when I return to Peru, he would have several agents keep tabs on me, follow me everywhere, at least until they got their hands on Hansi. The International Police wanted Hansi even more than the Peruvian authorities, and they had first dibs.

The flight to New York was made longer for me by the fact that there were several international agents onboard, making sure I was either protected, or perhaps keeping their eyes on me at the same time. Was I under suspicion, I thought.

For the next three days I spent the hours working at my desk at the Herald. Although I needed to return to Peru for the hostages sake, I had to get some work done at the office revising my files and making sure my security codes had not been tampered with.

The time had come that made my skin crawl. I had to leave for the airport for the flight to Peru and my nerves were at an edge. Suppose Hansi finds out about the international agents and kills the hostages anyway. My question would be answered soon enough. With the plane having landed in Lima, I had no inkling that soon things would become even hotter and more dangerous than I could even dream of.

As my taxi arrived at the hotel, I unpacked my belongings and waited for any kind of response from Hansi. I was sure he had his men tail me from the airport to the hotel. My nerves were at an edge. Suppose Hansi has already killed the hostages after torturing them for hours to get the information he desired? It only took another four hours before my telephone rang. It was Hansi himself and he was in no mood for any head games. He began by asking me what took so long to return and I assured him that my editor had me fly to Belgium for an important assignment. Hansi's reply was, "What's more important to you? The lives of your friends or some baloney assignment your editor had you take?" I vainly tried to explain that although I wanted to help him, I still had my job to perform.

Hansi then started by saying that because it had taken me to long to return and the three hostages refused to comply, he had no choice but to kill one of the hostages. I screamed as loud as I could and yelled at Hansi, "You did what?" A silent minute went by before Hansi said, "Just kidding. I wanted to find out how much of a rise I could get out of you, however, if I don't get something great this time, Father Ligouri will be the first to die."

Hansi instructed me to bring one of his men another scroll, but this time he wanted me to bring it personally, along with his man. Although I was apprehensive at first, I agreed and asked when and where we should meet. Hansi instructed me to take the scroll and meet his man at the village of Callao, a town just a tad west of Lima. There I was to meet him at the train station. Hansi explained that his man will have a brown shirt with blue pants. I was to give him the package containing the scroll and the two of us would be driven to an undisclosed location. I must admit the idea of getting into a car, from a train station, with someone I don't know quite scared the heck out of me, but I had to do it no matter what. My main concern right now was n't the scrolls but rather trying to think of a way to prevent Hansi getting more scrolls before he discovers the ones I gave him are fakes and also rescue the hostages.

Tomorrow was the day I had to meet with Hansi's man and incredibly just as I was laying down on my bed pondering this situation, there was a knock at the door. Rising to my feet and slowly walking toward the door, I looked through the peep hole and there stood three agents from the International Police. They were the agents responsible for capturing Hansi and his men and help me free the hostages.

As I opened the door, out there stood one of the most handsome men I ever laid eyes on, but should I mix pleasure with business, I wondered.

As the men entered the room, I asked the top man how he knew I'd be here. Turns out Hansi wasn't the only person following me from the airport outside Lima. The man asked me whether I was going through with Hansi's demands. When I asked how he knew about the phone call, turns out he had my phone bugged. All he needed was for me to meet the man tomorrow with the last fake scroll I had and leave the rest to them. Somehow I had a feeling of utter dread that things weren't going to go as planned. Things never do, you know.

As the night continued, all we did was plan and re-plan what we were to do once I was with Hansi's man and how we were going to capture Hansi. My main question was, will we get to actually meet Hansi or are we being led to another one of Hansi's destinations?

Daylight had come and I was very tired from being awake all night thinking and planning. The time had come for me to take the taxi to the town of Callao to meet with my contact. The other men would follow closely behind yet not too close as to raise any suspicion.

My nerves were at an edge. What if something goes wrong and I never see the hostages again, I wondered. As I approached the designated place, the shadowy figure of a man came walking towards me. Once he stood in front of me I saw it was nobody other than Hansi himself. I was shocked that Hansi would be the one to meet me, however, the first thing he said was that if something happened to him, the hostages were to be killed and his men would track me down no matter where on earth I was. He was determined to have either his way or we'd all die because of it.

As I produced the final fake scroll and handed it to Hansi, I looked around and noticed the International Police were hidden behind some trees, yet I could see them. I tried to motion to them to stay put, that if they made their move now, we may never find out where the hostages are located and I could potentially lose my life in the process. With my right hand behind my back, I motioned to the police to stay put and then when Hansi told me to follow him, I motioned the police to follow. Hansi was satisfied and was taking me to see one of the hostages. God, I thought, he has them at three different locations. How in God's name are we going to rescue all three hostages? Feeling quite helpless, I let my mind believe that the police will find the hostages and arrest Hansi and his men before things get out of hand.

As I walked beside Hansi, I asked him why he was doing this. I said, "I thought you said you were on my side and you didn't want anything to happen to me." Hansi just laughed and replied, "Stupid woman."

Finally, after walking for at least a half hour, we approached a warehouse on the outskirts of Lima. Opening the rusty door, Hansi said, "Well Miss Chamberlain. I have brought you to one hostage and if you want to see the other two, you'll do exactly as I say or you'll live to regret it. Upon entering a darkened room, I saw a person, tied to a chair, gagged, blindfolded, and appeared to have been beaten. Hansi stood next to the hostage and pulling off the blindfold I saw it was Pedro. I ran over to him, touched his face, and tried to assure him that everything would be all right. Hansi abruptly said, "Well, Sue. You have done well and have deserved to be reunited with your friend, but this isn't over yet. There is something else I want and you're going to get it for me before I release another hostage." In my mind, to myself, I wondered whether this nightmare will ever end, and then I realized that outside this warehouse were several agents of the International Police. I didn't want them to make their move yet; I had to find out what else Hansi is up to.

As Hansi instructed me to sit at the wooden table in the center of the room, he told me that he had heard that a burial plot outside of London contained a hidden scroll. I asked Hansi, How do you know there's a scroll buried there?" Hansi only replied that one of his connections had tortured a Catholic priest until he talked and revealed that there is a scroll somewhere beneath or near London and that's when Hansi said, "Miss Chamberlain. You are going to find me that scroll or I will kill a hostage." I replied, Hansi, how in God's name and I going to find a ancient scroll beneath or near London?" That's when Hansi said, "Miss Chamberlain. That's your problem. You'll have two weeks to find it or else something very unpleasant is going to happen to Father Ligouri.

After saying what I was to do, Hansi demanded I get moving so I turned toward the door with Pedro by my side and left for the hotel. Once we were safely at the hotel, we washed up, packed our belongings and took a taxi to the airport. Our first destination was New York City then onto London. I didn't know that the police were tailing us everywhere and certainly to London. I was certain that this adventure was going to become more deadly and confused. Who could be trusted, I thought. Although my editor was upset that this assignment was taking so long, I begged him to understand that soon I would bring him the story of a lifetime.

CHAPTER 7

The flight from News York to London was long and very tiring. Pedro and I have been through so much already and I'm beginning to think this adventure is a never ending story. As I relaxed in my seat, I remembered that at one time Father Ligouri had mentioned a priest he knew in London by the name of Father Dixon. Father Dixon and Father Ligouri knew each other since their seminary days and were quite close. Father Ligouri had stated that if I ever went to London, Father Dixon was the man to see. Father Dixon had studied Roman culture and knew England's history like the back of his hand.

Once we finally landed, Pedro and I decided to go to the church on the outskirts of London to check with Father Dixon before going to the hotel. I was curious about this priest and just had to meet him before we settled in for the night.

As the taxi pulled up to the small, quaint church, I saw the lushness of the property with it's beautiful trees and gorgeous flowers. Spring was in the air and the place was in full bloom. I rang the small bell hanging outside the door. It was the way to summon Father Dixon that someone was at the church. It was Father Dixon's way of letting the Lord know someone was at the sanctuary. Waiting for a minute the door finally opened and there stood a tall, hairy man. At first I thought it was the caretaker but when he introduced himself I nearly fell over. I certainly wasn't expecting such a tall, handsome man.

I introduced Pedro and myself as two people in search for a valuable scroll and asked if he could be of any assistance. Having us enter the church, he sat down on one of the pews and asked how he could be of any help. Pedro and I sat in front of Father Dixon and told him the whole story about our quest. When I told him that I had heard rumors that a scroll was buried near or in London, his face went white. He replied, "My child, you're in the wrong place. The only place I know where a scroll could be hidden is somewhere along Hadrian's Wall, up north." That's when it hit me. Of course someone back in that era could have taken a scroll and hidden it right under the Roman's noses. Never would they think to get their hands on a scroll, so well hidden yet in plain view. The problem I knew I was going to have was finding the exact location of that scroll. How, I thought, will I locate the exact location, knowing it's been buried for twenty centuries without anyone having found it sooner. Father Dixon then said, "Miss, I assure you that there must be some historical record, perhaps in London at the Museum of History." I told him that if there was a record at the museum, then perhaps it's already been found and taken somewhere. Father Dixon was sure that the rumored missing scroll had to be either well hidden at the museum or perhaps having never been found.

Father Dixon ended our conversation by inviting us to stay the night, and that the three of us would eat dinner then we would pour over every record book the church possessed, going back as far as the fifth century. It would be a time consuming task, but we had to do it in order to discover perhaps the last three scrolls.

The next morning Pedro and I went to the main library in London to look up as many records as possible pertaining to the scrolls, whether there was some sort of record or anything that mentioned the scrolls and possibly where they could be hidden. Centuries have passed since the scrolls were lost but now there was this opportunity to finally discover all of the Book of Abraham.

After nearly four hours of searching through the records, a man came into the library telling everyone about what's been going on in the news. Apparently, several volcano's around the world have exploded at the same time, from Asia, to Europe, the Pacific Islands as well as North and South America. The ash from the volcano's are reaching toward the sky, blocking out the rays of the sun. Even here in London the day was turning dark and ominous. While everybody was concerned about the volcano's, Pedro and I continued our search for anything mentioning the lost scrolls. Finally, after seven hours, I came across an article written by an Italian monk in the year 1477. He writes that he had discovered an ancient scroll and that knowing it's potential value, took the scroll and buried it near Hadrian's Wall. That bit of information practically did no good. Hadrian's Wall was miles long and trying to find something like a scroll could prove not only difficult, but impossible.

As I turned the pages, I came across what appeared to be a coded message. I took out my tablet, wrote down every word, and stuck it in my purse. I knew then that I had to have Father Dixon look at the paper and determine whether it was valuable or not. Perhaps I had to find a code breaker, but where?

Night has fallen and still I was busy searching. I decided to stop for the night, grab something to eat, and get some much needed sleep before visiting Father Dixon.

Upon entering the cathedral in central London, I was very agitated that I'm supposed to hand any scrolls I find to Hansi back in Peru. If I didn't, another hostage would die and I didn't want to think of that. There wasn't enough time to make any fakes and I was sure that sooner or later Hansi's going to figure out that the scrolls I've handed to him already are actually fakes, and then God knows what he'll do. At one point Hansi convinced me that he was actually on my side, then no sooner was I convinced, he turns around and once again becomes my enemy.

Father Dixon took my writing pad and read the code. For the next four hours Father Dixon was deciphering the code and finally after waiting so long, Father Dixon told us what it said.

Apparently, a young man, perhaps a shepherd, had been giving two scrolls from a dealer in pottery that had sailed from Jerusalem to Rome, then to Great Britain. The dealer went on to tell the lad to take the two scrolls and hide them from the Roman's and that nobody should ever find them because of what was written on them by Abraham himself, led by God.

Father Dixon told me that the scrolls could possibly be hidden somewhere near the present day town of Carlisle, near Hadrian's Wall. Pedro asked Father Dixon if he had a car we could use and Father Dixon was more than pleased to oblige. Tomorrow, I said, Pedro and I will drive to the town of Carlisle, up north, to begin searching for anything that appeared ancient. I must admit that I was beginning to think that soon all my questions will be answered, but as Father Ligouri once told me was if I discovered all the scrolls, especially the last scroll, could my mind deal with what the scroll told. I thought that when God revealed all the information to him to write the Book of Abraham, perhaps

Abraham had a hard time dealing with the prophesy, and I was no different.

Pedro and I drove all night, trying to find our way through the thick ash that had made it's way from the volcano in Iceland. It also had exploded it's lava high in the sky, making Great Britain and almost all of Europe in what seemed like a nuclear winter. The moon did not give it's light and wherever wasn't covered with ash, the moon I was told appeared as blood, a dark red.

After a very long drive, we came to the town of Carlisle. Hadrian's Wall was a short distance away but since it was dawn and I was extremely tired, we decided to spend the day relaxing at the small mom and pop type of hotel. It was a quaint little place and had that feeling like one was relaxing at their own home. The food was great and the other guests gave the place a sort of ambiance.

Morning of day two and Pedro and I were well rested and after a quick breakfast, we made our way farther north. Finally in the clearing I saw what were the remnants of what I believed was Hadrian's Wall. It was a crumbled area; not much to really see, but I decided this place would be the first to check out.

According to the files in the library, there was mention of a kind of rock, a special rock at that. I was said that it had a bluish tint and appeared as though it glowed. Looking around I found no such thing but decided to begin our dig at this spot, then work our way westward. The documents gave a hint that the Roman's had also tried to find the scroll but gave up once it became too dangerous for them. Bandits had permeated the whole area, fighting between the two armies made searching for the scroll that much more difficult. One thing we had going for us was there was no fighting and we had special equipment capable of penetrating the ground.

If our meter was correct, we might find something if not the scroll. Any clue would do for now.

After digging and scanning the area for more than four hours, Pedro and I decided to drive several miles west, near an abandoned village that had it's heyday beck in the seventh century. Perhaps this would be the ideal place to search and I couldn't give up. I had to find the scroll, have it analyzed, and turn it over to Hansi in order to have another hostage released.

Over the next three days all we did was search and dig, then finally after all our labor the scanner turned onto something below us. According to the meter, what was buried below was some sort of metal device. Pedro grabbed a shovel and dug a hole so deep I could hardly see the top of his head. The hole was so deep it actually looked as though he had dug a crater. Slamming his shovel into the earth, he had struck something.

At this moment I began to become quite nervous. Had we really stumbled upon a portion of the Book of Abraham? Taking his trowel, Pedro slowly removed the dirt surrounding whatever it was. Suddenly, the light of the sun showered the top of the unearthed metal. It was long and very old. The lid was decorated in some sort of graphic design. Once Pedro had finished scrapping the loose dirt around the box, he gently lifted it up, handed it to me, and said, "I think we found what we came for." Just as what was said in the records back at the library, the box was bluish in color and the designs were etched with gold.

As I started to open the box, Pedro asked if I thought we had found the elusive, bluish box that supposedly contained what was believed to be the last chapter in the Book of Abraham. I wasn't sure but one thing I knew was that I wasn't about to hand this precious document over to Hansi, even if I died in the process. I couldn't think that Hansi and his fellow Nazi's should be the inheritors of such a historical artifact.

I gently closed the lid and placed it in one of my cloth sacks. Securing it tightly to our car, I had Hansi fill in the hole while I called Father Dixon, telling him I had a surprise. Father Dixon informed me that according to his research, there was another Latin scroll buried somewhere on the Island of Patmos. Although we had found a Jewish scroll there, Father Dixon told me that when Saint John went to the island to write the Book of Revelation, not only did he possess one of the Jewish scrolls but also the final scroll written in Latin that revealed where the final three scrolls could be found and a hint at what they contained. That means that Pedro and I have to return to Patmos and once again begin digging.

I no sooner hung up the phone when a call came in and it was Hansi. Hansi started by saying, "Well Miss Chamberlain. Have you found what I wanted?" I didn't know what to say. I couldn't let Hansi know what I had found yet I was concerned about the remaining two hostages. My quick thinking saved the day, at least for now. I told Hansi that once I found the scroll, I would meet him in Rome, near the Vatican, and hand the scroll to him. In return I wanted one of the hostages set free but would it be Father Ligouri or would it be Rabbi Berman? Knowing how much Hansi hated Jews, I believed that he would save the Rabbi for last or perhaps kill him regardless. I asked for four more days before meeting him and thankfully Hansi agreed, but he'd still warn me if I tried anything stupid that would force him to kill a hostage.

On the return to London, my anxiety churned up a bit. Pedro, driving like he was on a race track, noticed three cars tailing us as we entered the outskirts of London. It had to be the International

Police, especially since they admitted they were going to follow us, but do they know what I have found.

I was afraid that the powers that be at the World Federation Council might try to get their hands on the scrolls as well, especially knowing how Adrian wanted total power and until he had the scrolls, his power was limited. Since Adrian came to power about seven years ago, much has happened. As of now numerous volcanos are erupting not to mention that Japan is in the line of fire with a tsunami headed their way. Los Angeles reported that there have been tremors lately and even places like the southeastern United States is reporting that Atlanta and even Miami have experienced small tremors, the kind that usually begin before a major earthquake. Reports are also coming in that there is a massive storm taking shape along the African coastline, headed for the United States or perhaps Mexico. It seems that mother nature is spewing everything rotten that it has. Some people are beginning to say that it's the wrath of God while other's just pass it off as nothing to worry about. I must admit that these things concern me, especially the storm forming near Africa. If it strikes land, especially New York City, it would be devastation unheard of since our country was formed.

Four days passed and it was time to meet with Hansi. I had the scroll checked out by Rabbi Epstein, the head Rabbi of London. His translation gave proof that Abraham was told by God the time frame from Noah through the last days. This particular scroll mentions the two world wars, naming such people as Hitler, Stalin, Lenin, and countless other twentieth century leaders. Rabbi Epstein told me that according to his calculation, there should be at least three or five more scrolls yet to be discovered. That meant that there was still a journey to take and danger was still an issue.

As I stood at the western side of the Vatican, I wondered to myself why these scrolls were being discovered at this point in time. Was there a reason God had hidden the scrolls for four to five thousand years, then allowed a lonely woman like myself to finally find the scrolls and have them taken to Jerusalem. It was a question I have pondered ever since Pedro and I found three scrolls in the cave near Puna, Peru.

As I glanced toward the setting sun, the silhouette of a man was walking toward me. It was Hansi himself followed by two bodyguards. As I looked into his eyes, I felt as though I was looking at pure evil, and calmly stood there, frozen in terror. Once Hansi asked for the scroll, he told me he would release Father Ligouri tomorrow and he would contact me again after I returned to Peru. As Hansi and his men walked away, suddenly five police cars sped towards us. It was the World Federation Council Police. They have finally managed to grab Hansi. Hansi had avoided capture for several years but this time he couldn't escape justice. One of the officers handed me the scroll and told me to leave London as soon as possible. He was sure that once Hansi's men find out that Hansi was set up and captured, they would kill the hostages and come looking for me.

Pedro and I were packed and ready to leave for the airport when a policeman knocked on our door. He had a message for me from Hansi. Hansi said to the officer, "Tell Miss Chamberlain that she has just sealed the fate of the priest and the rabbi. If I don't return to Peru in three days, they have been instructed to kill the two hostages and come looking for me." The only thing that concerned me was not my safety, but of my parents and sister. What if Hansi had given orders to kill them before getting their hands on me. Hansi was determined to make this a personal vendetta and he'd stop at nothing to have as many people killed as possible.

Before Pedro and I returned to Peru, I spent the next few days at my office typing a report to hand to my editor about how I had trapped Hansi, an international fugitive. My editor was impressed but he still didn't like the idea that my investigation still wasn't finished. He desperately needed me but I wasn't about to give up, not after coming this close. If the priest was correct, there are only three scrolls still out there, but where. Father Ligouri still had one of the Latin scrolls to decipher and I was sure by now he would have translated the document. The problem was that Hansi's men still kept him hostage and I had to come up with a plan to rescue the hostages and search for the last three scrolls.

Tomorrow was to be a special day and my editor wanted me to cover the story for the Herald. There's to be a top level meeting between President McNair and the Israeli Prime Minister, Eban, to sign an agreement protecting Israel from being attacked by the ever growing eastern forces. Years ago Adrian had promised the Jewish people he would protect them but recently he has been saying that the Israeli's have reneged on a deal he had signed with them seven years ago. Now it was only the United States that could protect the Jewish state.

As I was prepared to leave my office, the telephone rang. It was a Colonel with the Peruvian Police. They had been following Hansi's men and were able to discover where the hostages were being held. Father Ligouri was found at an old perfume factory while Rabbi Berman was found in downtown Lima at an old movie theater. I was relieved that they were found safe and sound but the Colonel informed me that Rabbi Berman had been tortured, extremely tortured. They had gouged out one of his eyes, cut off two fingers, broke his kneecaps, and practically broke every bone in his body. Rabbi Berman was taken to the hospital and placed in the cardiac ward. They weren't sure he would make it but I still had faith that Father Ligouri and Rabbi Berman would recover from their ordeal.

As I landed in Washington, D.C. I prepared my notes, such as what should I ask the President about his meeting with Prime Minister Ebon. I didn't want to make a fool of myself like the last time I had the opportunity to ask a question. While I was in Washington, Pedro returned to Peru and the caves outside of the town of Puna. Pedro was sure that the man named Joseppa had smuggled more scrolls than the one's we have already discovered. At least this time we didn't have to worry about Hansi and his men from interfering, at least I thought so.

Tomorrow is the press conference that President McNair and Prime Minister Eban will give. As I sat at my desk at the Herald, Thomas came rushing into the room. He screamed out loud, "There's a storm headed our way and everyone must evacuate and leave the city." I had no idea what he meant but within a few minutes, even my editor came rushing in. He yelled as loud as he could saying. "There's a wave of water headed for New York. The waves are about two hundred feet high, enough to blanket the entire city." I grabbed as much asx I could and headed straight for the door. It was then that I had to get to the airport before I couldn't leave for Washington. I assumed that all air transport and trains, buses, and cars would be impossible to use.

I had to get to Washington no matter what but as I arrived at the airport, we were told all flights have been cancelled and none were leaving anytime soon. Now what do I do, I thought to myself. As I pondered my situation, an announcement was made saying that the storm is one thousand miles long and five hundred miles wide. That meant only one thing. The entire east coast was in danger of being submerged and even as far as Chicago they were saying could be affected. I was trapped and with the storm making it's way ever so rapidly, there was very little time to flee.

Just when things seemed impossible, Jerry, my camera man pulled up and told me to get in, that we were leaving for Memphis. At least there I could catch a flight to Peru. I was abandoning the press conference in Washington in favor of my safety. I was sure the press conference would be cancelled and the President and Prime Minister would be evacuated and flown to perhaps Colorado.

David, my cameraman, drove so fast I was sure we'd either crash or get a speeding ticket but even the police were busy keeping the traffic flowing. It was hours before we arrived in Memphis. I was tired and totally exhausted but I had to persevere. I just had to catch a flight to Lima, Peru. At least in Peru I'd be safe and be able to conduct my investigation into how the scrolls were taken there. I had already discovered that a man named Joseppa had traveled from Palestine and that he had taken a wife named Shedaya but other than that I hadn't found out whatever became of Joseppa and his crew.

This time instead of investigating the caves of Puna, Pedro and I would begin digging outside the town of Tarma. Rumors had it that a man many centuries ago had brought valuable items from Jerusalem and had even sold some of the items in order to pay his crew and live on for a few years before returning to Palestine. According to the local population, Joseppa never returned home and lived outside of the town that's now called Tarma. Would I discover more scrolls or perhaps the grave of Joseppa?

Once Pedro and I arrived in Tarma, I had a call on my cell phone. It was an agent from the legal department of the World Federation Council. When the agent told me why he was calling, shivers went up and down my spine. It seems that Hansi and his men have broken out of jail and couldn't be found. The agent told me that every airport and train station in Europe has agents searching. Could Hansi somehow find a way back to Peru? Once again danger seemed to follow me, and this time the danger level was even higher. The agent believes that Hansi could be making his way to China. The Chinese have a reputation of harboring wanted international criminals and if that was the case, there was nothing the agency could do.

I told Pedro what the agent said and I insisted we return to the caves outside the town of Tarma right away. If there was anything there, we had to find it, retrieve it, and take it to Lima so Father Ligouri and Rabbi Berman could decipher the scrolls.

It didn't take long before we had a hit. About five feet below us was a silver chest. Apparently nobody ever found the chest which made me excited. Pedro lifted the chest, slowly opened it, and found two scrolls hidden inside. One was written in Latin, the other in ancient Hebrew. By this time of my investigation, I knew the two languages almost as good as being capable of reading them.

As we arrived in Lima, two truckloads of army troops blocked our way. The soldiers disembarked and an officer approached our jeep. "Papers please." He wanted to check Pedro's identification and my passport. As he slowly looked over the documents, I could hardly swallow. My nerves were on edge. Had we done something wrong, I wondered. The last thing I needed was to end up in a Peruvian jail. After checking our papers, the officer asked what we had in the jeep. Only Pedro's quick thinking saved the day. Pedro, the man he is, told the officer he was only checking the caves, looking for anything of value he could sell, then Pedro opened a nylon bag, took out a bottle of expensive cognac and gave it to the officer. "Here, it's for you my friend." At first I thought he'd arrest us for bribery but he took the bottle, said thank you, and had his men return to the trucks and drive off. I asked Pedro where he got the booze and why he gave it to the officer. Pedro could only reply, "Sue, I could tell that he'd want the cognac and that he'd leave us alone." Even in Peru, bribery is rampant.

Finally arriving in Lima, our first stop was at the cathedral for Father Ligouri to translate the Latin scroll.

Before he began to read the scroll, Father Ligouri did some research of his own. He had found out that there was a total of thirteen Hebrew scrolls. Eleven apostles had spirited them from Palestine, but one of them, named Judas, didn't live to take one of the scrolls. This is where Joseppa come's into the picture. Joseppa was given three Hebrews scrolls and several Latin scrolls. Joseppa was able to pay one thousand gold coins to a Roman officer to purchase three Roman vessels and take them far from Palestine for safekeeping. It was believed that Joseppa was to hide the scrolls somewhere in Africa but the seas had him arrive in South America, months after leaving Jerusalem. Now I know how Joseppa made his way to Peru. He had no idea where he was other than knowing he had made a long and arduous journey and that there was not only danger for him and his crew, but there was the language barrier as well.

Father Ligouri continued by saying that Joseppa had taken the chance that the Roman's would discover what he was going to do, but, Joseppa was friends with the Roman officer who made it possible for him to spirit the scrolls out of Palestine. Had it not been for him, Joseppa would have tried another way of preventing the scrolls from being discovered.

Saint Peter was given the task by Jesus himself to spread the scrolls to the four corners of the world. One thing I did know was that Saint Paul had taken three scrolls and hid them in first Damascus, then onto Asia, possibly having hidden one in Korea and perhaps another in what would become French Indo-China. That meant that one could have been taken to either Vietnam or Cambodia. That had me concerned because none of those countries would permit me to conduct a digging and further research. I had already been to China and North Korea and the dangers they presented was of great concern to me.

Father Ligouri then began to read the Latin scroll I had brought from Europe. Father Ligouri told me that the scroll contained the exact location of the three scrolls that Saint Paul had taken. The first scroll, according to this scroll, was buried in a tomb with a Syrian General, at the place where the Syrian monarchy was buried. In present day Damascus, it could most likely be found on the outskirts of the city, perhaps the western gate. The scroll revealed that the second scroll would be found along the border of China and North Korea, perhaps on the Korean side of the border in a town that once existed along the Chinese and Korean border. That meant that I would have to once again take the risk of performing an excavation in North Korea and I'd need my Chinese connection to make the dig possible. It would take a lot of cash to bribe the border guards and still not be guaranteed that any border guard would accept a bribe.

Father Ligouri continued by revealing where the third and final scroll could be found. According to the Latin text, the final scroll was taken to perhaps present day India rather than Vietnam or Cambodia. India, I thought. How strange that these scrolls were taken hundreds and even thousands of miles from Palestine just to keep the Roman Empire from obtaining the scrolls that once together made up the Book of Abraham. Hidden for centuries, the Book of Abraham revealed God's plan for mankind from the beginning straight through to the final age of mankind.

I was excited by the fact that so far every scroll I found contained historical evidence by revealing names of important people, places, battles, and numerous historical events such as earthquakes, floods, and even mentioning the discovery of electricity and other inventions that at the time of these writings had yet to become reality. I was certain that when God spoke to Abraham, he must have been blown away by what God had revealed to him. Abraham, the father of three major religions, was presented with a gift by God to let him know future events and how his name would last thousands of years yet to come.

As I was prepared to leave, Father Ligouri warned me of the dangers yet to happen, especially that we had learned that Hansi and his men had escaped from jail and probably would be trying to locate where I was. My main concern was my parents safety. Perhaps Hansi would use them in order to have me do his bidding. Hansi was capable of anything and that worried me.

When I left the cathedral, I heard people talking about the great tsunami that was unleashing it's fury on Japan, Australia, Vietnam and Korea. This tsunami was unlike any other in recorded history. It's massive waves could devour everything in it's wake and I had to go to Korea once again but would this great tsunami prevent me from searching for another scroll, I wondered. This storm is so vast that China is bracing for it's wrath. While this was going on, six volcano's around the world were also erupting. Thinking to myself that the worse had come, I learned that a great earthquake had devoured Los Angeles. Hundred were killed and thousands more missing. It struck me that all this is of biblical proportion. Even way back thousands of years ago nature had unleashed itself, but nothing like this. All this worried me since I had to return to China, try to find the remaining scrolls, and get them to Jerusalem for translation, and at the same time avoid Hansi and his men.

As I took the next flight to New York, we learned from the pilot that most of New York City was buried with the water from the massive hurricane that made it's way from the coast of Africa. We were told the closest we could land was Philadelphia, then make our way north. It then struck me that the building where my office is located, could be underwater as well. Here I am working for the New York Herald and that may not exist anymore.

The only way out of Philadelphia was by bus or train. No flights were leaving the city for New York City or even New Jersey. Atlantic City was being deluged with massive waves and the boardwalk no longer existed. Why is this all happening at the same time, I thought. Mother nature had gone insane and there seemed to be no stopping the fury.

I wanted to get to Newark to catch a flight to Rome via Paris to see my friend at the Vatican, Cardinal Catelli. He had one of the Hebrew scrolls that I had given him the last time I was in Rome. He had his friend, Rabbi Cassini take a look at the scroll before he would tell me what it revealed. Luckily for me I had arrived in Newark on the train, made my way to the airport, and managed to buy the last seat on the plane.

On the way to Paris I was thinking about Pedro and how much he had helped me in my quest, despite the dangers. As I drifted off to sleep, I thought about Damascus and what awaited for me there.

MY layover in Paris lasted for nearly one hour which gave me a chance to watch the t.v. monitor in the lounge. The news flash was reporting the devastation not just in New York City, but also Los Angeles and other populous countries around the globe. There were numerous earthquakes, floods, fires, and volcanic eruptions, all simultaneously, not to mention the downpour of rain pounding itself here in Paris. Although it is winter, parts of Europe are experiencing warm temperatures while other spots are being hit hard with mountains of snow.

As I boarded my flight to Rome, I wondered whether Pedro was making any progress in his search for more scrolls. Perhaps we had found all there was to find, but somehow I had a sneaky suspicion that there was more to this story. I was unaware that Hansi was also on his way to Rome and our encountering each other was very possible.

Rome is beautiful this time of year, even with the snow blanketing the ground. Once I checked into my hotel room, I walked the several blocks to the Vatican. Even with the bitter cold, I enjoyed the stroll taking me to the Vatican.

As I entered the vast halls of the Vatican, I searched for Cardinal Catelli's office. Since I was last here, Cardinal Catelli was promoted to Assistant Chief to the Pope. I thought how great it must be for him to have himself within earshot of Pope Peter, the greatest Pope the church has ever had.

Finally I found his office, entered the formal entrance and told his secretary that I was here to see him at his request. Having a seat as I waited, I scanned the room, looking at the beautiful artwork hanging non the walls and the various statuettes of the saints scattered about. As the door to his office opened, Cardinal Catelli held out his arms and gave me a warm, welcoming hug. Cardinal Catelli was almost a father figure to me. His warm heart and loving countenance made him the man that he is.

Seated in front of his massive desk, I opened by asking, "Cardinal Catelli, what have you learned since we last spoke?" "Well," he said. "I have had the last scroll you gave me to a friend of mine, perhaps you may have heard of him, Cardinal Mohanni, the Catholic Cardinal from northern Africa, primarily from Libya as well as Egypt." I affirmed that I had heard of him and his greatness but never had the honor of actually meeting him. Cardinal Catelli continued saying, "Sue, this last scroll you gave me is the third last scroll. It has mentioned important events leading up to and including the second world war, actually naming Hitler, Stalin, Roosevelt, and other key players during the war." How incredible I responded.

The last sentence was the one that nearly gave the Cardinal a heart attack. According to this scroll, Pope Peter is mentioned as the last Pope. Perhaps there would be a breakup of the church or could it mean that Pope Peter would be assassinated leaving the linage of Saint Peter vacant. Perhaps it meant that no Cardinal could ever succeed Pope Peter? According to the Hebrew text, there was coming a man who would solve the earths crisis so much so that all the nations would yield their power to him. Will he be responsible for the end of the church as we know it, I wondered.

At the very end of the Last Latin scroll, it mentions that there are three scrolls separated by boundaries that no man should tread. Where could that mean. I knew that there was a possibility that one could be found somewhere in Asia one in Africa, and the other one somewhere near India. This was early February and I wanted to have everything together by the time Easter rolls around in late April.

Back at the hotel, I received a call from Pedro. Pedro had managed to discover buried pottery, not the Peruvian type, but more like the kind discovered in Israel years ago. Could they be connected to the arrival of Joseppa centuries ago?

Two days later, I returned to the Vatican to see Cardinal Catelli one last time. I was taking the scroll to Israel before catching a flight back to China. Little did I know that there was even a greater chance of danger than worrying about Hansi. The Cardinal handed the scrolls over, blessed me, and thanked me for giving him the opportunity to personally see the scrolls pertaining to the lost Book of Abraham. He had heard of such a book in his early years of the priesthood, but nobody knew whether the scrolls actually existed and if they did, where could they have been found.

Making my way to the airport, I wondered to myself, Is this journey I've undertaken the right thing to do, or have I unleashed something that should have remained hidden? I was even beginning to think that perhaps there might even be a curse to anyone who finds them. I was willing to take the chance since this was a story of a lifetime and I was thankful to be a part of it.

As I arrived back in Israel, I made my way from Tel Aviv to my good friend Rabbi Rybinski, a Russian Jew who made his way to Israel after the collapse of the Soviet Union. I have known the Rabbi for many years and I knew I could count on him to preserve and protect the scroll. Rabbi Rybinski warned me about the Russian Mafia. They may pose a danger to me and the scrolls. The value of the Book of Abraham had everyone wanting to possess them for their personal gain, even if it included murder.

I also had to visit the head Muslim cleric, Imam Mehrdad. If anyone could guarantee my safety, he was the one. He hated not just the Russians, but most Asians as well. He may seem to be a bigot, but at least I could trust him, especially whenever I journeyed to a Muslim country.

Once I met with the Imam, I returned to the hotel to prepare for my journey to China. I called my Chinese friend, Gou Feng Jong. I needed his protection and expertise in making my way throughout China as well as my returning to North Korea. The Chinese part didn't frighten me as much as the thought of returning to North Korea did. Besides, all the reports coming through the wire revealed that the Eastern Alliance was preparing for war and as a westerner, I was somewhat hesitant to return to the region. If war does break out, I will be in a precarious situation.

The flight from Tel Aviv gave me a feeling of impending doom. Something inside me gave a feeling that this time I would have to wheel and deal for my life. As the plane landed in China, I wondered whether I would make a new discovery or was this just a wasted trip. The Cardinal did tell me where the scroll said to look and I wanted to find the last scroll before someone else gets their grubby little hands on it. Besides, the final scroll would reveal the last days man would govern the world and a new age would blossom from it. As I took a taxi to my favorite hotel in Beijing,

I was hopeful that my contact would be there. True to his word, Gou Fe Jong was at the hotel waiting for my arrival. His gave me the courage I needed. His face was glowing with utter excitement and the smile went from ear to ear, a good sign I thought.

Jong informed me we were take the train from Beijing to the southern city of Dandong. From there a guide would take us just a mile from the North Korean border where, according to Jong, a cave had recently been discovered. I knew that if the authorities discovered what we were doing, we could face arrest and a long imprisonment. No matter what, I thought, it had to be done and I was prepared to do it.

Once at Dandong, Jong and I went to the hotel in the center of the city and waited for our contact to arrive. His name was Shen Li and he was the city's deputy of the local Communist Party, and if anyone could help, it would be him. Li had the authority to conduct and digging in and around the city so I was grateful for that.

The very next day was day one of our dig outside the city of Dandong. It was winter and the bitter cold made me shiver. This wasn't the best weather to be going on a dig, but it was necessary and besides, spring is right around the corner. Mister Li took Jong and me to the entrance to the newly discovered cave. It was discovered by a local boy playing nearby. As the boy was playing with his marbles, one of the marbles got caught between a rock and some dirt. The boy struggled trying to grab the marble and in doing so had loosened enough dirt to cause a cave in, thus the entrance had been discovered after being dormant for perhaps centuries.

Taking our shovels and other gear, we began to dig. It seemed as though we would never make any discovery, but after several hours had passed, we found the entrance large enough to drive a truck through. I wanted to go deep inside right away, but Li advised me that I should wait until tomorrow for safety's sake. I had to agree, especially since the sun was setting and the city limits were several miles from town. As I laid on my bed, I dreamed about the glory and acknowledgment that would certainly come with my discovery. I thought about my editor back in New York City who was practically screaming down my throat about being away from the office for so long. While I drifted off to sleep while watching the television, I was so tired that it didn't take long for me to sleep.

As the morning sun shined through the window, I got a phone call from Pedro. He told me that he had discovered ancient pottery dating back to three centuries before Jesus. There were other trinkets and various metal wine goblets. Also, there was a vast amount of precious stones, much like the stones Pedro and I discovered in the cave a few miles from the town of Puna, Peru. I was so excited I dropped the phone but I could hear the excitement from Pedro as well. Pedro told me that tomorrow he was taking a ride to a small village in Argentina. There, he said, was a possible location of ancient writings, at least that's what the natives had said.

After a hearty breakfast, Mister Li, Jong, and myself were on the journey to the lost, well hidden cave. I was sure that I would discover another scroll since it was well known that the Apostles had dispersed throughout the world and I was sure that two or three had been to China and possibly Korea.

As we entered the dark cave, Jong led the way followed by me and Mister Li. The cave was deep and had a peculiar smell. I asked

Jong what that awful smell was and the only thing he could say was that over the decades, people had disposed of their trash, making the air fowl. Slowly making our way deep inside, Jong, flashlight in hand, came across a chest. It was laden with gold and silver and had what appeared to be cherubs. Perhaps the cherubs were placed on it as a way of protection? It measured a good three feet by five feet and weighed so much that the three of us could hardly move it. Taking out his survival knife, Jong began to chop away at the ancient lock. It was secured better than what we use today, but Jong continued twisting the knife until the lock snapped. Now I would get to see once again what had been hidden for centuries and revealing another part of the Book of Abraham. I was overjoyed that I had come this far and found another chest, much like the one Pedro and I had discovered deep in the cave outside of Puna.

As Jong opened the heavy lid, I saw a vast amount of precious stones and digging through them, I grabbed onto something round and heavy. As I raised my hand, revealing what I had grabbed, another scroll appeared. Thankfully, this trip was not wasted and I wanted to find that little boy who happened to find the entrance while playing with his marbles. Jong and Li closed the lid and carried the heavy chest to the car. We wanted to place the stones in various bags so to prevent anyone from taking the entire stash. Overjoyed, I didn't realize that I now had to return to North Korea and take a chance I could be arrested, or even executed by the Koreans.

Jong insisted that we put off any attempt entering North Korea. He had heard that the border guards had been changed. The new border guards were capable of shooting first and asking questions later. Now that his Korean connection had left, how were we going to ever enter Korea again, I thought. Jong assured me that with his connections it wouldn't take but a few days to a week or two before he would be able to bribe another border guard.

As I waited at the small hotel in Dandong, China. I wondered how Pedro was doing back in Peru. The cave that Pedro had discovered held a vast treasure of precious stones, gold and silver coins. Within a few days, my journey would take me places I really didn't want to be.

On the third day I had waited for something to present itself, Jong returned to my hotel room and this time he had his nephew with him. His nephew claimed that he had a cozy relationship with a North Korean border guard known only as Pheng. If anybody could help, he said, it would be Pheng. Unknown to me was that things were going to become as dangerous as could never imagine.

The next morning we loaded up the car with items the Korean guard had demanded and drove the few miles to the border. Once there, Jong and his nephew took out their binoculars, peered across the border, trying to see if Pheng was on duty, but he had no luck. Perhaps its Pheng's day off or was it too risky as of now to make the attempt to cross over?

As the two continued their search, three trucks rolled up and once parked, ten men per truck got out, rifles pointed at us, and demanded we explain ourselves. Their apparent leader, a man names Sergei Yazlov, began asking questions. Yazlov I would learn later, was a Russian mafia hit man and he had learned of our quest. Knowing how valuable the treasure would be, Yazlov wanted a piece of the action, but at the price of our lives. Yazlov demanded that Jong, his nephew, our driver, and myself line up and raise our hands into the crisp air. How did Yazlov discover what we were doing? Who gave away the information, I wondered.

As we stood in that line, Yazov began to question all of us, starting with Jong's nephew. His nephew tried to convince Yazlov that he was only the driver and that his uncle had promised him a weeks wages to help. As Yazlov stood there unconvinced, he drew his revolver, pointed it at Jong's nephews head and said, "Would you like to change your story?" Jong's nephew's legs were shaking uncontrollable and he had that all well so noticeable fear in his eyes. He tried to tell Yazlov he knew nothing, and that's when Yazlov responded, "Wrong answer." Suddenly, the revolver had discharged a bullet, and with pinpoint accuracy, the bullet entered his head, killing him instantly. Yazlov then said, "Anyone else want to lie to me?" I was so scared I collapsed, falling to the ground sure that my life was over, but Yazlov approached me and said, Don't worry Miss Chamberlain. I'm saving you for last." Fear gripped my ever soul. How did Yazlov know who I was and how did he find out?

The next person Yazlov asked was Jong what we were doing and that's when Jong said, "Yazlov, we have found nothing." Come to discover that Jong had told Yazlov all of what I had told him, placing me in a very uncomfortable situation. Jong even sacrificed his nephew to convince me that he was on my side. Now I knew I was in a deep hole with no hope of ever getting out.

No sooner had I heard what had just happened, Yazlov told Jong to escort me to his truck for the long journey back to Russia. As I was placed in the truck, I heard Jong tell Yazlov, "She will bring a pretty penny, won't she?" At that moment, I was gripped in total fear. What were they planning to do to me, especially once they get the information out of me when we return to Russia?

It took four days of virtually nonstop driving before we crossed the border into the southeastern tip of Russia. Yazlov instructed his driver to get to the airport for the flight that would take us to Moscow where I would be interrogated at great length, then sold into the sex industry in either eastern Europe or even in Russia. Yazlov even threatened me with an injection of heroin in order to keep me in line. Just hearing him tell me that made me even more frightened especially since there was no hope of rescue. What would Pedro think. Would he ever be able to find out what has happened to me, I thought.

As I was placed into the jetliner that would be a direct flight to Moscow, I pleaded with Yazlov but he only ignored my pleas.

Hours later, we arrived in Moscow. Yazlov had a limousine waiting for us near the gate. As I walked down the steps to the car, I noticed there were several, perhaps as many as fifteen men standing guard. I knew my fate wasn't going to be very good, but I still had faith that somehow I'd find a way to get out of my predicament.

At least two hours had passed as we approached a large estate. The guard opened the gates and as we entered the massive courtyard, I saw a vast amount of men standing guard. This meant that escape was nearly impossible. Yazlov ordered me out of the car and to walk inside the house. As I entered the vestibule, I could only say I was in awe. The walls were made of the finest marble and the many vases that were filled with flowers got my attention. Yazlov then said, "Miss Chamberlain. Your personal maid will show you to your room."

As I followed the beautiful young woman up the marble stairs, I couldn't believe that Yazlov lived in such a fine house. He must certainly be worth a small fortune.

Once inside my gorgeous room, I took off my shoes and immediately laid on the king size bed. I was exhausted and swiftly fell off to sleep.

After four hours had passed, I was awaken by my personal maid. Yazlov sent word that I was to join him for dinner in his massive dining hall. The maid took out a beautiful gown for me to wear for dinner and once I was washed and ready, I followed the maid down the stairs and into the dining hall where Yazlov, along with several other people, were waiting.

Yazlov was treating me as though I were an honored guest. Sitting at the table I saw at least several dishes of the finest meats and game. Yazlov began the evening by saying, "Sue, please accept my generosity. Tonight we relax and tomorrow we will get down to business." I thought, what kind of business is Yazlov referring to.

After dinner, Yazlov escorted me to his private smoking room. As Yazlov began smoking a Cuban cigar, I began to gasp for air. The stench of that cigar made me sick to my stomach. I never could take anyone smoking anything, much less a cigar. Yazlov then sat in his favorite couch and said to me, "Miss Chamberlain, please sit down on the couch with me. Let's get acquainted." I just stood there, shocked that Yazlov would be so informal. I refused to sit with him so I took the chair that was farther from the couch. I didn't want Yazlov to lay a hand on me, but little did I realize that it wouldn't be the only thing Yazlov would do, and that had me upset. I could only imagine what he was capable of and what he really wanted. Yazlov is a monster and I was sure that whatever he wanted, he'd have a very good chance of obtaining it.

For the next hour or so, all I heard from Yazlov was how rich he is and how his grandfather was murdered by the Soviets many years ago. The night felt as though it would never end and after he had informed me about his family and wealth, Yazlov said goodnight to me, left the room, and departed, leaving me there to ponder my fate.

As the morning sun began to rise, I opened my eyes and prepared myself for the day. The maid had a beautiful dress waiting for me as well as the whole ensemble. Apparently the maid had checked my clothes to get the proper size and although I felt as though I was being prepared to be fondled and perhaps being dressed for a sexual encounter, I had no choice but to dress in what was prepared for me.

As I walked down the vast hallway and then down the stairs, I saw Yazlov, along with three other men, waiting down the stairs for my arrival. I felt as though I was being showcased and being treated like some sort of prize. Yazlov, along with the other three men, began to walk to Yazlov's private office, with me in tow.

Yazlov sat behind his huge desk as the three men stood guard. I sat in the chair closest to the desk and just waited for Yazlov to begin asking questions. After about twenty minutes, Yazlov then got to the meat of his questions. Yazlov had heard about my quest and that I had discovered the long lost Book of Abraham. The longer I sat there, the more questions he had. I couldn't let Yazlov get his hands on the scrolls, even though most were by now, well hidden in Jerusalem. I knew that there were three more scrolls yet to find, but I wasn't telling Yazlov about that. I decided to string him along so I began to make up a story that I had hoped he would believe.

Five hours had passed and my story, even to me, was bizarre to say the least. Finally, I did tell Yazlov that there was a possibility that one scroll was in China, another in North Korea, and the final scroll might be found in Central America. Two of the three countries were true and I was hopeful he would buy into the whole bit. Yazlov then said something that shook the daylights out of me. Yazlov said a very influential man he knows has Pedro locked away and being interrogated. "So far," Yazlov continued, "He will talk and when he does, we will know where the scrolls could possibly be found, then we will deal with Pedro."

As Yazlov continued his questions, I tried to contain myself but I was worried about Pedro and what they would do to him. I then came up with a plan, one that would prevent Pedro being killed, and could result in my escape from Yazlov. I told Yazlov that I was prepared to talk but not until his connection was in the room, only then would I reveal any information. By this point, Yazlov was willing to do anything to get the information I held inside my head.

Several days had passed before Yazlov summoned for me. As I entered his office, Yazlov said, "My South American friend has agreed to come to my estate to hear for himself what you have to reveal. He will even bring your friend Pedro with him, just as insurance, in case you renege on the deal."

A few more days passed and still nobody showed up. Is Pedro still alive or did they torture him enough that they managed to get the information from him rather than dealing with me. If that was the case, what would happen to me. Would Yazlov have me killed or would I ever escape from his clutches. It then dawned on me that Yazlov had threatened to sell me into the sex industry form where I'd never escape. That thought put more fear into me then being murdered. The shear thought of being forced into being a prostitute made me want to puke.

Finally, after waiting for so long, I was summoned to Yazlov's private office. As I entered the darkened room, I tried to adjust my eyes so I could see clearly. Yazlov ordered me to sit in the chair closest to his desk. A minute of utter silence made me ponder what is really happening. Suddenly, the room lit up and I saw a man standing next to someone bound and gagged in a chair. The man appeared to be either Central or South American, but I will soon discover something else.

Yazlov told the man, "Introduce yourself to Miss Chamberlain." Once my name was mentioned, the man bound and gagged in the chair began to struggle against his bindings. Who is this man, I wondered. The man introduced himself as Pietro Alvarez. That name sounded very familiar. As Alvarez began to speak, I only thought of his name and if it was connected somehow. After a minute or two and never hearing what he was saying, it dawned on me. Pietro Alvarez is a well known terrorist who was wanted by the World Federation Council for hundreds of murders and other violent crimes. Once I knew who he was, I began to tremble. I knew that Yazlov was a dangerous man, but Pietro Alvarez was well known for being a violent man who would stop at nothing to get what he wanted, and the scrolls were the kinds of thing Pietro would love to get his hands on.

As I trembled in fear, Pietro walked over to the chair with the man sitting with a cloth over his head. Yazlov then said, "Miss Chamberlain. I have a surprise for you that will be interesting for you to see." With that said, Pietro grabbed the cloth and raised it high in the air. It was none other than Rabbi Berman, himself. Pietro went on to say, "I have the right man. He will translate the remaining scrolls for me or I will kill him." My response was simple. Kill Rabbi Berman and you will never get the scrolls translated. I felt I had Pietro and Yazlov by their necks. Yazlov replied, "Don't be so sure of yourself Miss Chamberlain. I still have another hostage which I will reveal to you later." As Yazlov finished, my mind began to go in circles. Who, other than Rabbi Berman, did Pietro and Yazlov kidnap?

Pietro was threatening the hostage with severe torture unless I agree and take them all to China and North Korea to find the two scrolls believed to be there. Having no choice in the matter, I agreed. Yazlov said, "Good. Tomorrow we will all go to China and begin the digging." Yazlov apparently knew just where to look. He had heard about how the city of Kunming, a place in Yunnan Provence, had developed during the first century and that a man known to the Chinese as a man from the west with good news about the heavenly one. Perhaps this is the place where another scroll could be found.

As the flight to China began, I was thinking about how I could get my hands on the scroll, yet, prevent Yazlov and Pietro from obtaining it. I had to try to prevent anyone other than the head Rabbi in Jerusalem from possessing them no matter what, even if it cost me my life.

The flight was long and I was beginning to tire. This was going to be the most arduous journey I will ever undertake. Once we land in China, Yazlov ordered the gear to be unloaded including rifles and plenty of ammunition. This guy is serious, I thought. They really were capable of killing anyone who got in their way. Rabbi Berman's hands were tied behind his back, preventing him from trying to escape while I was closely guarded.

On the outskirts of Kunming was a very small village whose name I didn't know. In this village was a place considered sacred by the citizens of the village. Yazlov, preoccupied with what to do next, was unaware that the citizens of the village were keeping a watchful eye, suspicious of all of us. I was sure the villagers would do anything to protect what we were about to discover, but I was hopeful that somehow I could convince them that the scroll had to be taken back to Jerusalem where it's journey began.

The small dwelling that housed the sacred scroll was unassuming. There were three men standing at the entrance to the building. Yazlov questioned the men and once they refused to let us inside, Yazlov ordered his men and Pietro to shoot the men dead, thinking that would scare the villagers and cause one of them to give it up. The doors to the building were locked and only the head man of the village had the keys.

Yazlov roared out to the people, "Who is going to be next. Give up the keys and the scrolls and I might spare you your lives." By this time word had gone out about Yazlov and Pietro. Suddenly, we were surrounded by at least thirty men, armed with automatic weapons and an assortment of other military weapons. This was now the perfect Mexican standoff. Who would shoot first and would I survive the outcome?

Yazlov, as bold as he was, threatened the villagers if they didn't drop their weapons and allow him to accomplish what he set out to do. By this time a large crowd had gathered. We were outnumbered and I was curious to see how Yazlov and Pietro would get themselves out of this situation.

Without warning, Pietro fired his rifle, killing one man. Threatening to kill somebody else unless they had achieved what they came for, Yazlov waited several minutes, then without hesitation, killed a man and a woman from the village who were unarmed. Thinking he had frightened the people, Yazlov walked up to the doors, fired his weapon, and the doors were now unlocked. With a gleam in his eyes, Yazlov entered the building, and after a couple minutes had passed, came out, holding up one of the scrolls. I ran towards him, lifting my arms in the air, and grabbed the scroll and collapsed.

At this time as I laid on the ground, I heard the sound of gunfire. Crouching as low as I could, I witnessed a slaughter. Yazlov collapsed next to me, dead as dead could get. Pietro, on the other hand, managed to get to the truck and drove off as bullets penetrated the truck. Unbelievably, Pietro was able to escape all the gunfire to fight another day.

Once Yazlov and his men were dead, I rose to my feet, thanking the villagers for rescuing me. As I looked around, I saw Rabbi Berman on the ground and his body was riddled with bullets. Yazlov had murdered the Rabbi and now I was in a predicament. Without Rabbi Berman, how would I get the scroll translated for the people of the village? The head of the village walked towards me and said, "Please, give me back the holy scroll." I had to beg the man to allow me to return the scroll to Jerusalem to join the other scrolls that made up the entire volume of the Book of Abraham. It took some time but once he knew I wanted to return the scroll rather than keep and sell the scroll, he finally permitted me to return the scroll. Before I left the village, I thanked them for killing my kidnappers and showering me with their generosity.

As I sat in the plane returning to Jerusalem, I thought of Rabbi Berman and what if something bad happened to Pedro. I had tried numerous times to call Pedro without success.

Handing the scroll to Rabbi Goldstein, I told him about Rabbi Berman and how Yazlov and Pietro wanted to get their slimy hands on it. Thanking me and telling me that in about two weeks, he would have the entire scroll translated, Rabbi Goldstein shook my hand and told me he would call me when his work was complete. I really wanted to know what the scroll revealed and I only had to find perhaps just one or two scrolls to complete the book of Abraham.

CHAPTER 8

With Yazlov dead and Pietro on the run, I flew back to New York City. I had to return to my office at the New York Herald to file everything I kept in my journal and also my head. My editor was pleased to see me yet he had the look of utter anger. I knew he was beginning to get even more angry as the days turned into weeks and then into months, but I assured him that the wait would be worthwhile. At this time I had no idea how elusive that last scroll would become. That was the final chapter of the Book of Abraham and it contained everything that dealt with the end of the world. What would it reveal and was it right for me to know. I was always taught that only God should know what's to take place, yet he revealed his plans to Abraham, the father of us all.

As I spent the next few days working at the office, my parents had a surprise for me. I didn't know what it could be but I had an idea that it had something to do with my upcoming birthday. Mom and dad always celebrated my birthday as though it was my first, but I thought what the heck, if it makes them happy then I'm all right with that.

As I was relaxing during a long day in my favorite lounge, the doorbell rang and I was shocked when I saw who it was. With excitement in my eyes, it was none other than Pedro himself. Pedro hardly ever comes to New York City, but I had an inkling that tonight my parents are taking us out on the town to celebrate my birthday. It's my twenty ninth birthday and just the thought of turning thirty next year has me somewhat depressed. I guess as the years move forward and we get older, just the thought of time passing us by gives me an unsettling feeling.

My parents showed me a great time. We ate at my favorite place and took in a show on Broadway. It was an evening to remember, but tomorrow begins another day of work.

Once I returned with Pedro to my apartment, we celebrated with a little wine and some soft music. I was beginning to fall in love with Pedro and I was unsure whether he felt the same way. We had spent so much time together, it's no wonder that I felt this way. After all the torture Pedro has been through, I wondered whether he ever intended to get involved with a woman or was his work preventing him from having a relationship. As Pedro relaxed, I made my move. Unbelievably, Pedro took me by the hand and walked me to my bedroom. It was to be his birthday present to me by making love like I never would have dreamed. Pedro was the perfect picture of masculinity what with his gorgeous mustache, curly black hair, and his wonderful demeanor. He was a perfect gentleman and always willing to let me have my way most times.

As the sunshine's rays came through the window, I woke up just in time to see Pedro standing in the doorway holding a cup of java. "Good morning Sue. How do you feel today?" Affirming I felt well, I ate breakfast, got dressed for work, and left for the office. While I was at the Herald working, Pedro was at the library doing some research, not just about the elusive Book of Abraham, but also about anything he could discover about the man who started this journey from the start, the man we learned who's name was Joseppa. It was Joseppa who made the long journey from Palestine to South America and we wanted to know more about him. If we could only obtain that last scroll, we would possess the greatest discovery ever, even since the beginning of time.

Tomorrow, Pedro and I will be returning to Peru, at least I thought. As we laid back watching some television, there was a knock on the door. I was too exhausted so Pedro went to look. As Pedro opened the door, there was a crash. Three men flung the door open, grabbed Pedro then me. As they dragged us to their waiting car, I noticed another man inside. It was Pietro Alvarez himself. At this moment, fear came over me as though someone had covered me with a sheet. As we drove off, Pietro only said, "You two are going to tell me everything or else I will cut out your tongues." Now I was really scared. I knew from my last encounter with Pietro and Yazlov, that he was capable of anything.

Over an hour later, we arrived at a cabin somewhere in the deep woods. As Pedro and I were shoved inside, Pietro told us, "Relax you two. There is plenty of time for us to get acquainted." One of his men turned on the television and that's when I first heard the broadcast that the Eastern powers seemed to be preparing for war against the Western coalition. The Jewish state of Israel has been threatened for several years now and their great protector, Adrian, was losing his patience with the Israeli Prime Minister, Moshe Eban. I felt like I was about to lose the story of a lifetime, but being forced here and not knowing where we were, made me vulnerable. Besides, I was powerless and I had no idea what Pietro had in mind for Pedro and I.

We were somewhere in New York, deep in the woods as Pietro grabbed my arms, walked me to a cabin, and threw me on the sofa. As I sat there trembling, I saw the other men tie Pedro to a chair, gag his mouth, and place a blindfold over his eyes. Pietro then stood before me and said, "You will tell me everything I want to know or each time you refuse or lie, I will torture your friend here until there's nothing left to him, then I will start on you." Just by the tone of his voice and what he said made me realize this guy wasn't fooling around.

Before I could utter a word, Pietro said, "Let me show you what I mean." Pietro walked over to Pedro who couldn't see anything, and began by breaking one of his fingers. Pedro screamed in agony right through the gag in his mouth. I thought, poor Pedro. He was suffering because of me. Once Pietro broke one of his fingers, he walked over to the sofa, sat down, then began to question me.

The first question out of his mouth concerned the first five Hebrew scrolls as well as the first three Latin scrolls. I told him they were safely tucked away in Jerusalem. I thought if I was honest about that it would stop him from hurting Pedro, but I was wrong. Standing to his feet, Pietro said, "Where in Jerusalem?" I told him I didn't know and that's when Pietro walked over to Pedro, took another finger, and broke it so loud I could hear the crack across the room. Once again, poor Pedro tried to scream in agony through his gag and all I could do was watch Pietro torture him.

I could see that Pietro was enjoying himself, and that he was wishing I wouldn't talk too quickly. He wanted to torture Pedro some more and I felt that no matter whether I told the truth or lied, Pietro would cause Pedro a whole lot of suffering.

Once again Pietro asked me where the scrolls are and once again I told him I didn't know. That was my third mistake and Pedro was to suffer another broken finger. By this time Pedro was in such agony his screams began to go through the gag and reverberate the room. Pietro then told me, "Tell me, who has the scrolls?" I knew if I told him exactly where they were, terrible things would happen to the Rabbi, but yet, poor Pedro was suffering just the same.

I began to tell him that a man named Hansi had stolen them from my hotel room the last time I was in Jerusalem. Pietro stood silently for a moment, snapped his fingers, as one of the men came over to him. Pietro whispered something in his ear, then the man left the room just as Pietro said, "We will find this Hansi and he will give us the scrolls or else you will be the next person to suffer some pain. That statement alone made me sick to my stomach, but what he said after that was worse, at least in my mind. Pietro leaned down to my face and said, "You have something your friend doesn't have." I just sat there wondering to myself what Pietro meant, then it dawned on me. Not only was Pietro going to torture me as well, but he had plans to rape me, perhaps by him and the three men with him. As I started to gag, Pietro told me to get to the bathroom to puke., he didn't want me to vomit on his beautiful rug. As I ran to the bathroom, I could hear him say something to Pedro but I couldn't make it out.

As I began to vomit, I started to look around the bathroom for something to use as a weapon. I had to do something or else Pedro and I are going to die. I started by rummaging through the bathroom vanity, then the linen closet. Unbelievably, I found a plastic letter opener. Wondering to myself why a letter opener was in the bathroom, I tucked it snugly in my pants. The opener may be made of plastic, but it was sharp enough to hurt someone and if they were going to rape me, it would be the last thing they'd ever do.

Back on the sofa, I sat there pondering my fate and thinking of a way to escape. Several hours had passed before Pietro allowed me to eat. As I ate, I saw him take some food to Pedro. He loosened his gag, released one of his arms, and put the spoon in his hand and left him there to figure a way to feed himself. I was so hungry I ate everything in front of me, but as I ate, I looked over at Pedro and saw him struggle to feed himself, especially since Pietro released the arm with the broken fingers.

As I finished my meal, the man returned and whispered something in Pietro's ear. I could see on Pietro's face that whatever the man said upset him immensely. Now what, I thought. What could the man have told him to cause a look of anger on his face. I was about to find out.

Pietro resumed the interrogation, retying Pedro's arm to the chair. "Now" he said. "Let's try this again." As Pietro walked over to the sofa, I knew I had a look of terror in my eyes. He started by saying," This time I'll do one of his feet if I catch you lying to me." Pietro continued to ask me who had the scrolls and I continued to tell him that Hansi had them. "Well then," he said. I guess I'll have to break a toe or two since I know you are lying. Having said that, Pietro walked over to Pedro, took off one shoe, and began to break a toe. Once again poor Pedro was suffering because of me. Pietro screamed at the top of his lungs, "I know you're lying and do you want to know how I know?" All I could do was look him in the eyes with utter fear. Pietro loudly said, "Do you want to know how I know? I had my colleague check on this guy Hansi and he discovered that he is wanted by the World Federation Council and that he too is searching for the Hebrew scrolls and that he nearly had his hands on them. Tell me, why are you lying? Don't you care about your friend here suffering because of your silence?"

I began to tear up and that's when I was broken. I told him that the Hebrew scrolls were taken to one of the museums by Rabbi Goldstein. I wanted to make Pietro think that they were safely tucked away, preventing anyone from getting their hands on them. Once again, he whispered something to the man who left before, and as before, the man left the cabin while Pietro just sat on a chair, staring at me, perhaps thinking of a way to make me talk.

Pedro, still tied to the chair and suffering from the pain his broken fingers were causing, tried in vain to say something. I asked Pietro to allow Pedro to speak and to untie him from the chair. Pietro at first kept silent, but after I continued to plead for mercy, Pietro finally gave in to my request. As I watched Pedro struggle to sit straight, Pietro cautioned us that if we tried anything, like attempting to escape, the both of us would be tied to a chair and he would be forced to ask more questions and if needed, torture us. Pietro apparently was waiting for the man he sent to return, but I was wondering why. What is Pietro up to and where did he send the man? After waiting for three hours, the man returned and whispered in Pietro's ears something I couldn't make out.

As Pietro turned to look at me, he had the reddest face from anger that I ever saw. Pietro started out by saying, "My man here tells me that he found out that Rabbi Goldstein never took the scrolls to the museum like you said. Now, tell me where they are or else somebody's going to suffer extreme pain." Although I knew where they were, I didn't want Pietro to know, no matter how much pain we had to endure. Once again Pedro was tied to the chair and this time Pietro took his lit cigarette and proceeded to burn Pedro's arms. Pedro began to scream from the pain, even more than when Pietro broke his fingers. "Now, tell me where the scrolls are or your friend here will truly find out how much pain I can cause." I still didn't want to tell him, but after several minutes had passed and Pedro continued to suffer the pain from the cigarette, I began to talk.

Pietro had the look on his face of feeling he had won, and I began to tell him that Rabbi Goldstein had hidden them in the wall safe in his office. Pietro immediately had two of his men leave the cabin and go to New York City to purchase five plane tickets for our impending flight to Jerusalem. Now it was only Pietro and one other man guarding us.

About an hour later, the door of the cabin burst open and several men quickly disarmed Pietro and the man and said they were under arrest. I didn't know what was going on and that's when one of the men told me he was Detective Ramos Vincenza from the World Federation Councils criminal department. He had received a message from one of his agents that Pietro was in the United States and once they discovered where he was staying, they began to pursue him, thankfully trailing him right to this cabin. Pedro and I were returned to my apartment after I took Pedro to the hospital to have his wounds checked. Other than the broken fingers and cigarette burns on his arms, Pedro was doing a lot better then I would be feeling.

For the next week, Pedro stayed at my place while I returned to my office at the Herald. My editor was pleased that I have finally returned, but, I informed him that once Pedro was better and able to travel, we would be returning to Peru. Pedro wanted to get back to his house so he could do more research about where the final scrolls could be hidden away. We had to investigate where Joseppa had bc to on his journey southward. I was sure Joseppa had come ashore somewhere in either Central America or perhaps even in

America, centuries before the United States was discovered and settled.

As news spread that the Eastern Alliance was preparing for war, I had asked my editor if I could cover the story before returning to Peru. I'm usually not a foreign correspondent, but I had to get my paws on this crucial event. When my editor agreed, I was overjoyed and told Pedro about my assignment. I told Pedro to help himself to anything while I was gone, but Pedro only wanted to return to his hometown.

As I packed my bags, I once again told Pedro to stay put until I return. I had to get back to Jerusalem and contact Rabbi Goldstein. I had to be sure the Rabbi was safe, especially since the two men who left the cabin were still on the loose.

I was glad to be back in Israel. The culture and people gave me pleasure I couldn't have imagined. The warm days and cool nights reminded me of New York during the springtime.

I had a friend that works at the Jerusalem Times. It's a small newspaper but it somehow manages to survive despite being a small operation. I have a friend, Henry Maxim who works there and if anyone could help me cover this story, it would be Henry. The first thing Henry did when we met was take me in his car and drive to the Valley of Meggido, the place where the final battle is to be fought. Henry was sure that the Eastern Alliance was preparing for that battle. Millions of soldiers were preparing for such an event and even the Western Alliance could be planning something as well. Would these two forces clash in this valley or were they going to reach some kind of agreement. The Eastern Alliance hated the Israeli's and the Muslim nations had long wanted to destroy the Jewish state. Pope Peter had negotiated an agreement with the World Federation Council, meeting with Adrian it's leader several times to somehow have his assurance that the W,F.C. would always secure a peace agreement with the Israel's. The Israeli's needed that assurance that the Western Alliance would come to their aid if they were ever attacked by overwhelming numbers, however, recently Adrian has displayed displeasure with the Israeli Prime Minister, Moshe Eban. The Pope had even gone as far as to send his personal emissary, Cardinal Manci to help the two leaders reach a new agreement, but the emissary wasn't having much luck persuading the two sides to come together. The Eastern Alliance, led bu China and Russia were causing the countries in the western world to be cautious about what they have been saying recently.

As we were leaving the valley, Henry said, "I want to show you something Sue. You'll never believe what I have discovered on a recent excavation during my time off of work." I knew Henry was a part time archeologist, but I had no idea what he could have found. Just the suspense gave me chills with excitement. By this time even I was becoming a professional digger.

Henry took me to his house and revealed what he had found. It was an ancient Hebrew wine vase and it had the inscription of it's owner and when Henry told me who it was, I nearly fainted. The name on the vase was, Joseppa. My God, could it be the same Joseppa that had traveled to South America? When Henry saw the look on my face, he had to ask me why I had a puzzled look on my face. I began telling him about what Pedro and I had discovered in Peru and that a man from the time of Christ had taken Hebrew scrolls from Jerusalem and took them across the vast ocean. Even Henry couldn't believe whether it was the same man, but when he showed me a piece of jewelry buried with the vase, I was convinced that it was the same Joseppa that had hidden the Hebrew scrolls.

The piece of jewelry was inscribed with a woman's name. It was inscribed, Shedaya, wife of Joseppa. I nearly fainted. Henry had stumbled upon something that belonged to the same Joseppa I had discovered. I was overjoyed so much I wanted to tell Pedro as soon as possible, but first there was a story to cover.

I took a flight to Rome to cover the latest developments in regards to the Eastern Alliance's threats of total war. The Israeli government is in an emergency session, trying to iron out some sort of agreement that they hoped Adrian and the Western Alliance would agree to. Prime Minister Moshe Eban was in the United States, holding meetings with President McNair and the United States Congress. Not only is the subject concerning the Eastern Alliance in the table, but also sending emergency aid to several countries that have been devastated from the recent natural disasters. China, Japan, Korea, and all of Southeast Asia were practically wiped out from several typhoons that crossed their paths. Then there were those countries that are reeling from the volcano's that have spread so much ash into the atmosphere that it nearly has blocked the sun from appearing. Los Angeles had such a volatile earthquake that roughly eighty percent of the city is destroyed, including Hollywood.

As I landed in Rome to cover the story my editor had assigned me, I couldn't help but think of the massive loss of life in New York City when it was overtaken by a storm now being called, Tropical Storm Edward. Two hundred foot waves slammed into the city, taking out all the docks and even damaging the bridges. Even my office didn't escape the wrath.

Feeling comfortable, I rested before I left the hotel to go see my friend, Cardinal Catelli. I was always excited to see him. He always had a joke or two to say and at times I had a hard time believing he was actually a Cardinal, and a high ranking one at that. The taxi driver informed me that Adrian was expected in the morning to conduct his conference with Pope Peter II. It made me wonder why Pope Peter II was having a rather large amount with Adrian. Adrian had power, of course, but usually the Pope only conducts a meeting between himself and any other head of state when it concerns the Vatican's ability to aid whomever asks. I didn't like Adrian because there was something about him I couldn't put my finger on, but perhaps it was my own paranoia.

Cardinal Catelli told me that he would be transferring to Europe in a month or two, replacing Cardinal Foustino from Spain who had died about two weeks prior to our meeting. I thought, shucks, now I'll just have to force myself to visit Spain sometime. I was never there but I was sure I'd bring Pedro along to act as my translator. It would sure be an adventure, I'm sure.

The time had come to head to the Vatican the next day to cover the story of Pope Peter II and Adrian. Adrian needed the pontiffs support if the Western Alliance was to go against the massive army that the Eastern Alliance had assembled. Could they actually have nearly two hundred million soldiers ready to attack? I thought, yes, it's possible because not only was China, all of Asia, Russia, and the Muslim countries able to achieve such a massive amount of soldiers, but their threats were being taken very seriously by the west. The only country in the western world that had the ability to take on the Eastern Alliance was the United States. President McNair had gone on the record as saying that America, Canada, Australia, New Zealand, and the South American's were all willing to come together to prevent that alliance from overtaking Jerusalem.

Cardinal Catelli had offered me the position as his personal secretary but since I wasn't Catholic and not a priest, I graciously rejected the offer. As I left the Vatican to have dinner before the evenings event, I called Pedro to find out what he's been doing. Pedro said he never did find anything again in the caves in Peru, however, one of his friends, Ricardo Montenero told him that there was a very good possibility that when Joseppa arrived from Jerusalem, he could have first settled in Mexico. To me that made perfect sense. But then I knew there was the possibility that he could have made his way to America or even Canada as well. Pedro told me he'd do more research before heading to Mexico for a dig. I only knew I had a very important assignment and I was running late.

As I was seated for the news conference, I saw an old friend of mine who I haven't seen in years. Her name is Sally Farthmoor, and she's been a reporter for many years at the same television station in Chicago. Sally is the kind of person who regularly can be seen searching almost everywhere for a good story and believe me, this assignment is probably one of the best stories to cover in years. Sally was tickled pink to see me and all she could say was, "Where have you been all these years. I surly didn't want to let the cat out of bag so all I told her was I was investigating a story down in South America, never mentioning to her that the story I was doing was in Peru and in the Middle East.

Sally chatted with me for nearly twenty minutes before the news conference started to begin. As Adrian took the podium, seated behind him was President McNair. President McNair had a look on his face as though he had just come through the bowels of hell and soon I would begin to learn why he had that look. I always knew there was something about Adrian but I could never put my finger on it. Even Pope Peter II had a strange look on his face.

When it became time for me to ask a question, I started to get butterflies in my stomach. I was so nervous I could hardly breathe. My only question to Adrian was, "President Adrian. How come the Western Alliance has yet to respond to the crises in the Middle East such as the Eastern Alliance's threat toward Israel?" Adrian responded that he had always kept his promise to the Israeli's that the Western Alliance and the World Federation Council in particular had always kept it's word. I thought to myself, what a fake. I had a feeling that Adrian was about to do a double cross but perhaps that was only my assessment of him.

Once the conference ended, I wished Sally well and returned to my hotel room for the night. Tomorrow I return to the states, but not before wishing my good friend Cardinal Catelli before leaving Rome.

As I arrived in New York, I saw the devastation that the hurricane had done. The entire coastline of the city was gone and the waters were still as deep as a five foot man. The waters were receding, but not fast enough so the people could begin the rebuilding. That will take months or even years. Even the building that the New York Herald had it's offices was damaged so much we were afraid we wouldn't be able to return to our offices.

Although I wanted to return to South America, I had to type out my story and prepare it for tomorrow's edition of the Herald. My editor began to show signs of weariness and even pure exhaustion. I would learn later that his wife of twenty seven years was killed in the flooding of the city. He has been putting very long hours in at work, not to mention cleaning out his condo. He was already nearing retirement and I began to suspect I'll have a new editor to deal with very soon and that person may not be as understanding as he is. I had to continue my research concerning the elusive

Book of Abraham and I was so close to discovering the final two or three scrolls. The last Latin scroll had written inside that the final scroll could be found near a stone covered mound somewhere in the Spanish hills. The question was, did it mean that the final scroll is somewhere in Spain, or is it as Pedro's friend suspects, it is somewhere in Mexico?

For the next three weeks, I devoted my time researching anything that may give me a clue about where the final scrolls could be found. I'd spend those weeks mostly at the library as well as the recently opened Museum of Jewish History here in Manhattan. If there was any possibility that they would have some information that would help in my research that would be very rewarding.

One day while I was leaving the museum, a man approached me an sarcastically said, "Come with me you whore." What was this guys problem and why was he calling me such a derogatory name. He roughly took my arms and shoved me inside a waiting car. I was blindfolded, my wrists tied behind my back as well as my ankles being tied together and told to keep quiet and stop struggling. I was so nervous I had crazy thoughts running through my mind. What if this guy was a part of an international crime ring or even worse, suppose he's a terrorist and I've just become a hostage to be auctioned off to the highest bidder. I knew that lately women were disappearing and never seen again and I wondered is this my fate. Soon I would find out why I was chosen.

It seemed as though hours had passed before the car came to a stop. My ankles were untied, but my arms remained behind me and I was led blindfolded inside a house somewhere far from New York. I was placed on a chair and my ankles and arms were tied to the chair. Remaining blindfolded, I heard several men whisper something I could barely make out, but one word in particular scared the daylights out of me. All I could make out was something about chopping a body in pieces and burying the limbs and head somewhere nearby, a place the police would never discover the remains. Changing my thoughts I wondered not only who these men are, and what do they want from me.

Hours seemed to pass before the men opened the door after what was a secret knock and although I couldn't see, I heard a man enter the room and order them to take my blindfold off. The light of day nearly blinded me after being unable to see for so long. The man introduced himself as being a friend of Hansi's. I thought, "Oh my God. Hansi has found me and I now knew why I was kidnaped. Hansi apparently discovered that I was about to find the last scrolls that would reveal everything that God told Abraham would happen in the final hour of man's reign on earth. I was sure that whatever was written, could never be told, and that it would have to be kept a secret so no person could make it sound as though he was God himself. Would that person try to convince the world that he is God, I thought. Then I began to remember that what I had learned from the Christian Bible was that in the last days a man would come into power and cause everyone on earth to believe he is God and demanded they bow and worship him, but were these the days that were prophesied. Could the Book of Abraham contain the name of this individual?

As I sat in the chair, the man began to ask questions about Pedro, Father Ligouri, Cardinal Catelli, and Rabbi Goldstein. I was shocked at the thought that these people knew I had any contact with them and would Hansi kidnap them as well to gain access to the scrolls? One thing was certain and that is the scrolls already discovered were tucked safely in a museum in Jerusalem and even I couldn't get my hands on them. The head man said, "I think I'll leave you here to ponder whether the scrolls are worth your life before I begin to question you." Before he left, I asked him if he could feed my since I haven't had anything to eat for several hours. He left me alone with one man who cooked a bowl of stew, then untied me to allow me to eat without struggling. As the man sat across from me at the small table, I started to slurp the food and when the opportunity presented itself, I threw the bowl of stew in his face causing him to scream in pain from the hot stew burning his face. While he attempted to wipe himself, I ran for the door and made my way to the road down the small stretch of trees lining the way. I hitched a ride with an old couple and had them take me to the police station. I had to report his incident so I would be safe and be able to make my way to Mexico tomorrow to meet Pedro and his friend, however, I had no idea that once again I would be diverted to somewhere else.

As I made my way back to New York, I thought that perhaps Pedro was in more danger than I was. Hansi knew his way through all of Central and South America and just the thought of once again having to deal with him made my skin crawl. I had just escaped from his men and I had no intention of having that happen again. I had a detective friend of mine have a couple of policemen keep tabs on me, at least until I leave for Mexico in three days.

By the time it came to head out for the airport to reunite with Pedro, a phone call came in. It was an old, very old friend of mine who also was an archeologist, specializing in Columbian artifacts. His name is Roluno Maxim, a very well educated and admired person in the world of archeology. Roluno informed me that he had found some amazing artifacts in Columbia and he wanted me to fly down to see him and give me first chance at this unique story. I had no idea whether I should go, but he was adamant that I come. I hesitantly agreed and after calling Pedro letting him know where I'd be. I bought a ticket online and headed for the airport. I have never been to Columbia and I was sure this would be a great adventure, especially since Roluno always found something interesting.

After the long flight from New York to Bogota, I was to go to the Hotel Garviella. It was a posh hotel and Rolundo paid for all my expenses, so now one should know why I just couldn't refuse the offer. Once I was at the hotel, I checked in and called Roluno as instructed. Roluno told me to stay put until two days would pass then he would arrive in Bogota to meet with me. I was apprehensive of the idea of waiting two days but I knew Roluno had his reasons.

As the time slowly went by, I found myself drifting off to sleep and was awoken by a knock on the door. I slowly walked over, peeked through the opening in the door, and saw it was Roluno. He looked magnificent. His dark wavy hair and those eyes that seemed to penetrate the soul made me desire him all the more. I thought perhaps he would take me by the hand and walk me to the bed where we would make passionate love, but I came to my senses when I remembered that Roluno was all business.

As we both sat at the small table in the corner of my room, Roluno explained that he had found a treasure outside the coastal town of Santa Marta. Roluno stated that for nearly four years he has been excavating, looking for a treasure he knew had to be there and then he laid it on me. He had stumbled across a statue that to him had funny inscriptions. I asked to see the statue but Roluno told me he had it in a safe place back in Santa Marta. It was a long drive to the town and the sun baked down on us, a light breeze surrounding my body.

Santa Marta is by no means a small town, but yet it did have a small town charm to it. As we drove to the outskirts of town, Roluno had to show me the place he had found the statue, perhaps hoping that I could explain why it was there. The place was dusty and had the appearance of having loads of bugs. Even the dirt had a foul odor. Roluno took me by the hand and led me to the spot where the statue was found. It couldn't have been fifteen feet from the surface and I was astonished that it had been well hidden and preserved for so long, but I still had no idea why Roluno thought I'd be interested in a statue he found in Columbia.

Roluno took me to a small house located just yards from where he has been digging and once we were inside, Roluno said, "Wait here. I'll show you what I have found." As I was by now totally confused, it didn't take long before I'd have my answer. As he entered the room, he showed me the statue and offered it to me. It had to be at least eighteen inches in length and made of pure gold and quite heavy I must say. As I gave it all my attention, I saw it had inscriptions surrounding it. I immediately noticed the inscriptions were ancient Hebrew. Wow, I thought. Could this statue have any significance with the scrolls we discovered. I asked Roluno if I could take the statue to a friend of mine back in Jerusalem for further study. Hesitant at first, Roluno agreed but not before showing me something else. Along with the statue was one of the scrolls I had been searching for. When Roluno came into the room holding a scroll, I nearly collapsed. He had found a scroll where I never would have guessed one to be and now I began to put two and two together. The statue and the scroll could be connected to Joseppa and soon I'd have my answer and a stunning one at that.

I decided to join Roluno in another dig, at least several hundred yards from where the statue was found. Roluno figured that whoever placed the statue and scroll at the spot discovered, there certainly had to be more and I didn't want to miss out on further discoveries. I called Pedro to let him know that I would stay here, in Columbia for several more days, then fly off to Israel to had over the scroll and statue to Rabbi Goldstein.

As we were digging, a news flash came over the radio. The Russian president, President Alexander Krychkovski and the Chinese Communist Party leader, Xo Lin had a summit whereby they continued to agree to keep the Eastern Alliance together. More countries were joining that alliance and that made everybody in the west extremely nervous. They already had a very large amount of allied troops between them all and the western nations would need a formula to counter that alliance. Adrian was beginning to tire of the Israeli's being stubborn and I must admit that even I was beginning to get anxious. If total war breaks out, what will become of my many friends in the Middle East, from both sides of the conflict. My mind thought of Hakim in Egypt, Rabbi Goldstein, and even Bill Butler in Iraq not to mention all the other people I had met and made friends with. If hostilities broke out, it would create another world war and nobody would be able to claim victory in the end. I was sure it would involve nuclear weapons and I thought of the destruction it would create.

As we continued our digging, I heard Roluno's shovel strike something hard. He was down about twenty feet when he stumbled upon a metal chest. Taking his hands he began to wipe dirt away from the chest and I helped as much as I could since the space was so small. Finally, after digging for hours we had discovered something. Roluno bent down and lifted the chest, struggling to place it high above his head to the ground. As soon as I saw it, I knew it wasn't any metal but another silver chest. It also had precious stones on the outside similar to the others

Pedro and I had found. Roluno pushed himself up and asked if he should open it. I took it upon myself to slowly lift the heavy lid and once it was completely open, we both awed in amazement at how the sunlight made it sparkle. It contained all sorts of precious stones along with another scroll. I have found perhaps two of the final three scrolls we assume are left. That means there's possibly one more scroll or even more and I know that the last scroll will be the most elusive one to date.

Along with the stones and scroll was some kind of paper, parchment I believe. It was written in ancient Hebrew and was unlike the scrolls. Totally satisfied with what we had come across, As the birds and other creatures were stirring around, I took the next flight to New York City to jot down my notes on my computer at the Herald before continuing on to Jerusalem. It would also give me some time to spend with my parents, something I haven't had the opportunity lately.

Pedro had continued with his search, but somehow I felt he was wasting his time, but then who knows. After spending some time with my parents, I took the taxi to the airport to take the next flight to Tel Aviv, then from there to Jerusalem. I was certain Rabbi Goldstein would be thrilled to see what I was bringing this time. I was extremely tired and dozed off to sleep, hardly waking up in time for the meal onboard.

I no sooner arrived in Israel when I received a message from the office back in New York. The new editor wanted all reporters back in New York in three days for a special meeting. There would be no excuses so I knew I had to complete what I set out to achieve before returning to New York especially since I didn't want to lose my job.

My editor was retiring and soon a new person would be chosen for the coveted job.

I had to place my faith in the new editor, despite the fact that I had a sneaky suspicion that Greta Fox was the chosen one. Greta and I go way back and there has been times when we didn't see eye to eye, however, she could play fair at times and that was the same quality my present editor possessed. I had to hand the small, heavy chest to Rabbi Goldstein, then have him give me some information concerning the chest, make a dash for the airport, and return to New York.

At the specially called meeting, my editor introduced the new editor and I was right, it was Greta Fox. Greta assured the entire staff there would be no changes to how the office would run, which gave me some relief. The only thought I had was, would Greta agree to have me continue with my investigation without hindrance?

Easter was seven weeks away and I wanted the investigation completed by then. Since I had a new editor, I decided to take a week or two staying at my desk in New York. I felt I could do some investigating online for a while, then return to Israel to meet with Rabbi Goldstein concerning the chest of precious stones and two scrolls. I was so close to finding that elusive final scroll, but I was motivated by the fact that if I was able to gather all the scrolls, there could be a Pulitzer Prize waiting for me down the road.

It's my father's birthday and I planned a special celebration. He was turning sixty and I wanted to make that day special. Granted it's not the same as turning seventy-five or so, but I wanted to make him feel good nonetheless. Mother will probably wear her favorite dress and I made arrangements to have dinner at my father's favorite place, The Cove in downtown New York. The Cove was well known to make the best steaks this side of the Rockies and I wanted to make this evening very special.

While eating, my father wanted to know what I've been doing lately and why I've been gone so long from home. I assured him that although I couldn't reveal the story yet, it would be an earth shattering story to date.

As I prepared to leave for the office, my cell phone rang. It was Pedro and he sounded very enthused about something. Pedro mentioned that he has been exploring near Bogota, Columbia and that there's a possibility that there is buried treasure from the first century. According to local legend, during the centuries, some famous and not so famous explorers had searched for the final scroll. Rumor has it that Cortez, Montezuma, and various notables had searched to no avail. Could the final scroll be near Bogota? Anything is possible I suppose, but Bogota? Pedro had come across ancient writings that had mentioned a stranger going by the name Joseppa and that he had taken a woman named Shedaya in Mexico and had traveled throughout the land spreading a new religion. He was known as a wise man by the natives, and had made new friends that helped him travel south, finally ending his journey in Argentina.

Although Pedro had discovered that valuable information, I thought it would be better to search somewhere in Mexico. Something told me that was where the last scroll was hidden. It had to be far away from Palestine to prevent the Roman legions from taking that treasure to the Emperor in Rome. Even legions from other countries fighting the Roman's would be very interested in having the scrolls to use to their own purpose.

The time had come for me to return to Israel. Rabbi Goldstein called to tell me the good news. I had found the two scrolls that were possibly written a couple years before the entire manuscript was completed and was completed by Abraham to be a beacon of light to the children of Israel. The Book of Abraham had been feared lost and now, thousands of years after being written, I of all people had discovered the book. It was now that I came to my senses and realized that I wasn't there yet. There was still an investigation to perform and that last scroll has been so elusive, I was afraid I would never find it.

Jerusalem was the kind of city I always thought was fantastic. It had it's fascinating history of course, but it also had it's nightlife and especially it's Jewish culture. I had become close friends with many Israeli's over the years, even the Arab Israeli's. I felt secure in the knowledge that I had gained the respect from the people that at times could be trying. Some of the people I had met were quite suspicious of me, but for the most part I blended well with the people.

As I arrived at the Synagogue, I could only imagine what the Rabbi was going to tell me. Had I found the most important scrolls to date, the one's that revealed things that would happen in the twentieth century and beyond?

As I entered his office, I could tell he had tons of enthusiasm regarding the scrolls I had given to him. Rabbi Goldstein explained that these two scrolls covered the years 1647 through 1977. It gave not just dates, but also names of notable people throughout the period. I named scientists and their discoveries, and also covered the period of flight. Important world leaders such as Hitler, Stalin, Kennedy and his assassination were also covered. I was in awe that the scrolls were written thousands of years ago by Abraham and that it was all revealed to him by God. Even the Christian Bible and the Torah didn't contain such information. Rabbi Goldstein told me, "Sue, what you have discovered no man before you has found. It may be God's purpose that thousands of years would pass before their discovery. The remaining question is, where is the last scroll and what does it contain?" I shivered in my bones that I was so close to discovering the final scroll but at the same time, as I said to the Rabbi, do I really want to find that scroll since it may contain information that God has kept secret for so long and does it mean that as the final scroll, it has the last writings of the fate of man.

For nearly four hours, Rabbi Goldstein and I poured through the two scrolls, hoping to learn even more. Deciphering the remaining texts proved difficult. There were words describing battles and elements that we were still unaware of. The scientific writings became elusive and at times appearing impossible to understand.

As we finished going over the scrolls, Rabbi Goldstein said, "Sue, do you realize that you have found the Book of Abraham that even makes the Bible and Torah seem insignificant. Saint John was given visions of the last days by God, but the Book of Abraham covered the ages from the great flood to perhaps the final day of man's reign on earth. Was Rabbi Goldstein correct in his assumption, I thought.

As I left the Synagogue, I returned to the hotel to have dinner and give Pedro a call. I had to know whether he has found anything since our last conversation. I remembered that Pedro told me that he had found tablets that had the name Joseppa on them. Could that be the same Joseppa I knew had arrived in the America's so long ago, or was it just coincidence? The it dawned on me that Pedro told me that the other name written down was the name of

Joseppa's wife, Shedaya. There certainly couldn't have ever been two couples with the same names throughout history. The odds were slim to none.

Pedro had done so much digging that almost every day something presented itself. I informed Pedro I would be arriving in Bogota in three days and help him dig for more treasures, but I was still leaning toward Mexico. That country was perhaps the first country Joseppa anchored his boats when he arrived those two thousand years ago.

By the time I arrived in Columbia, Easter Sunday was now seven weeks away and I was soon to be given the story of my lifetime, but first I had to complete my search for that elusive final scroll.

Pedro met me at the airport and the sun was very hot and the smells of the city permeated the place. As we drove for what seemed forever, Pedro told me that the place he has been digging is the town of San Jose del Guaviare, a place along the road that snakes it's way to Peru. It made perfect sense. If Joseppa and Shedaya arrived in present day Columbia, they would certainly arrive at this city which might have been just a little village back then before continuing on to Peru and then even traveling through Argentina as well.

As we pulled up to the place he was digging, there must have been fifty tents scattered around. Pedro said, "Sue, I believe I have found the final place where the most important scroll is hidden and I have hired the people here to help with the digging. If we did ourselves, we could easily be here for many years and perhaps without success. No matter what Pedro said, I still believe the final scroll is somewhere in Mexico, I just had a hunch.

As the days passed, all we accomplished was making more holes in the ground and I was exhausted. On the tenth day I received a phone message to go to Berlin, Germany to cover a story about some historical documents discovered in the heart of the city. Although I was tired of all the digging, I still preferred to remain here rather than go on an assignment to Germany, but my new editor insisted and I really valued my job, so off I go, leaving Bogota for New York, and get to the Herald for final instructions.

While I was returning to New York, I got a call on my cell phone from a detective in Paris. It seems that Hansi was spotted in the seedy part of town and was asking questions related to me. Why would Hansi be asking anyone a question about me, especially in the seedy part of town. It then dawned on me that a few years ago, I met a woman, living in Paris, who contacted me about a man she had concerns about. Although he didn't reveal who he was, he did have questions, such as, "Where is the man Sue Chamberlain met while in Paris?" I then remembered that several years ago I was working on a story about women being held captive by a group of east European men, being sold as sex slaves, and were beaten about the face so bad that one woman's jaw was not just dislocated, but shattered. It took surgeons five operations just to be able to get the woman to eat without any pain.

According to the detective, the woman asked for me by name, but I had no idea which woman it was considering that I had contacts with several of the former sex slaves. When I asked the detective what her name was he refused to reveal her name because her life could be on the line. I told the detective I would be in Berlin for a few days and after the assignment was finished, I would take a quick stop over in Paris. I was very curious but yet at the same time feeling cautious. If Hansi and this woman were connected,

I would certainly be in extreme danger and Pedro would have no idea where to find me.

As I arrived in berlin, I checked into the Adlon Hotel, a very expensive yet glamourous hotel. Even during the Nazi era, the Adlon was the place to be whenever in Berlin.

Tomorrow a special conference was to be conducted at the Berlin Museum of Ancient Studies. I had no idea what I was about to cover since all my editor told me was to be here. I was confused. Why did my editor have me come to Berlin when a colleague of mine, Randy Miles usually covered any stories from western Europe. I guess she knew that I was the proper person to cover this event and soon I'd know why.

I spent the evening taking in the sights and sounds of Berlin. I visited the place where the old Berlin Wall once stood and I couldn't get over the fact that what the wall represented was not just divisions, but also a period of time when both sides distrusted each other. I, of course, am to young to remember the building of the wall and as a young child, I was also to young to know the meaning. All I remember was seeing people standing on top of a wall, yet had no idea where it was or what it was about.

Relaxing on the bed in my hotel room, I concentrated on my assignment and became so tired, I drifted off to sleep, waking up without knowing how long I had slept. I showered, dressed, and took the stroll from the hotel to the train station. The area of Berlin that housed the museum was in the far eastern part of the city and I wanted to be one of the first to arrive to obtain one of the best seats since it was first come first served. Nobody had an assigned seat. The part of the building housed a large auditorium, which I understand could seat more than five hundred people. I managed to arrive in time to seat myself just three rows back. That was a good thing since there were numerous rows behind me and I had such a good seat that hearing the conference wasn't going to be a problem.

As the conference began, an old friend of mine, Erik Shoustein took a seat at the podium. I haven't seen Erik for many years and he had aged substantially. Erik was the kind of guy who would shower a girl with utter kindness, yet he did have a dark side which I witnessed shortly after I met him. He was having an argument with a young man, barely out of college, about something Erik had discovered in Egypt during one of his diggings, The young man accused Erik of falsifying an article that Erik had written for a well known journal about what he had discovered. He had accused Erik without the proper documents that would suggest Erik had done such a thing and nearly ruined Erik's reputation.

As everyone sat quietly, Professor Von Shymer began his lecture about something he discovered in the ruins of Berlin. What he had found has been missing since the destruction of the city toward that end of World War 2. As Von Shymer continued his lecture, he surprised me with the words I had known for so long, yet unaware that other's knew of it's existence. When Von Shymer said the words, "The Book of Abraham has been discovered." that statement floored me since I have been on this case from the get go and I didn't know that a well known respected professor knew of it's existence. Does the professor know of my work and could this be a trap just to reel me in to cause my reputation to be soiled?

Once Shymer finished his news flash, he allowed the press to come forward and look at the document for ourselves to prove he had found the last scroll. The scroll was encased in a glass covered frame and when I saw it, I felt I had seen something that resembled a scroll, yet I was sure the parchment wasn't from the period. How can I prove Shymer was passing off a fake? How much has he insured the scroll for and where was it headed?

I realized I had to get to Jerusalem to let Rabbi Goldstein know of Shymer's discovery. If anyone would know about Shymer it would be Rabbi Goldstein. I packed my bags, headed for the airport to take the next flight to Israel, unaware of the danger that was following me.

As I arrived in Tel Aviv, I called Rabbi Goldstein asking to see him to let him know what I have learned. I was afraid for Pedro because if this document was a fake and could be proven, Pedro was in more danger than I was.

As my meeting started with the Rabbi, he listened cautiously, not batting an eyebrow until I had finished my story. Now it was time for Rabbi Goldstein to begin. He started out by saying, "Sue, I have known for some time about Shymer and his so called discovery." According to Goldstein, Shymer had been to Egypt, Libya, and Turkey in search for that elusive scroll. Shymer was so desperate to find the scroll and display it for the world to see feeling that would give him the fame he so desperately needed, that he resorted to contacting Hansi to have him find a forger who could do such a good job of faking the document, Goldstein knew that Hansi and Shymer were of the same mold. It seems that Shymer's father was a high ranking Nazi during the war and that he wanted to please Hitler so much that he, as well as Hansi's grandfather, searched the four corners of the world, looking for the Book of Abraham.

Shymer, Hansi, and other people wanted to get their hands on the final scroll so bad they would stop at nothing and I already knew Hansi was capable of doing just that. I already had to deal with Hansi, but I had no idea how bad Shymer could be. He would make Hansi look like a saint compared to his capabilities.

CHAPTER 9

Rabbi Goldstein cautioned me that perhaps I wouldn't want to know what the final scroll said and could reveal just what all the time from Adam and Eve to the present really meant. What was God's purpose, he said. I even began to dwell on the subject myself but always put it in the back of my head. The final scroll that would be the completion of the Book of Abraham would prove to be the most elusive. I had false trips to China, North Korea, Manchuria, and Southeast Asia, with nothing presenting itself.

Once Rabbi Goldstein was finished with his interpretation of the two scrolls, I decided to return to New York for the long, much needed rest I needed, but somehow I had a suspicion that my little period of rest wouldn't last long.

After a few days passed, I was having dinner with my parents when I was interrupted with a call coming through my cell phone. It was Pedro, calling to inform me that he may have found something very profound concerning the Book of Abraham and the connection between Joseppa and Mexico. Although I still needed more rest, I agreed to leave for Mexico in three days so I could at least finish transcribing my notes into my computer at work to have at the ready for this earth shattering story I was sure would win me the Pulitzer Prize.

Before I knew it, I was on a flight from New York to Mexico City. Pedro would meet me at the airport then we'd take the long ride to the outside of the town of Veracruz, then a day later meet up with Pedro's friend Alejandro for the final leg of our journey to the town of Chiapas. At the town of Chiapas we would pay for our hotel rooms and then prepare our gear for tomorrow's drive about twenty five miles south to an area where Pedro and Alejandro had been doing some excavating. So far they have found pottery and a few other trinkets dating to perhaps the fourth or even third centuries, but Pedro was sure that further digging would produce even more older treasure, perhaps something left behind by Joseppa himself on his was south.

The hotel in Chiapas was what one could describe as shabby chic. It had some charm but yet wasn't the kind of place I would have chosen, I assure you. Even my makeup didn't want to be here. Although the room appeared clean, I still felt like there were creepy crawlers running under the bed and between the sheets. No matter, I decided a hot bath would at least take some of my concerns away. Besides, tomorrow was going to be a hot sweaty day and I wanted to at least smell good.

When I left New York, people were preparing for spring to arrive, but winter still had it's grip on much of the nation. With snow still on the ground, it was hard to imagine that Easter is only six weeks away. I had no idea at this point, but on Easter Sunday, my life and everyone else's would dramatically change forever.

Daylight and bugs scattering throughout the room. I dressed as fast as possible, grabbed my gear, left the room and placed the gear into the truck. I was so repulsed by the filthy room that I found it difficult to even think of having breakfast but Pedro insisted, especially since it could be hours before lunch and with the heat I could possibly faint.

As we approached the area where they had begun to dig I saw the various holes spread throughout the area. Pedro and his friend have really been busy, I must say that. I didn't know where to start digging and after some thought, I decided to dig a few yards south from the southernmost part of Pedro's last dig. Taking out my trusty shovel, I started the boring task of digging and after several minutes I realized I was getting nowhere fast. I asked Pedro, "Pedro, are you sure there is anything here?" Affirming he had already found treasure at this location, I tried to believe him so I continued my share of digging but as the day wore on and we were getting nowhere, I told Pedro, "Perhaps we should try some place else tomorrow when we get a fresh start." Pedro was still adamant that something was here that would yield proof that Joseppa was here and that there was a good possibility that the final scroll could be buried here.

I felt Pedro was imagining things. I said, "Pedro, why would Joseppa bury the final scroll here in Mexico and yet take the other scrolls to Peru and perhaps Argentina?" By now even Pedro had to agree that what I said made sense, yet he still wanted to continue the digging. Alejandro agreed with me that we needed to do more research at the library in Lima, Peru before we continue to dig anywhere. Standing in front of me, Pedro had that dejected look and after some time thinking, he eventually agreed. The three of us returned to town, gathered our clothes from the hotel, left for Mexico City for a flight back to Lima, Peru. I was now going to probably finish my quest at the very same place it had started.

Once we were settled in, I left for the Cathedral to have a chat with Father Ligouri. It's been a long time since our last conversation and I needed some quality time with him. Father Ligouri was the kind of man I felt easy bearing my soul to. I was by this time tired and frustrated. This journey has taken everything out of me and yet after all of this time, I still had to go on and complete the task at hand no matter what. There was not only the difficult task of digging and doing research, but there was also the constant fear of danger lurking at every corner. I have been taken captive, nearly murdered, almost raped, and have been thrown to the ground by someone in a fit of rage.

Father Ligouri asked me how I was doing with my work and I told him how I had been dealing with dangerous people and being in terrible places. Father Ligouri was even held captive at one point because of me and nearly lost his life.

I told Father Ligouri that it was good to be back in Peru but yet I yearned for New York and the bright lights of the city. Father Ligouri told me that he had heard a rumor that Hansi was seen in Lima as well as in Argentina. That sent chills down my spine. What if Hansi finds out, I'm back in Peru? I knew Pedro would want to know but what could he do about that anyway.

After talking with Father Ligouri for three hours, I left for the town of Tarma to meet up with Pedro. I had to convince Pedro that Peru was not the place to search but there was the possibility that we could discover something in Mexico instead. I had already journeyed there awhile back and had discovered some small treasures. Once I had a long talk with Pedro, he had to agree that Mexico was the proper place to continue our research and our digging. This time I thought we would dig outside the town of Tabasco. Tabasco was a port city and could possibly yield some treasure nearby. Tabasco has historically been known to be the port where merchant ships have docked throughout the centuries. I have been told that even Spanish explorers have been known to have buried some of their booty nearby. Perhaps I'd find some Spanish bullion?

The flight to Mexico City gave me the chance to catch up on some reading. I had taken a book on ancient Jewish writings with me that I had purchased some time ago while I was in Jerusalem. I wanted to study and learn as much as I could, almost immersing myself in it, so once I discovered any more writings, I could at least have some idea what I was looking at. I must admit that the ancient Jewish script was difficult at best, but I was determined to learn the language. As my eyes closed from exhaustion, I drifted off to sleep and dreamed of a simple time when I could have been a Jewish Princess during the time of King David.

As the plane landed in Mexico City, Pedro nudged my shoulder, waking me out of my sleep. Time had passed by so quickly I could hardly believe we had arrived at our destination. I had no idea that this time, I would have a life changing experience like no other.

Pedro and I rented a car for the long drive from Mexico City to Tabasco. Once there, we'd get a room at the hotel, change clothes, then drive outside the city to a place Pedro learned is called the area of souls. Apparently, hundreds, perhaps thousands of years ago, there was a village that was attacked and ransacked by an army of strangers from another land that murdered the people, taking the female survivors as slaves, and leaving the town abandoned forever. The survivors were never heard from again and the town became known to others as the town of souls or area of souls to some. It had a spooky feeling about it. Some say the place is haunted and that anyone who goes through the area becomes possessed by the spirits of those who were murdered. I told Pedro I didn't believe in such nonsense but Pedro had an inkling about such things. I had no idea that Pedro was superstitious.

I was fascinated by the appearance of the town of Tabasco. Is this the place where tabasco sauce was created, I wondered. I was told that outside the city limits was a farm where hot chili peppers are grown and sold and I usually don't eat hot peppers but Pedro insisted I give them a try, besides, he said, what could it hurt. As we drove up to the farm, they had a stand loaded with their produce. There were all types of chili peppers. There were red, green, yellow, and even orange one's. As I scanned over the table, Pedro took a red one and insisted I try it. Little did I know he had given me one of their hottest peppers. As I took it in my mouth and bit down, my tongue and lips began to burn. I spit the pepper out while Pedro laughed so hard I think he nearly farted. Why did you do that, I responded. Pedro, laughing so hard said, "Sue, that wasn't even their hottest pepper." Well, that was the hottest one to me and I walked back to the car and waited for Pedro to finish his business.

Driving for several miles, we came to a spot that appeared to have been searched before. Pedro assured me that nobody had been here, yet I felt as though someone had beaten us to this place. To the right was an open field, to the left was a mountain, not a large mountain, but large enough to perhaps hide something of value. As Pedro and I unloaded the car, I looked over my shoulder and noticed that the trees seemed out of place. Why were these trees here? They weren't the kind of trees that were native to Mexico and that puzzled me. Pedro thought I was losing my mind but somehow I felt I was right about this. Paying no attention, Pedro began to walk up the mountain toward an area that seemed to be void of vegetation. Gathering my senses, I started the journey up the mountain right behind Pedro. Those trees still consumed me, but soon I'd have my answer.

Finally, after an hour had passed, we came to the summit. Low and behold, there was a small opening that led through a darkened hole. This was when Pedro told me he had been here before and wanted to keep this place a secret, even from me, until the last minute. This was one of the places where he has found buried treasure that Spanish explorers had hidden their booty so many years ago. Pedro believed that buried beneath the Spanish treasure could lay something from the first century, perhaps from Joseppa himself. He was sure Joseppa had sailed here at Tabasco, docked his ship, and made his way inland, going as far south as Peru.

Although I thought Pedro was losing his mind, I still believed that there was a possibility that there could be something buried in this mountain.

Making our way inside the mountain, all I could see were hundreds of bats flying about and the total darkness that permeated the place. Without our flashlights, the place would be totally dark and rather spooky. It also smelled very dank and I could here what sounded like running water. Pedro told me that he had discovered a small stream making it's way through the mountain towards the southern exit and into the river.

Once we had found the stream, Pedro suggested we follow the path of the stream then start to dig about two hundred feet deeper than our present location. We would be around four hundred feet below the surface and the only thing we have to worry about was a cave-in, not Hansi or anyone else. Pedro assured me that he had taken every precaution that nobody was following us, but I had my doubts. I remembered his assurances about that same promise in Peru when Hansi showed up at the caves. I wanted to find that last, elusive scroll that would make up the Book of Abraham. Once I found that last scroll, I would at last complete my assignment and be able to write my column for the New York Herald. I was certain my editor would be pleased and this article would probably get me a promotion and maybe even that Pulitzer Prize I so desperately desired.

As Pedro checked his map, he loudly said, "Sue, this is the place we have to dig at first." I thought to myself, "Is he nuts? Why would there be anything here?" Well, if Pedro thought this was the place, then this must be the place after all, he's been here before. Taking a shovel in hand, I began to dig, and dig, and dig, until my hands had calluses. I was beginning to tire and I begged Pedro to leave the mountain, return to town, then come back the next day to resume the digging. I wasn't use to this manual labor, I must admit, as much as I wanted to find that last scroll, I didn't know if I had it in me to continue the quest the way I've had to do it. The question surrounding my mind was, am I doing this for nothing, or better yet, am I at the wrong place? Although Pedro wanted to continue, he agreed that it was getting to be to much for me to go on so we packed up our gear, left the dark, deep, mountain, and drove back to the town of Tabasco. My hands were chaffed, and my legs were sore, yet, I wanted to have a night on the town. Pedro and I both showered, got in our good clothing and had a great dinner and dancing before retiring for the night.

The morning sun beamed in my eyes, causing me to wake up. I felt refreshed and ready to take the day by the reigns. Pedro appeared to be more sore than I was, but I didn't want to let him know how sore I was from yesterdays event. I shook his shoulders, causing him to awaken, then poured both of us a hot cup of coffee before we were dressed and on our way back to the mountain.

Once inside, we continued our digging and it didn't take long before we struck something in the ground. It was hard and sounded like metal, yet it also had the density of wood. Scooping the dirt surrounding the object, Pedro was finally able to see what it was and he ecstatically yelled out, "It's a wooden chest with metal straps around it." Now I became excited. Pedro said, Sue, this thing is very heavy, come help me." As I grabbed onto the chest, I used all my strength and could hardly budge the thing. It was too heavy for both of us to bring out of the hole and onto the surface. I suggested we slowly empty the chest little by little, placing the items in the three bags we brought with us.

Pedro saw the chest was locked and also noticed there was some writing below the lock. It appeared to be ancient Hebrew but neither one of us could translate what it said. I had studied some Hebrew but not enough to decipher what this writing said. Pedro said, "What are we going to do? I don't want to break the lock until we find out what these writings say." I suggested I write down the words, take the paper to Israel to have Rabbi Goldstein translate them before we attempt to open the chest, then at least we'll know whether or not we should proceed. Pedro agreed, so I wrote everything down, we scattered some of the dirt over the chest, put a marking over the location and returned to Mexico City. Pedro would remain here while I returned to New York, then take a flight to Tel Aviv, then a bus to Jerusalem.

My arrival in Tel Aviv led me to a marketplace where there was a bizarre that sold cheap items for the tourists. I decided to take a look to see if there was anything I could buy for myself, something that wouldn't cost much, yet wouldn't appear to cheap. As I scoured through the jewelry, I noticed something that caught my eye. It was made of nickel, but gold plated, and it was very fancy. Engraved on the one side was a symbol, the exact same symbol that I had written down from the chest I had discovered in Mexico. How peculiar, I thought. I decided to purchase the item and was even willing to pay extra which pleased the merchant. I guess he thought I was a crazy American but I really wanted this piece of jewelry.

As I arrived in Jerusalem, I got to the hotel, unpacked, and headed straight for the Synagogue to see Rabbi Goldstein. The young lady who cleans the place answered the door and said the Rabbi would return in an hour so I asked if I could wait inside. Although she was hesitant, she did allow me when I pleaded with her that I had come a long distance to see the Rabbi.

As I waited, I took out the piece of jewelry I purchased in Tel Aviv and held in tightly in my hands. As I inspected the item, the cleaning lady passed by and once she saw the piece, she quickly ran away, screaming out loud, "My God, Take that cursed thing out of here before someone dies." I was puzzled. What was it about this piece of jewelry that caused her to run away screaming and saying such things? Perhaps Rabbi Goldstein will be able to explain. I placed it back inside my purse and just sat quietly and waited for another few minutes for the Rabbi.

Once Rabbi Goldstein saw me, his eyes lit up and he gave me a tight hug. Rabbi Goldstein was always glad to see me and when he asked me what brought me back to Jerusalem this time, I told him I wanted to have him translate something for me that I found on a chest I discovered in Mexico and that before I open the chest I wanted him to translate the writings. As always, he agreed.

In opened my purse, took out the piece of paper, and gave it to him. As he sat at his desk, he read the writing and began to have a fearful look in his eyes. He glanced up at me and said, "Sue. Did you open that chest yet?" I told him I haven't and that's when he said to me, "Good, because if you do, you will die." I said, "What do you mean, I'll die. ?" He walked over to me and said, "See here. This is the ancient Hebrew word for curse. Apparently whoever placed any scroll, perhaps the final scroll inside that chest placed a curse that whoever opens the chest and discovers it's contents and reveals it, will die."

Damn it, I thought. Now what. How can I open the chest now. I'm so close to discovering what no man has ever discovered throughout the centuries and yet so far away. I certainly didn't want to die, but I wanted to find out, at least for myself, what was inside the chest. As I opened my purse, the piece of jewelry I purchased in Tel Aviv fell out on top of the table. When I reached out to pick it up, Rabbi Goldstein grabbed my hand, preventing me from picking it up and asked, "Where on God's green earth did you get this?" When I told him that I was at a marketplace in Tel Aviv when I arrived, he said, "Goodness gracious Sue, do you realize what you have here?" Naturally I didn't but I was sure he was about to explain.

Rabbi Goldstein went on to say, "Centuries ago, the story goes that during the time the Jewish people were slaves in Egypt, they were forced to wear that symbol around their necks as the Egyptians considered them to be a cursed people. After Moses liberated them, they took off their necklaces and pledged from that day forward that anyone whoever reveals what is contained in the final scroll of the Book of Abraham will inherit the curse. Even in ancient Egypt it was well known about that book." Apparently it was to be well hidden until the last days when the Messiah arrives and also it will be at the same time that the Ark of the Covenant will be discovered. This symbol, a winged demon, cradled by Satan, is the curse. Only when the Messiah arrives will the curse be broken when Satan is cast into the lake of fire which many believe to be our sun.

When Rabbi Goldstein told me that, I decided to throw that thing away, but not inside this temple. Now I know why he had that fearful look on his face. My one question was, "Why did that man sell me this piece of jewelry?" Rabbi Goldstein told me that he probably thought that as a tourist you'd most likely never know and you would suffer some sort of twisted fate. That made me decide right then and there never to go to another marketplace and buy any neat looking jewelry ever again.

I was saddened that the chest Pedro and I had found couldn't be opened but I also believed that somewhere there was another chest waiting to be discovered with the same revelation. Rabbi Goldstein's only response to that was, "Be very careful. You never know what you will release."

The flight back to the United States was very depressing. How am I going to tell Pedro what I've learned and can I convince him to keep his hands off that chest? I know Pedro, and at times his curiosity can get the best of him.

When I returned to my office at the New York Herald to do some computer updating on what I've already achieved, Rabbi Goldstein called. He told me that he may have given me some wrong information concerning the chest Pedro and I have found. Yes, there is a curse, but, only if the chest is opened by someone other than a Jewish Rabbi and whatever is inside must be translated or read by a Rabbi. Rabbi Goldstein told me to return to Mexico, retrieve the chest, and bring it to him in Israel for not only to open it, but also for safekeeping. He certainly didn't want anyone other than himself to open the chest and see it's contents and naturally that had to have meant Hansi.

I was happy as a lark to hear such good news but my main concern was trying to convince Pedro not to open the chest and what is more important, get it out of Mexico, across the border by land or through customs at the airport. The chest is only about thirty inches by twelve inches by seven inches but still large enough to cause someone's curiosity. It also seems quite heavy for it's size which brings me to another thought. Suppose there are more precious stones inside and a customs agent decides to open the chest, discovers the stones, and arrests Pedro and me. Then what? All sorts of thoughts raced through my head while I made my way back to Mexico City, then on to the city of Tabasco.

As I arrived in Tabasco, Pedro was on another dig so I checked into the hotel and went to the local bar for a few cold one's until Pedro returned to town later in the evening. I had to report to him what Rabbi Goldstein had told me and also learn whether he could come up with some sort of an idea of how to get the chest out of Mexico and then on to Israel. Certainly, even the United States Customs Agents would be curious as well.

When I laid my eyes on Pedro, I was excited to say the least. I think I'm beginning to fall madly in love with him. He's very charming, handsome, and very gracious. Tonight we will celebrate our latest find and hope that this is the final chest and scroll that we have be pursuing for so long, but somehow I had a sneaky suspicion that this little adventure wasn't quite over yet. I still had that devil Hansi to worry about and not just him, but also his men or any of his connections around the world. He was involved with the Chinese Mafia, the Italian Mafia, and the neo-Nazi underground. Any one of these organizations would love to get their hands on this chest, especially if it contained the last scroll that made up the Book of Abraham.

For the next four days Pedro continued to dig, hopeful that more could be found but I felt it was futile. Even if there was something still to be found, would it be of the same quality as this latest chest we have discovered? While Pedro continued his work, I on the other hand had to come up with a plan to get the chest out of Mexico and onto Israel without being discovered. After hour after hour had passed then day after day, I finally came up with an idea and I hope a brilliant one at that.

This evening when Pedro returned to town, I told him of my plan. I said, "Tomorrow I'm going into the marketplace to make a liquor purchase. I'm buying twenty cases of tequila to have shipped to Israel for an upcoming wedding. Along with the cases of tequila, hidden between them, will be the chest. I will have them shipped by boat. The manifest will state that the pallet contains the cases of liquor and unless someone opens the crate, they'll never know." I could see the fear in Pedro's eyes. His response was, "Do you have any idea what will happen to us if anybody gets wise to what your plans are? I don't think I could take twenty years in a Mexican prison, could you?" I had to admit that thought had crossed my mind but I also asked Pedro whether he had a better idea.

The next day I went down to the marketplace, made the purchase for the tequila, had the booze crated with the chest inside the middle, bound and placed on a pallet. Luckily for me when I handed the foreman the chest along with a chunk of money, he was a man who could do anything for the right amount of money. His silence could be bought, the question was could one afford his silence. Once I saw the package was safely placed on the ship and had passed inspection, I returned to the hotel, brimming with satisfaction, and informed Pedro, mission accomplished. He could hardly believe what I had achieved.

In three days we would be in New York, celebrating all we've accomplished so far and continue waiting a few weeks before returning to Israel to retrieve the chest, and hand it over to Rabbi Goldstein. By that time it will be Easter and perhaps I could be so lucky as to celebrate Easter Sunday in Jerusalem. I had no idea how ironic that would turn out to be.

Pedro would spend his time waiting at my parents house while I worked at the Herald, at least that would keep him out of trouble, but as usual, trouble would find Pedro.

It was right after I had lunch that my phone rang at the office. A man's voice quietly told me to return to my parents home immediately and be sure nobody knew where I was going. When I tried to ask why, the phone went dead. That raised my suspicions. Who was this person and why did I have to return to my parents house? I left the office so fast I forgot that I was supposed to meet with my editor in an hour to discuss my assignment on Easter Sunday in three weeks in Jerusalem to cover Pope Peter's special meeting with World Federation Council President Adrian at the Jewish Temple. It was to be the world's most special event, broadcast live throughout the world even though there was a threat of all out war from the eastern alliance.

As the taxi pulled up to my parents apartment, I noticed the curtains were drawn together and the lights seemed dim. That was so unlike my parents. They always had the curtains opened and the lights shining brightly. I was almost afraid to go up but yet I was curious. My knees were shaking at the thought of the potential danger awaiting me. I was just hopeful that everybody was safe and not being hurt.

I knocked on the door and as my mother opened the door I asked if everything was all right. As she stepped back, a man grabbed the door, slammed it shut and pushed my mother to the chair near the fireplace. As I stood there in shock, I was hustled to the dining room, shoved on one of the chairs, and waited a few seconds in silence until the kitchen door opened and in shock saw none other than Hansi walking toward me.

"Well, Miss Chamberlain. We meet again." I then asked Hansi what he wanted and why he had my parents get involved. With a grin on his face he answered, "But Sue, they've always been involved." I responded, "What do you mean by that?" Taking a few moments to answer, he then responded, "You see Sue, they gave birth to you and you have given me trouble so therefore they have been involved from the very beginning. You have decided their fate. One of them are going to die tonight, unless you give me what I want."

By this time I was starting to get quite concerned. Giving me trouble was one thing, but my family was another. I pleaded with Hansi to let them go and I would do anything he wanted. He laughed and told me I would do anything anyway just so he doesn't kill my parents.

I asked Hansi what he wanted. He once again laughed and said, "Surely Sue. You must know what it is that I want. I want the final scroll and the jewels from that last chest you found in Mexico. That Jew in Israel you gave them to will die unless you bring them to me. I will let you leave this apartment, go to Jerusalem, retrieve the items, bring them back to me within seventy two hours, and if you tell the police or anyone else, your parents will die, understood." Hansi had me over a barrel but I knew I had to come up with a plan or something bad will happen. I know Hansi and even if I gave him what he wanted he will kill my parents anyway and perhaps even me.

As I packed my bags and called the airlines for a flight to Israel, I hugged my parents and told them I will do all I can to help them get out of this predicament safely. Three of Hansi's men drove me to the airport, walked me to the security gate and watched as the plane took flight. I was on my way to Israel not knowing whether Hansi would kill my parents while I was gone or if he had other plans.

When I arrived in Tel Aviv, I phoned Rabbi Goldstein to let him know I was on the way and that I had to see him, it was of the utmost importance. He was glad I was in town since he had good news for me. The train ride to Jerusalem gave me the opportunity to relax and take in the sights of the country and also the time to think of a way to handle Hansi once and for all.

As I entered the temple, Rabbi Goldstein was finishing making arrangements for a wedding in three days but he did have some time to spend with me, thankfully, since this was a matter of life and death. As I sat in front of his massive desk, Rabbi Goldstein said, "What is it you wanted to tell me so badly?" When I told him I needed to take the chest back to the United States with me and that it was a matter of life and death, he became quite concerned. He replied, "I don't understand. Why do you have to take it back home with you?" I tried to make up a story without telling him exactly what was really going on for fear it would endanger the lives of my parents. Rabbi Goldstein replied, "I can't let you take it back home. It belongs here in Israel, you said it yourself."

I knew he was right, but I had to persuade him somehow. After several attempts I gave up trying to convince him and then asked him what he wanted to tell me.

Rabbi Goldstein said, "Wait here a minute. I'll be right back." Several minutes passed before he returned to the office holding the golden chest. As he laid it on his desk, it glittered in the sunlight. It was the most beautiful thing I ever laid my eyes on. As he sat down, he began to translate the inscriptions on the chest. Taking his fingers, he began scanning, saying, "This inscription gives the name of the apostle who was given this chest. His name was in English Thomas. He then gave it to the man named Joseppa for safekeeping. This part describes that the contents of this chest can only be seen by the high priest of the temple and nobody else otherwise that person will become blinded by the light and suffer a painful death. The contents of this chest contains the exact location of the final scroll which will only be revealed two weeks before the final hour of the time of man."

I said, "Does this mean that this chest cannot be opened by anybody at anytime other than the high priest?" His response was, "Yes." I thought to myself, well that stinks. How will I ever find that elusive scroll. No wonder no one has ever discovered it's location. God himself must have surely buried the scroll, much like he has buried the Ark of the Covenant.

It was at this time I had to reveal to the Rabbi why I had to return to New York with the chest. When I told him that Hansi was holding my parents hostage and had threatened to kill them, he unwillingly agreed to let me take it home, on the condition that once Hansi was dead, I would return to Jerusalem with the chest and return it safely to him so the Head Rabbi could open the lid to see what it contained and when that happens he would call me to let me know. When Rabbi Goldstein told me that, I felt very relieved and made my way back to New York, chest in hand.

As I stepped off the plane in New York, I could only imagine what Hansi would be capable of once he had his hands on this chest. Would he still kill my parents or even kill me, or would he take me hostage for further use? Those are questions that could only be answered once I returned to my parents apartment.

As I slowly made my way to the building, I looked up at the apartment's darkened windows, and felt as though something terrible has happened while I was in Israel. Did I take to long to return or was Hansi tired of waiting and killed my parents anyway, or did he take them some place else? The only way to find out was to open the door to the apartment and as I slowly did so, the room was dark, but I could see shadows of people in the room. As I entered the room, someone grabbed me by the arm and shoved me to the center of the room where who I believed was Hansi sitting in an armchair. As the man turned on a small lamp, I saw it was Hansi and as he stared at me, he whispered, "Did you get what I wanted?" I opened the package and slowly took out the chest and held it in my hands, As he saw the golden chest, Hansi gasped, excited at the fact that he had what he had been searching for almost as long as I had been.

Rising to his feet, he walked over to me, his breath blowing in my face and wrapped his hands around the chest and my hands. He ordered me to let go of the chest and as I did as ordered, Hansi held tightly to the golden chest and closed his eyes and acted as though he was having a sexual orgasm. His excitement was felt throughout the room, even his men acted as though they were experiencing the same feelings.

I stood there feeling tense, then said to Hansi, "Now that you have what you wanted, don't you want to open the chest to be sure that I have given you exactly what you wanted and didn't cheat you." Realizing that possibility, Hansi took the chest and placed it on the table next to the small lamp shining in the room. As he laid the chest down, I slowly made my way to my parents and asked them if they were all right and once they said they were, I told them that when Hansi began to open the chest, they were to close their eyes until the chest was closed again or they would go blind. As we watched Hansi slowly open the chest with his men surrounding him, the three of us closed our eyes and felt the electrical impulses surround the room. Hansi and his men screamed in complete horror then pain as their eyes were melting in their sockets and their bones began to crack. One by one they fell to the floor, Hansi closed the lid to the chest and as he fell to the floor, his last words to me were, "What have you given me, you bitch." Once I was sure the chest was closed, I opened my eyes and saw the four of them laying on the floor dead as dead could be. Their eye sockets revealing their melted eyes.

I then told my parents they could open their eyes. My mother told me that Hansi had threatened to kill her first and when I came through the door she only had one hour left to live before Hansi was going to kill her. I had made it home just in time.

Once we regained ourselves, I made the call to Rabbi Goldstein and told him what happened to Hansi. Rabbi Goldstein knew that Hansi couldn't help himself and that at least now he was out of the picture but somehow I knew there were other's who wanted the elusive final scroll that this chest revealed where it was located. I had to return this chest to Rabbi Goldstein as soon as possible before something bad happens again.

As I returned the chest to Rabbi Goldstein, I had a text message from a woman from a museum in Germany requesting I come see her as soon as possible. Apparently she had learned about my research and needed to see me so I left Israel and flew to Berlin on the next chartered flight.

I had been to Germany before to research information about what the East German Government had kept hidden from the west for decades but what the woman had wanted to show me was something I was unprepared for.

As I entered the museum, I asked for Ruth Keptner. As I waited, I looked at the many paintings in the room and was in awe at the beauty they held. I didn't know at the time the awful history they held. Many of the works were confiscated after the war from the collections of Hitler and other Nazi's, perhaps, and they may belong to numerous dead Jews.

As the clicking of shoes approached, I turned and saw this beautiful woman approach. She introduced herself as Ruth Keptner. I shook her hand and told her I was Sue Chamberlain. She walked me to her office, then as we sat down, she told me she has something of great importance to tell me. I was curious. What could this lady possibly tell me here in Germany that required my presence. She started off by explaining that she was aware of what I've been doing lately. I thought to myself, how could she possibly know about my research.

Mrs. Keptner said that she had come across a document written a few years ago by a German Jew who survived the death camps during World War 2. He had hidden away in his apartment here in Berlin a Jewish document dating back thousands of years. It was written in ancient Hebrew text and had been missing ever since he had hidden the document, until a young couple had purchased the apartment after the end of the communist era, and began to remodel the place. As they tore apart the walls, they found this document.

As she continued telling me the story, she opened the drawer to her desk and produced the old document. As I looked the document over, it appeared to look exactly like the ancient scrolls I had found in Peru and Mexico as well as in Egypt, Syria, and Damascus, not to mention Israel. After seeing so many scrolls over the time I've spent searching, I could almost read most of the text. I told her, "According to this, it tells of a great man who would conquer most of Europe, create a living hell on earth, and nearly destroy the holy people. Soon after another will come to destroy the holy people and he to will fail for I will come to destroy the evil one's."

Ruth asked me what the text meant. I told her, "Well, I think that the great man who would conquer Europe could be Hitler and the one after could be the anti-Christ but I'm not sure. Let me take this document to Israel and have my good friend Rabbi Goldstein take a hard look at it and see if he can discover what the document actually says." Ruth, although reluctant at first, agreed. Ruth wrapped the delicate document in a cardboard box lined with tissue paper, handed it to me with stern instructions to guard it with my life and return it safely to Berlin. I didn't know whether I had something of great importance or whether this is a fake document. Only Rabbi Goldstein will be able to tell, besides, I wanted to find out from him whether he had learned what was inside the chest that caused Hansi to go blind before he was killed by the light from the holy chest.

Easter is two weeks away and time was going fast. I had an assignment to be in Jerusalem to cover the meeting between Pope Peter II and President Adrian at the Jewish Temple on Easter Sunday and I was wondering if this trip would keep me there in time.

Rabbi Goldstein, as always, was happy to see me, but yet he was unhappy to give me the news he had for me. He told me that the High Rabbi opened the chest and saw what was inside. There was another scroll, but this time, the scroll revealed where the next scroll could be found that would give the clue to the location of the final scroll. The scroll also stated that the final scroll was closer than anyone could have ever realized yet many have stumbled not realizing the importance of their foolishness. I must admit I didn't know what that meant but I was here for another reason.

I told Rabbi Goldstein I was here to show him something. I took out the document and explained to him how I came across it. I needed to not only have the thing translated, but also have him authenticate it to be sure it was real and not a fake document. He told me to give him three or four days then he will know. I told him I'd return but not until I made contact with Pedro in Mexico City. I was on a time crunch and I wanted to see Pedro before having to cover that meeting between the Pope and Adrian. Off I was to Mexico City and perhaps another adventure.

CHAPTER 10

I arrived in Mexico City to meet up with Pedro to discover that he had found another important document as well as some treasure, but not anything made of gold like before, but rather something made of clay. What could possibly be worth anything of value made of clay I wondered.

As I waited at the hotel for Pedro, I called Rabbi Goldstein to inform him of my whereabouts and to let him know that Pedro may have stumbled upon something of great importance. In the meantime, the head Rabbi was busy trying to decipher the golden chest I had left behind, the same chest that made Hansi go blind right before it killed him and his men.

I knew that time was fleeting and I had to have the final answer before going back to Jerusalem to cover the major story of that meeting between Pope Peter II and President Adrian of the World Federation Council. According to my sources, it was to be the most historical event in world history and I certainly didn't want to miss it and besides, it was my assignment from my editor at the New York Herald.

As I waited for Pedro to arrive, I turned on the television and watched the news. The news had nothing but terrible things to report. There were still catastrophes world wide including floods, volcanic eruptions, oceanic devastation, earthquakes never seen before in world history. Millions have died in the last decade alone and cities have ceased to exist. There were small wars throughout the world, but there were fears that a major war was about to break out in the Middle East. The Eastern Alliance, which included China, Russia, Eastern Europe, and the Muslim countries were gathering for a major push to invade Israel to destroy the country and kill every Jew they could find. Then there was the Western Alliance, which consisted of Western Europe, Britain, and Scandinavia, gearing up for a push from the west toward Israel. It was to be the final squeeze to crush the country and bring it to it's knees once and for all. The lone country that allied itself with Israel was the United States, but the United States has been virtually destroyed from all the calamities that have plagued the world, leaving even that country vulnerable to attack.

Finally, after waiting several hours, Pedro came knocking at the door. He appeared disheveled and also appeared as though he hasn't slept for several days, which he hasn't. He has come across a vast wealth of treasure that was placed at a location near Mexico City nearly two thousand years ago by none other than Jossppa himself and Pedro had the proof.

Pedro was beside himself. It was the happiest I ever saw him and he could hardly wait to show me. "Come," he said. "Right now," I responded. Shaking his head, he took me by the hand and down the long corridor we ran, down the steps to the waiting car, and off we drove. The warmth of the sun made me even more tired than I was, but Pedro wanted me to see what he had discovered, so I had to please him.

When we arrived at the place where he had found the treasure, I could see piles of pottery scattered all over the place as well as what appeared to be wooden chests, having rotted somewhat.

The closer I got, the more I saw. How could all this stuff been sitting here for more than twelve centuries and never having been seen by anyone, I thought. Surely someone had seen or taken something over the years. I got out of the truck and walked gingerly over to one of the piles of what appeared to be nothing more than a heap of trash. There were broken pottery dishes, pots, pans, and an assortment of other items such as cups and saucers.

One item that seemed to catch my attention was a large jar with some type of inscriptions surrounding it's oval shape. It stood about two feet tall and around one foot wide. Believe it or not but I could actually smell something like wine that had fermented even more so over the years but was that possible. The smell became stronger as I unplugged the jar. It's plug was tightly inserted inside making whatever was inside still there and lo and behold, liquid poured out from the top of the jar. I yelled to Pedro, "Quick, come here. I think I've found two thousand year old wine." Pedro was flabbergasted at the suggestion that I had actually found wine still inside one of the jars but did warn me not to even think of taking one sip. Although the temptation was there, I assured him I had no intention of imbibing that sweet smelling liquid.

The jar had many inscriptions around it's circumference. As I studied the inscriptions, I recognized one of them as meaning, "The one who appears as God will consume the earth." Was this jar one of the many that Joseppa had left behind with written warnings of what was to come in the distant future?

As I continued to look over the jar, Pedro had discovered another item that interested him. It was a utensil, but unlike any other utensil one would use to eat. It was something like a fork yet appeared as though it was pointed like a knife. What could it have been used for we wondered. Pedro and I didn't have a clue but we knew who would so we packed it in our bag to take it to Jerusalem to Rabbi Goldstein. If anyone would know, he would.

I decided to place the large jar inside the truck for safekeeping until we return to Mexico City, then pack it in a large container and ship it to Rabbi Goldstein for further study. By the time Rabbi Goldstein get's the package I will be in Jerusalem to cover the meeting between Pope Peter II and President Adrian. That will take place on Easter Sunday and is to be a momentous occasion.

It was starting to darken so Pedro and I gathered as many of the good pieces as possible and leave for Mexico City. Arriving at the hotel, we placed our stash in my hotel room, took inventory of everything, had a wonderful dinner, and even made love. I must say it was a fulfilling and rewarding day.

Thirteen days until Easter and I must return to New York to finish the fine details of my research and prepare for my assignment. My family will be thrilled to see me, something they haven't had the pleasure of for a very long time. Several months have passed including Thanksgiving, Christmas, New Years, and Valentines Day. The time spent in Peru were fascinating and Pedro was very helpful and polite. I have fallen madly in love with him and each day I was hopeful that he would pop that very important question, but he still seems to avoid asking. Does he know my true feelings, I wondered.

Two days have passed and it was time to return to the states. I managed to pack some of the treasures we've discovered to take home, claiming they were only trinkets I had picked up at a tourist trap. Pedro was staying behind but promised he would come back to New York once my assignment in Israel was over after Easter and I must admit that perhaps he might just ask me that very important question.

As the plane took off and I looked out the window watching Mexico City appear smaller and smaller, I wondered whether I had done the right thing by pursuing these scrolls. Have I unleashed a terrible curse or have I given the world something they have wanted for thousands of years? I guess soon we would have an answer.

My arrival in a devastated New York City convinced me that my work was worth the effort. The entire eastern and western coasts of the United States have been severely flooded from the massive ocean waves that penetrated the coastlines. One hundred to two hundred foot waves took out Long Island and practically every community along the coasts, and then there were the inner states that were consumed by tornado's and the southern states by massive hurricane's. California not only endured massive flooding from the Pacific Ocean, but Los Angeles and other cities have been wiped out by massive earthquakes as well. The entire country has suffered great loses, and then there are other countries around the world that have been devastated as well. It's as if God almighty has unleashed his mighty hands across the globe as punishment for man's evil deeds.

As I made my way through the flooded streets of New York, I kept thinking about what Rabbi Goldstein had told me some time ago. He had warned me that once the last scroll was discovered, it's power would bring nothing but trouble. God himself had written the scrolls by Abraham's hands and all the scrolls that have been discovered, had everything that history had recorded through the ages including names and places, but the one thing that has eluded mankind, was the last chapter that would mention the name of the anti-Christ and the false prophet. Perhaps when Saint John wrote the Book of Revelation in the Holy Bible, he used coded words instead, whereas Abraham's book, mentioned actual name's of people and places yet to come at the time of Abraham.

When I arrived at my office at the Herald, I hade a voice message on my phone. It was from Pedro and he had more news for me. His voice was filled with excitement as he said that he had discovered another wealth of precious items, buried several feet below the surface just twenty miles south of Mexico City. This time, however, it wasn't just pottery and utensils, but another small, yet golden chest, with what appears to be ancient Hebrew writing on it. Next to that was a small cup with Latin phrases etched on it's surface. Pedro held them in his hands, rubbing them gently to be sure he had actually found something useful, then he placed them in his basket and returned to the capital.

I knew I had to get my hands on those two items but yet I had to spend some time at the office before returning to Jerusalem to cover the story on Easter Sunday, which by the way, is only eleven days away.

Rather than go to Mexico City to meet Pedro, I text him to have him ship them next day air to me so I could see them for myself before taking them to Israel when I return to cover the story of a lifetime. By late tomorrow I should have them and just thinking about them filled my with joy and excitement.

I spent several hours at my desk transferring everything I had written down in my notebook into the computer. There must have been more than two hundred pages at least. I knew I had jotted noted down, but God, so much of the stuff. I have traveled to several countries, been kidnaped, shot at, had to eat food that would make an animal puke, and suffer from extreme temperatures. Yet, I was undeterred. I promised myself right from the beginning that once I started this project, I was going to see it through, no matter what.

I spent so much time at work, I drifted off to sleep and when I awoke, it was seven o'clock the next day. I stretched, grabbed my purse, and left for home to take a shower and eat something. I wanted to be home when the package arrives from Mexico City. I could hardly contain my emotions, that's how much I wanted to see these objects for myself.

The time had finally come. As I was relaxing on my sofa reading the morning paper, the doorbell rang. Standing there holding a package was the UPS delivery man. I signed the paper and gently laid it down. Taking a knife, I gently opened the package, took out the bubble wrap, and for the first time I saw the two items Pedro had told me about. The cup was made of pure silver and had the Latin inscriptions on it. It was the most beautiful thing I ever laid my eyes upon, even though it wasn't made of gold. Then I took in my hands the golden chest. I dare not open it but I must admit the temptation had crossed my mind.

Laying the golden chest down on the coffee table, I once again held the silver cup in my hands. It was heavy and I began to try to translate what I could the Latin inscriptions that were inscribed on the cup. I knew some Latin from my days at Catholic school but that was a long time ago. According to the writings, it described something about the crucifixion of Christ as well as the crucifixion of Saint Peter. I thought right away that this cup had to have been made close to the second century since Saint Peter was crucified during the reign of Nero.

If that was the case, how could Joseppa get his hands on this cup. Was there a later journey perhaps? Joseppa was a man who was a trader who sailed the Mediterranean Sea between Rome and Jerusalem via Greece and modern day Turkey. He had many ships and was quite wealthy and I began to think that he may have had other vessels travel the same route he had taken when he arrived in Mexico and North and South America. If that were the case, then Joseppa could have beaten Columbus by several centuries in discovering America.

I knew that I had to take the cup to Cardinal Catelli in Rome for further analysis if there were to be any questions answered. I then made arrangements to take a flight to Rome tomorrow to go to the Vatican to see the Cardinal and spend a couple days exploring Rome for my own benefit and do some more research covering first century Rome. I still had ten more days left before I had to be in Jerusalem to cover the story concerning the meeting between the Pope and Adrian.

Before leaving for Rome, I called Pedro to find out whether he had discovered any more treasures, but as expected, nothing new has been found. I thing these two items are perhaps the last of the vast treasures that Joseppa hid while he was in Mexico as well as the America's.

As I boarded the plane, all I could think of was whether this cup would reveal anything that any of the scrolls hadn't revealed.

Cardinal Catelli was happy as always to see me. I sat in front of his massive desk, loaded with papers as always, and took out the silver cup, and handed it to him. As he looked it over, I explained to him that Pedro had found the cup buried near Mexico City. Puzzled, he lifted his eyebrows looking confused, but still looking the cup over. As he continued looking the cup over, I couldn't take the anticipation any longer and asked, "Well, Cardinal. Is this cup genuine?" Finally after another minute or two had passed, Cardinal Catelli responded, "Sue, what you have here is a late first century, perhaps early second century silver cup. It covers two crucifixions, Christs and Saint Peter's. It also explains Saint Paul as well as Saint John. The one thing it also says strangely enough is there is a book, the Book of Abraham that God has hidden and woe is the one who opens the book."

Cardinal Catelli went on to say that it could be the reason why there are twelve scrolls scattered throughout the world. "If anyone were to find all twelve scrolls and read all twelve, finally revealing God's plans from day one to that final day, he would unleash worse judgements upon the earth than God has already planned. Perhaps what has already happened with all the earthquakes, floods, and chaos around the world is the result of you discovering the scrolls, Sue."

Saying that to me sent a cold chill down my spine. To think that I could be responsible for what's been taking place throughout the world makes me feel like I'm holding a heavy load on my shoulders. Damn, if only Pedro hadn't found this cup. If this cup gave me bad news, what has the chest yet to reveal I thought. Thanking Cardinal for his time, I left with the silver cup in hand and returned to the hotel for the night. Tomorrow I'd spend the day researching at the Roman Library the history or ancient

Rome before boarding the flight back to New York City to prepare myself for Easter Sunday.

The Roman Library was a wealth of information and thankfully it even held English translations of everything it held, There were sources covering Rome from the first Emperor to the end of the Empire. The only time period I wanted to cover was from Emperor Tiberius, Caligula, and Nero. Emperor Nero was especially important since he was responsible for the crucifixion of Saint Peter as well as the burning of the city.

According to one account, Nero had one of his trusted persons executed for treason and attempted murder of his person. His name was Aristoteles, which translates from the Latin term, intelligent. Intelligent he was. So much so that it caused Nero to mistrust him. Nero felt that he had to be the most knowledgeable person in the empire and if anyone even appeared so, he'd have him murdered. Nero caused himself to have numerous enemies and by the time of his death, there were no tears shed for Nero.

According to the cast amounts of information, the first century was a very interesting period in human history. The most important was the vast amount of Roman trade throughout the empire and beyond. That's how I think Joseppa learned the many ways to make his way throughout the Mediterranean even trading with the Spanish. Perhaps after trading with Spain is how his ships had somehow made their way along the coast of Africa, then along the southern route, north towards North America first, then once again southward towards Mexico then South America. Joseppa most likely never was able to return to Palestine so he decided to settle in modern day Peru.

It was time to return to New York to begin writing as much as possible my column on this endeavor that's been eating up my time for several months. It is now seven days until Easter and I must crunch as much information into my article as possible so it will be in that Sunday's paper while I'm covering the story in Jerusalem at the Jewish Temple on Easter Sunday. To make matters even more complicated, I still had to meet up with Pedro in Mexico City for one final excavation before finishing my article and taking the last flight out of New York destined for Tel Aviv, then try to get the best hotel room I could get all things considered.

My editor caught me off guard when she saw me at my desk and began to ask questions about where I've been lately. I told her that my investigation concerning ancient scrolls had taken most of my time but that I was now about ninety-nine percent completed. I just had that elusive one percent, and that was discovering what that golden chest Rabbi Goldstein had that we found in Mexico locked away in his safe was written on the outside and what was, more important, inside.

Six days before Easter and I found my way on a flight to Mexico City to meet up with Pedro. This time my stay would be more interesting than ever before and take twice as long, almost to the point of making it a close call.

When I finally met Pedro, he had such excitement in his eyes and said, "You must come at once. I have something of great importance to show you." I must admit, I had no idea what he could have been talking about, but it didn't take long to find out. Once we arrived at his latest dig, we entered his tent and he walked over to a wooden chest in the far end, then gently opened the lid. Inside was golden scroll, unlike the others. Not only was it made of gold, but it also was laden with precious stones such as diamonds, sapphires, rubies, and many others, to numerous to mention.

I asked Pedro, "How did the Israelites ever manage to get their hands on such expensive stones and gold?" Pedro explained that centuries before the Roman era, King David as well as his successors built the first and second Jewish temples which were laden with gold and precious stones. Abraham whose book these scrolls are made from, was a very rich man of his time and by the time of King David, the Priests of the temples had enriched themselves of Abraham's wealth. The scrolls as well as the chests had been made during those time periods, then as time passed by and the Jews were being persecuted, the scrolls and chests were hidden for centuries until they were found again a few years before Christ was born, then once again after the crucifixion, they had to be hidden, but this time they were to be separated so nobody could ever possess the entire Book of Abraham again and know it's entire contents because unless they had all the scrolls, none of the scrolls would make sense.

That made sense to me now. That's why the Apostles as well as many other's including Joseppa each took one or two scrolls and taken then across the empire at that time and buried them, hopefully never to be found. I thought to myself once again, "What have I done. I have disobeyed God and discovered all the scrolls."

This time all the scrolls would be gathered together in Jerusalem and if any unscrupulous person ever found out, God help us all. I had no idea that at this point in time there was one particular person who qualified to fit that position.

As Pedro held the scroll up in the air, the light that shown from the sun made the scroll sparkle and a beam of bright light almost blinded any person looking at it. As he brought it down, I noticed it also had inscribed something in ancient Hebrew along the upper part of the circumference. I had no idea what it said, but I was sure I had to get it to Rabbi Goldstein as soon as possible. I didn't want to wait until Easter Sunday either, so I excused myself, took the scroll, placed it inside a small case I brought along, and left for the hotel to gather my things and return to New York in time to catch the next direct flight to Tel Aviv. At least, I thought, I'd be in Jerusalem in time for that special meeting between Pope Peter II and President Adrian at the rebuilt Jewish Temple to celebrate it's grand opening.

Five days until Easter and I'm in New York visiting my parents one last time before I return to Israel. My parents have been quite upset with me because of my absence for so long but in my line of work that often happens. Trying to explain didn't seem to help but I could understand their frustrations. After an afternoon at the theater and dinner with them, I returned to my apartment, packed my bags, secured the scroll in my carry-on, then took the taxi for the airport. As the bag went through the scanner, the scroll was quite noticeable. An officer had me walk to the side, took my bag, opened it, took out the scroll, and asked what it was doing in my bag. I told him my father is a Rabbi in Jerusalem and it belongs to him and the temple and if it isn't returned, he would become quite upset and it could cause an international incident. After a few minutes passed, they bought my whole story and let me go.

The sights and smells of Israel always made me feel as though I were home. I have been here so many times I felt as though it was home and even the people were beginning to call me by name.

As I made my way to Rabbi Goldstein's office, a young boy walked towards me and asked if I could help his brother who had managed to get his head stuck in an iron gate. Although I was nearly at Rabbi Goldstein's office and in a hurry, I felt compelled to help the lad. When we approached the young man, I started to touch his head to help release him when four men appeared out of nowhere, grabbed me by the arm, took the bag containing the scroll, and shoved me into a waiting car. As we drove off, I could hear the men talking in Arabic and although I didn't understand everything they said, I did know a few words and when I heard the Arabic word for beheading, I began to panic and started to scream. That only made them slap me harder so I decided to keep quiet and go along with anything they demanded. I guess kidnaping is something that seems to go along with this territory quite often.

After driving for nearly what seemed an eternity, the car stopped and the men took me inside an old warehouse, tied me to a chair and had me wait for another hour before a mystery man would arrive.

When the man arrived, he was seated in the darkened corner of the room and began to ask me all sorts of questions about where I've been and what I've been doing lately. Another question was concerning Rabbi Goldstein and how he was connected to all this. I refused to answer anything until I was assured that Rabbi Goldstein or anyone else would not be harmed. That's when the man replied, "Miss Chamberlain. I would be more concerned about my own safety if I were you." As I looked up, he rose from his chair, walked towards the light, and that's when I saw who it was, and the terror in my eyes had to be noticeable.

CHAPTER 11

As the man looked deep into my eyes and saw the fear in them, he need not introduce himself to me. It was none other than Xi Xian, the most feared man in Asia. Xi Xian was known as a man who would stop at nothing to get what he wanted and even if he had to kill an entire family, children included, he'd do it.

Standing before me, Xi Xian said, "Miss Chamberlain. I've found you at last and you had the last scroll with you. Now. You are going to go back to Jerusalem with my men and retrieve all the other scrolls and chests for me or I will kill your entire family back in New York, then I will split your tongue in half before setting you free. How does that sound to you?" I had to admit that he had me right where he wanted me. I feared him more than I ever feared Hansi. In fact as of now I'd give anything to be dealing with Hansi rather than Xi Xian.

It is five days until Easter Sunday and I've got my assignment to do, and now I have to scheme to get the scrolls from Rabbi Goldstein and hand them over to Xi Xian. Not only does Xi Xian want the scrolls, but he even wants the sacred chests as well. If there was only something Pedro could do to help but I couldn't contact him and put him in jeopardy. Enough lives have been lost and enough people have been put in danger so I agreed to get the scrolls for Xi Xian. "Good." He said. Once I agreed, his men untied me and four of them placed me back in the car and we all drove back to Jerusalem. In the meantime I had to come up with something that would deceive his men at least until I could come up with a plan.

One thing that bothered me was how did Xi Xian get the Arabs to work for him. I always knew Xi Xian was powerful, but how was he able to accomplish getting the Arabs to do his bidding? They aren't the type of people that are easily persuaded.

As we drove up to Rabbi Goldstein's residence, something didn't seem right. The doors were open and things seemed amiss. As we entered, the foyer had papers scattered about and there was trash everywhere. I called out, "Rabbi Goldstein, Rabbi Goldstein, where are you. Are you all right?" Complete silence. Just at this moment, several men came crashing through the door, guns drawn, and Xi Xian's men opened fire. Bullets scattering everywhere. I ducked behind Rabbi Goldstein's massive desk while men where shooting everywhere they could.

When it was all over, Xi Xian's men were dead and the other three remaining men grabbed my arms, lifted me up, and ordered me to their car, When I asked them who they were all they would say was that they were officials from the World Federation Council and that I was to be taken to Belgium for questioning. I thought to myself, now what have I done. Things were beginning to get extremely messy and I only had four days now to be at the rebuilt Jewish Temple for that historic meeting between the Pope and Adrian.

All during the flight from Israel to Belgium I had loads of questions, none of which were being answered. I decided to just sit in my seat, eat my meal, and get a few winks in before our arrival, just in case I go without sleep for some time.

My arrival in Belgium began with a motorcade to what appeared to be a castle on the outskirts of the capital. It was huge and was loaded with priceless art and other gems. I had never seen such beauty in my life other than perhaps in the Vatican and maybe not even there. A maid came and escorted me to a private bedroom that also had a connected sitting room and private bath. It's walls were made of granite and it had beautiful paintings on the walls. As I sat on the bed, the maid approached and said, 'You will spend the night in here. I will bring dinner to you and in the morning you will have breakfast before meeting the master of the residence." I thought, who in God's name lives here. The sheer opulence was a lot to behold.

The morning sunshine came through the sheer drapes and I noticed fresh orange juice on the table. Once breakfast ended, I dressed myself, and then was escorted to the main living quarters where I waited for the master of the house. I was very curious to see just who in God's name calls this place home. When the man came walking through the massive doorway, I nearly fainted. It was none other than President Adrian himself.

As I stood there stunned by the appearance of Adrian dressed in his finest attire, I was also quite confused as to why the most powerful man on earth would have me in his private residence. Adrian, hand out stretched, showed me to a beautiful yellow chair and had me sit. Walking to a cart full of the finest wine's and cognac, Adrian poured me a glass of red wine while he had a glass of the finest cognac money could buy.

As he seated himself in his favorite chair, Adrian stated, "I suppose you're wondering why you are here in my private residence. Let me just say that you have served me well and for that you will be rewarded." I had no idea what he was referring to and I asked, "What are you talking about Mr. President?"

Adrian responded, "Do you know who has been rescuing you from evil men such as Hansi over the last several months? It is I and with good reason. You see, it is I who has wanted all those scrolls you call, the Book of Abraham. It is the reason that I have had the power to lead the organization known as the World Federation Council. What is most important, I have had help." Lifting up the phone, he pushed a button and summoned his private secretary. As soon as he came through the door, Adrian said, "Show our guest in, please." In a few seconds, the guest came walking through the door and when I saw who it was I nearly fainted. It was Rabbi Goldstein. Rabbi Goldstein walked toward Adrian and asked how he could be of service.

I have found out that all this time when I had handed Rabbi Goldstein the scrolls and chests, he had handed them over to Adrian. Once Adrian possessed all the scrolls, he would have absolute power and nobody could touch him. Now things were beginning to make sense to me. That is why Adrian, as President of the W.F.C. could guarantee the Jewish state of Israel peace and security all these years if he had the Book of Abraham for himself. The Jews believed that if Adrian had the scrolls, he could be trusted to assure the Israeli's that there would be a lasting peace. Adrian then said to me, "Miss Chamberlain. You may return to New York to write your article but I want you to be front and center on Easter Sunday in Jerusalem in front of the rebuilt Jewish Temple for my announcement to the world." I had no idea what kind of announcement Adrian had in mind but I knew I had to be there in three days so I thanked him for his hospitality and had one of his drivers take me to the airport for a flight to New York City.

During the flight, all I thought of was Rabbi Goldstein. Was he a patriot or was he a traitor. Did he play a role in securing peace and safety for the Jewish people, or did he hand them over to a madman, much like Hitler who has nothing but evil plans for the Jews?

When I arrived at my apartment, I collapsed on my sofa and drifted off to sleep. I was so tired I slept for eleven hours until the telephone woke me up. It was Pedro. He had just arrived in New York and wanted to find out if I was home. I was glad to hear his voice and told him he must come right away because I had some news to tell him. I didn't know what sort of reaction Pedro would show once he learned that Rabbi Goldstein had betrayed our trust.

When I told Pedro what I had learned, Pedro just sank into the sofa, his face drained of his blood, and felt sick to his stomach. As we both sat there wondering what to do, the telephone rang. When I answered, the voice on the other end was a man who said he was an aide to Rabbi Goldstein. He said that the Rabbi had given President Adrian all the scrolls except the last scroll. Adrian doesn't possess the entire Book of Abraham, at least not yet. Rabbi Goldstein is to take Adrian and Pope Peter II into the Holy of Holies in the Jewish Temple on Easter Sunday and hand him the final scroll, thus handing him the entire Book of Abraham. It would then make it official.

The man told me that I had to return to Israel on the next flight and come to Rabbi Goldstein's office and steal the final scroll to prevent Adrian from obtaining it. Should Adrian get his hands on that scroll, he would have absolute power over all the earth including every King and President.

When I hung up the phone, I told Pedro to pack a few things as we're headed back to Israel to steal that final, golden scroll. Before returning to Israel, I had to enter my final notes into the computer at work, then complete the article and send it to my editor for final approval. By the time Easter Sunday arrives, the article should have final approval and I will have covered the story from the Jewish Temple in Jerusalem. Between the two events, I was sure I'd have a Pulitzer Prize this time.

As we arrived at the King David Hotel, my nerves began to get the best of me. Would Rabbi Goldstein catch me in the act of stealing the scroll or worse yet, does Adrian have a tail on me already? No matter, I had to do this at all costs and I was prepared to do whatever was necessary to achieve what I had to accomplish. I had to prevent Adrian from obtaining the final scroll, even if it meant losing my life and I was prepared to do it. Pedro, on the other hand, wasn't as willing as I was but went along with the mission anyway.

As we waited for this mystery man to arrive, we went over our plan on how to spirit the scroll out of Israel once the events of Easter Sunday were over. I was sure that Adrian would believe I had something to do with the scroll being taken so we had a plan that Pedro would take them first to Egypt, then to Greece, then to New York and my apartment. We would meet there until I could come up with a plan on what to do with it.

A knock on the door relieved me from thinking, yet made my nerves jump on edge. Pedro answered the door and saw a short, bushy haired Jewish lad standing in front of him. Pedro asked his who he was and when the lad told him, Pedro had him enter the room.

The lad said his name is Yahuda and he has been molested by Rabbi Goldstein for several years and has been too scared to tell anyone. He assured me that he knows where the scroll is and he is willing to hand it over to me on one condition. I said, "It depends what that condition is." Yahuda asked that I take him to the United States to be with his uncle in Chicago. He claims to have a passport but Rabbi Goldstein has it locked away, preventing him from leaving Israel. I agreed but said I had to have the scroll first, then I'd find the passport and get him to America tomorrow morning and he could stay at the King David Hotel with us tonight for safety sake. I could see the relief in his face shine immediately. Yahuda went inside first to be sure the coast was clear and once he was sure the rabbi wasn't inside, we entered his private office and began to search for the scroll. At the one wall was a small desk and it was locked. Pedro had a talent for opening locked drawers and safes so it was up to him to do the job. Just as Pedro began to pick the lock, we heard a door open and all three of us scrambled for cover. It was Rabbi Goldstein and he came into the office, unlocked the very desk that Pedro had began to pry open, took out a document, closed the drawer, then unwittingly left the room without locking the drawer.

Whew, what a close call I thought, but at the same time it was a stroke of luck on our part. As we shuffled thought the papers in the drawer, I told Pedro to make it a quick one before Rabbi Goldstein returns and locks it back up and perhaps even catches us in the act.

After spending close to half and hour searching for the golden scroll, we came up empty handed. Yahuda suggested we wait until tomorrow when the Rabbi takes his daily stroll around the city which usually takes him two to three hours, then we would have more time. I wondered why Adrian had me taken to his private residence and Pedro told me that it was his way of letting me know that Rabbi Goldstein was working for him and that I was after all a vital link in his cog. I must admit I felt used and dirty. How could I have allowed myself to be so used and not know, but I realized that Pedro was also being made a fool of as well.

Three days until Easter Sunday and I still had to return to New York to complete my article and submit it to my editor for final approval, then return to Jerusalem to cover the story of Adrian, Pope Peter II, Chief Rabbi Goldstein, and Muslim Cleric Imam Mehrdad. Also in attendance would be many world leaders including the Russian President Alexander Krychkovski, whose Eastern forces are poised to attack, Chinese President Xo Lin whose Eastern forces are also poised to attack, Israeli Prime Minister Moshe Eban, American President Joseph McNair, who leads the Western Alliance whose prepared to attack the Eastern Alliance north of Jerusalem. The one man that is absent from the event will be the Western Alliance Commander, General Harold Wexler. It is feared that if things don't go as planned, all hell will break loose and Israel could be destroyed by the Eastern Alliance. What will President McNair do and what is most important, what will President Adrian do?

As Rabbi Goldstein left for his walk, Pedro and Yahuda searched his office while I left for the airport in Tel Aviv. I had to take the next flight to New York, get to the New York Herald, do some final work on my story, submit the final draft, wait for the editor's final approval, then return to my apartment for some much needed rest and wait for a telephone call from Pedro in Jerusalem with what I hope is good news.

Two days until Easter Sunday and the newspapers were all reporting that the Vatican Emissary to Israel, Cardinal Manci had arrived in Tel Aviv to prepare for the arrival of Pope Peter II on Easter Sunday. Cardinal Manci was all smiles as he arrived in the Jewish Capital City, and the crowds were out in full force. Fearing there would be any disturbances, the security police had the roads leading from the airport to the city center closed. As I watched the television reports, the telephone rang.

It was Pedro and he sounded fearful. "Sue, please come back right away. The police have picked me up and I need bail money." I asked him why he was in jail but all he could say was for me to come to Israel and get him out of jail. According to Pedro the police also arrested Yahuda but Pedro has no idea where Yahuda was taken. I still had to submit my article and wait so I returned to the office, quickly went over my notes, and submitted the article. It would take another four hours before my editor sent me an e-mail letting me know she gave my article her final approval. It was now official. My story would be in the newspaper in five days with the final paragraph yet to be submitted. That paragraph concerned the final scroll and until I had my hands on it or at least had the proper person possess the final golden scroll, the article could never be complete.

Today, the day before Easter. I packed my bags, but before leaving for the airport, I went over to my parents apartment one last time. Somehow, I had an inkling that I might never be coming home or that there may never be a home to return to. I had to hug and kiss my parents one last time then return to what I believed was my destiny. I felt I was born for this very reason and that somehow, God had a purpose in my life for what was about to happen.

My mother pleaded with me not to go, especially hearing the reports that war could break out any second and that millions of soldiers were poised to attack from both sides. I assured my mother that if I had a feeling there was any sort of trouble, I'd catch the next flight out of Israel and head to Germany before returning to the United States. My father hugged me so tight I thought he'd break my back. I was always his little girl and he never let me forget that. As I opened the door to leave, I turned my face back, saw my mother's face with tears flowing down, my father's voice shaking as he said his final goodbye, and I felt as though they knew they would never see me again. Closing the door behind me, I slowly walked out of the building, took the taxi ride to the airport, and after a couple hours had passed, I was in the air, watching the city fade away below me in the darkness. I was now alone, and I was full of fear, unlike any time before.

As the plane landed in Tel Aviv, it was early Easter morning. The sky was just beginning to brighten from the sun. I summoned a taxi, then took the drive to Jerusalem. Taking a room at the Hotel King David I always stayed in, and had reserved for a month prior to this day to be sure I had a place to stay, I entered my room, collapsed on the bed totally exhausted. It then hit me. I couldn't rest. I had to get to the police station and bail Pedro out of the central jail.

The bail was set at one thousand U.S. dollars. To me it was a mighty steep amount but what was I to do. Pedro was glad to see me and get freed from that stinking jail cell. As for Yahuda, that was a different story. There was no way of finding him but Pedro told me that Rabbi Goldstein had the golden laden scroll and that today during the festivities at the temple, he was to hand over the scroll to Adrian as they were to ascend the steps leading to the interior of the temple and then to the inner chamber where the holy of holies is located. The three of them, President Adrian, Pope Peter II, and Rabbi Goldstein were to enter the Holy of Holies for the blessing, then once the blessing was finished, the three would come out to the plaza where Pope Peter II was to make an announcement to the people in the plaza as well as those watching by television. I was given a prime location to watch by order of Adrian himself when he had me in his private residence a few days ago, and I'm still wondering why he had me there in the first place. I had assumed it was because of my research and discoveries of all the scrolls and golden chests. Adrian was about to possess all of what Pedro and I have found and that thought alone made me tremble. For the first time in history, since Abraham himself, one man would have in his hands the entire Book of Abraham.

Pedro and I still had seven hours to get our hands on that scroll before the days events and I was as determined as ever of getting my hands on it. Once I had the scroll, I then had to find a way of getting it out of Israel without getting caught and that's where Pedro come's in. As I thought before, Pedro would take the scroll and make his way to Egypt while I head to Tel Aviv and the airport. I was sure Adrian would have all the airports, train stations, bus stations, and taxi's closed off until the scroll was recovered so I had to make my way out as quickly as time would allow.

Pedro suggested we give Rabbi Goldstein's office one more try, but I was somewhat leery about that idea. What if we were caught? I knew Rabbi Goldstein would turn us over to Adrian's security staff and then I'd never be seen or heard from again. Pedro would certainly be killed but I on the other hand could become Adrian's private plaything. Adrian had a mean streak about him and he was capable of anything. I saw it firsthand one time when he scolded one of his own men.

With just six hours to go, Pedro and I made our way to Rabbi Goldstein's office. I gently knocked on the door, waited a few seconds, then knocked again. After waiting a few more seconds, I slowly turned the doorknob, and finally after a second or two had passed, I entered the foyer. With Pedro behind me, I entered the dimly lit room. My eyes had to adjust to the darkness before I could find the doorway leading to the Rabbi's office.

Gently knocking on the office door, I waited a few seconds and with no response coming from the other side, I turned the doorknob and entered the room. Pedro stood guard on the other side while I rifled through the desk drawers. One drawer was securely locked. Now what do I do, I thought. I had no idea how to pick a lock so I continued searching other places for now, at least until I could come up with a plan on how to unlock and open the drawer.

It took me another half an hour searching every drawer and shelf until the only drawer left to search was the locked drawer. I ran over to the doorway and asked Pedro whether he knew how to pick a lock. "Of course." was his response. While Pedro picked the lock, I waited outside the office. Just as Pedro opened the drawer, the outer door opened and in walked Rabbi Goldstein. I wanted to faint but I had to think quick of what to say about why I was standing in the foyer.

When Rabbi Goldstein turned and saw me standing in front of his office, his words were, "What in God's name are you doing in my foyer?" At first I was at a loss for words but as usual I was thinking quick and told him that I wanted to see the golden scroll one more time before he hands it over to Adrian later today. I pleaded with him to give me this one more chance, after all, I discovered it and that should give me good reason enough. Thankfully, he agreed.

As we entered his office, I looked around the room trying to find where Pedro was hiding and while Rabbi Goldstein was unlocking the drawer where he kept the golden scroll and golden chest, Pedro made a dash for the door and just in time. Rabbi turned towards me as Pedro left the room taking his shadow with him.

Rabbi Goldstein had the golden scroll wrapped in fine linen and as he unwrapped the linen, I saw the golden scroll appear. It was magnificent. It was worthy of a king. It's ancient Hebrew script written in the silver band around the top edge made it even more beautiful then anyone could imagine. As Rabbi Goldstein re-wrapped the scroll and placed it back in his safe, locking it securely, I knew I would never see or handle it again. Then, in a loud voice, Rabbi Goldstein said, "Now be gone. I have work to do before today's events. I must prepare for the service in the temple." As I turned and walked out the door, all I could think was how much of a fool I have been to trust this man all this time rather than placing my trust to Cardinal Catelli in the Vatican. Had I done that instead, things might have turned out differently.

I returned to the hotel and met up with Pedro. Pedro still believed we had a chance of getting our hands on the scroll whereas I knew there was no chance. I guess things just had to run it's course and pray that we would live to see another day and return to our home's and families.

Four hours until the events were to take place. Pedro and I left the hotel and walked around the city one more time, talking about all the experiences we had searching for the scrolls and all the dangers we encountered. Not only did we have to deal with Hansi, but there was Gou Fe Jong, Madam Zara, Alejandro, and many others. It was quite an experience I must say. This adventure has taken me to many places including Egypt, Syria, Iran, North Korea, China, and other destinations. My passport was loaded with many stamps from numerous countries.

As we made our way to the square surrounding the Jewish Temple, it is now three hours until the event that will be telecast throughout the world. Every nation on earth will cover this major event and I will be fortunate enough to be here to witness first hand what is about to take place. It is the final chapter of my article and once the day is ended, I will leave Jerusalem for the last time, take a taxi to Tel Aviv, take the next flight to New York, and go straight to the New York Herald to submit the final draft of my article for final approval.

Crowds were starting to appear and as we waited, I heard in the distance something that sounded like thunder. It was actually farther than it sounded but it caused me great concern. It's still two hours until show time and I asked Pedro whether he heard the thunder like sound. At first he didn't, but about a few minutes later he also heard something earth shattering and then suddenly it stopped. Everybody heard it and then wondered what it could have been because as soon as it sounded it also stopped. Could there have been a small earthquake somewhere, we wondered.

Now with one hour before President Adrian, Pope Peter II, and Rabbi Goldstein appear before the crowd, the numerous dignitaries from around the world are beginning to make their way to their designated seats. Searching the area, I noticed the United States President McNair take his seat with his lovely wife. Israeli Prime Minister Moshe Eban sat next to President McNair but I noticed that the Russian President and Chinese President were absent. I thought, How odd. At an event such as this and with being invited, one would surly believe they would attend this event, but soon I would know why.

More and more people were crowding into the square until there was no longer anymore room. It is estimated that there are as many as twenty thousand people in the square and even more surrounding the plaza. Security is tight as the security for Pope Peter II is here as well as for President Adrian. Directly in front of the temple is situated the Israeli Orchestra. They will play three national anthems. The Israeli, the Vatican's, and the anthem for the World Federation Council.

The time has come and as President Adrian, Pope Peter II, and Rabbi Goldstein took their places above the steps leading to the Jewish Temple, the crowds broke out in cheers, and as the cheering grew louder, so did the tempo. The ground seemed to shake from all the cheering and foot stomping. Rabbi Goldstein raised his hands into the air as a signal to silence the crowd, then introduced first, Pope Peter II, then about two minutes after the crowd settled down, he introduced President Adrian of the World Federation Council.

After several minutes of speaking to the gathered crowed, Rabbi Goldstein announced that the Muslim Imam, Imam Mehrdad would also take his place among them, and as the Imam walked up the steps towards the three men, the Muslims began to cheer their leader. Now there were four men standing before the crowd.

As the four turned and walked towards the doors of the temple, the people continued their cheering, knowing the men would be worshiping in the Holy of Holies. Representing the three major religions of the world would solidify the solidarity of the world for the first time in human history. After two hours had passed, we heard the thunderous sound again in the distance, but this time the sound was followed by explosions in the far distance. The Israeli army has been exchanging gunfire with the Eastern Alliance and the crowd became concerned that perhaps the explosions could find it's way to the center of Jerusalem.

Within a few minutes, the four men came out of the temple and stood at their designated spot. Rabbi Goldstein spoke first saying, "Ladies and Gentlemen. Standing before you are the political and religious leaders of the world. I introduce to you Pope Peter II who will speak first before President Adrian gives his address."

As Rabbi Goldstein walked away from the microphone, Pope Peter II shuffled toward the very spot that the Rabbi had left. Coughing slightly, Pope Peter II began to address the crowd. His speech lasted around twenty minutes but what he said at the end of his address made everyone, including myself, left in shock.

Pope Peter II introduced President Adrian as the Messiah. He, according to Pope Peter II, is God in the flesh. Raising his arms towards Adrian, Pope Peter II walked toward Adrian and embraced him. President Adrian embracing Pope Peter II, then walked to the microphone and spoke to the crowd assembled in the square as well as those watching through television around the world.

Adrian began by saying, "Yes, I am the Messiah you and the Jews have been waiting all these centuries for. I have now possessed the entire Book of Abraham giving me the power to govern the world. You will fall down to your knees and worship me as your Lord. Anyone who refuses to worship me will be put to death."

I couldn't believe what I was hearing. Thousands of people in the square began to fall to their knees and worshiped Adrian. In the distance I heard the sounds of explosions and the sounds of death. Adrian announced he was about to destroy Jerusalem using the forces of the Eastern Alliance because the Jews have caused much misery to the people of the world unless they convert to him and him alone.

Just at that moment, the American President, President McNair was assassinated and the Israeli Prime Minister was wounded in the attack. Suddenly, it seemed like all hell had broken out. Pedro and I just stood there in utter shock. We had no idea what to do or where to go. Adrian was still at the podium demanding total obedience. As he commanded he be worshiped, someone began to scream saying, "What's that in the sky?" I looked up and saw what appeared to be thousands if not millions of bright lights headed toward earth. Were they meteors or something else falling from space? As I continued to look upwards, I could hear the crowd also continue to say, "My God, what is that?" It also seemed to not only be getting closer every second, but also larger and larger with the one light in front appearing to be the largest one of all.

Suddenly, it started to become darker and rain began to fall. The lights in the sky appeared even larger than before and even Adrian gazed at the lights. Within a few seconds, the lights became noticeable for being human in appearance. They were riding what looked like horses with wings and the person in front wore a crown of pure gold and silver. He held in his right hand a massive sword and to his left was what seemed to look like an angel.

It wasn't long before the millions of people were now on solid ground and were doing battle with both the Eastern Alliance as well as the Western Alliance, defeating them in a few seconds. The man in front of the invaders walked towards Adrian who was the anti-Christ, and Pope Peter II, and pointing towards them, commanded the angel to take the two, and as the angel did as commanded, the earth opened up with fire and brimstone spewing out from the core of the earth, and the angel threw Pope Peter II into the bowels of the earth first, then Adrian fell into the earth, never to deceive the people ever again.

Now, the man at the center of it all, walked up the steps to the temple, took the golden scroll and the golden chest which held the key to the temple, and entered the place of worship. The people who came with him had encircled the temple and began to sing praises unto him and after a few moments had passed, the angel escorted the man out from the Holy of Holies to the people and told the people, "Fear not, for the Lord hath cometh." The people who had come with the Lord are the saints, those who had lived on the earth and had died, and have returned to rule with him for the thousand years.

The man standing in front of the microphone then began to speak. As he spoke, everyone who listened was able to hear him speak in their own language simultaneously. I heard him speak in English while Pedro heard him speak in Spanish all at once.

He said, "I am the Lord your God. I am here to rule and reign for one thousand years and there will be peace. The time has come."

It was at this moment that the angel of the Lord spoke and said, "Great is the name of the Lord, your God."

It was at this moment I realized that my searching for the scrolls was meant to be and I was seeing for myself, The Christ.

<u>The End</u>

Printed in the United States
By Bookmasters